The Complete Idiot's Reference Card

Keys to Great Characterization

1. Create characters that you can fall in love with.
2. Make sure your hero and heroine react sensibly and heroi...
3. Make your characters strong, but give them a few flaws to ...
4. Give your characters goals to strive for.
5. Avoid stereotypes by understanding what motivates each character.

Keys to Exciting Pacing

1. Start with a bang—or at least with a compelling mood.
2. Don't overload the first chapter with "back story."
3. Edit your sentences until each one says only what you mean.
4. Be sure to include a healthy dose of dialogue.
5. Cut any scene that doesn't move your story forward or serve an important function.

Keys to Compelling Conflicts

1. Give your characters goals—ideally ones that clash.
2. Make sure the obstacles to the "happily-ever-after" get progressively worse before they get better.
3. Include both internal and external conflicts.
4. Don't solve the characters' problems by magically pulling a rabbit out of a hat.
5. Pick conflicts that will sustain you to the end of the book.

alpha
books

Keys to Creating Emotion

1. It's not enough to tell readers what your characters are feeling—show them through physical actions and choices.
2. Characters' emotional reactions must be consistent with their personalities.
3. Include specific details about the environment so that the reader feels grounded and involved in the scene.
4. Raise the stakes by making it difficult for your characters to choose love.
5. Use dynamic verbs and carefully chosen adjectives.

Keys to Building Sensuality

1. Write at the level of sensuality with which you feel comfortable.
2. Make sure that love scenes reflect the personalities of your characters.
3. Love scenes must move the story forward or add to the character development just like any other scene.
4. You can add to sexual tension by focusing on the sensual details in the environment.
5. Don't worry what Aunt Tilda will say! Write to your heart's content.

Keys to Research

1. Understand your subject thoroughly, but don't bog your story down with details simply to impress your reader.
2. Use just enough details to paint a picture that draws your reader into the right time and place.
3. Double-check your facts before and after you write and be prepared to do more research after you've written your first draft.
4. You don't have to be an expert researcher, but you must strive to make sure every fact is accurate.
5. Do the best you can to understand your subject, but don't be so paranoid about making a factual error that it keeps you from writing.

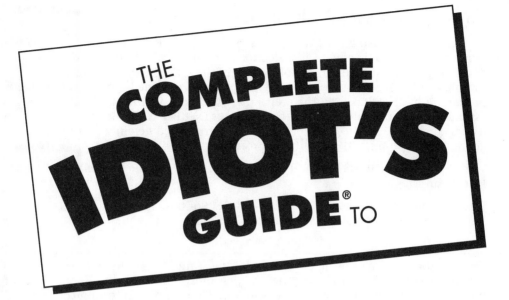

THE **COMPLETE IDIOT'S GUIDE**® TO

Getting Your Romance Published

by Julie Beard

alpha books

Macmillan USA, Inc.
201 West 103rd Street
Indianapolis, IN 46290

A Pearson Education Company

Publisher
Marie Butler-Knight

Product Manager
Phil Kitchel

Associate Managing Editor
Cari Luna

Acquisitions Editor
Randy Ladenheim-Gil

Development Editor
Amy Gordon

Production Editor
Christy Wagner

Copy Editor
Abby Lyon Herriman

Illustrator
Jody Schaeffer

Cover Designers
Mike Freeland
Kevin Spear

Book Designers
Scott Cook and Amy Adams of DesignLab

Indexer
Brad Herriman

Layout/Proofreading
Svetlana Dominguez
Terri Edwards
Mary Hunt
Ayanna Lacey
Heather Hiatt Miller
Stacey Richwine-DeRome

Contents at a Glance

Contents

Part 2: Seven Aspects of Highly Affecting Romances   71

6 Plotting: Fresh Take on an Age-Old Story   73

7 Characterization: Heroes to Die for and Heroines to Cry For   87

Part 3: After the Romance: Bringing Up Baby   161

13 Research Recap   163

24 Romancing the Industry 311

25 The Last Word (Or Why You Really Can Do This) 323

Appendixes

Foreword

In 1984, I was a 22-year-old baby writer who had just typed "The End" on her very first manuscript. After whipping the last page out of the typewriter with a suitably dramatic flourish, I popped the entire manuscript into an envelope, mailed it to the only romance publisher I'd ever heard of, and waited for the offers to come pouring in.

The silence from New York was deafening.

After a year of waiting for that mail Jeep to round the corner, I finally received my first rejection. I hadn't completely wasted that time, though. I'd spent many hours at the local library, desperately thumbing through the sources that would help me get published, many of them woefully outdated. When I was ready to submit my manuscript again, instead of mailing it "cold" (as I'd since learned it was called), I sent query letters to 22 different publishers, asking if they'd like to read all or part of the manuscript. I sold the book within three months, then went on to sell 10 more, all of which have become national best-sellers, won numerous awards, and recently enabled me to negotiate my first seven-figure contract.

Knowledge *is* power.

Now, thanks to Julie Beard and *The Complete Idiot's Guide to Getting Your Romance Published*, you won't have to waste a year of your valuable writing time poring over outdated writing references or waiting for the postman to ring. You can have all the knowledge you need to get started in this business right at your fingertips in a comprehensive and concise guide that's as fabulous and entertaining as the romance genre it celebrates.

And Julie's not just going to cover the basics. She's going to explore the enduring appeal of romance fiction and tell you exactly how much money you can expect to earn with your first book. She's going to help you decide whether or not you need an agent and explain why the most winning heroines would be a combination of Scarlett O'Hara and Melanie Wilkes. She's going to teach you how to empower both yourself and your damsels in distress.

Julie's not only going to tell you how to *publish* your romance; she's going to help you write it!

You may be a natural-born storyteller. You may dream in technicolor and think in prose. You may have one of the freshest voices to come along in years, but even the most angelic soprano needs some training and discipline. And that's where educating yourself about the craft of writing and the business of publishing comes into play.

I can't think of a more accomplished teacher than Julie Beard. She's not only a savvy professional who has worn many hats in her stellar career, but an author whose own romance fiction rises to the very highest standards of our genre.

Published authors are frequently bombarded with questions about how to get started in the business. The next time you ask me a question, don't be surprised if I simply smile and hand you a copy of *The Complete Idiot's Guide to Getting Your Romance Published*. As Julie points out, over 2,000 romances are published every year. With this book to guide you on your path to success, one of them may very well be yours.

Teresa Medeiros

Teresa Medeiros is the author of 11 romances for Bantam Books, four of them extended *New York Times* Bestsellers. Her first hardcover will be released in June 2000.

Introduction

If there is one thing that every romance reader can count on, it's a happy ending. Readers expect that by the end of every romance novel the heroine will solve all of her problems and get the guy of her dreams, too. Come to think of it, you have a lot in common with romance readers. You expect a happy ending as well. But for you, the happily-ever-after will come only when you achieve your dream of becoming published.

I've been writing romance novels for more than 15 years. My first historical romance hit the shelves in 1994. If you're good at math, you've already figured out that it took me a decade to become published. Why so long? I didn't have a book like this to show me the way, for one thing. I stumbled toward publication through trial and error. You're going to have an easier time than I did, because this book is a virtual road map to publication. It will show you the shortcuts I wish I had had.

Writing is an exciting and sometimes nerve-racking adventure. Of course, there's no guarantee that you'll ever be published. But I can guarantee one thing for sure: You'll never become published if you don't start writing that book you've been dreaming about ... now! The sooner you start, the sooner it has a chance of being published.

You don't have to do it alone. I'll take you through the process of writing and publishing from start to finish. I'll help you understand why the romance industry is so popular and how the best-selling authors tap into readers' hearts. I'll teach you how to come up with plot ideas, and I'll explain in detail the seven aspects of highly affecting romances: plotting, characterization, pacing, voice, conflict, emotion, and sensuality. Once you learn how to write a great romance, I'll show you how to get it published and how to promote it in today's tight market.

No one ever said getting published was easy, but it will be a whole lot easier after you read this comprehensive "how-to" book.

How to Use This Book

This book is easy to use because it starts with the basic concepts and progresses from there. While it was written to appeal to writers at all levels of experience, it's designed specifically to help those who know nothing about the romance industry and want to know everything.

There are four major steps to publication. Let's take a brief look at each one in turn.

In **Part 1, "Falling in Love with Love: Understanding the Magic of Romances"** you'll learn to see romances through the eyes of the readers. You'll understand their expectations and the genre's hard-and-fast rules. With an overview of all the subgenres, you'll be able to choose the kind of romance you want to write.

In **Part 2, "Seven Aspects of Highly Affecting Romances,"** you'll learn everything you need to know about writing a romance, from plotting and characterization to conflict. You'll learn how to heighten sensuality and tug on the heartstrings.

In **Part 3, "After the Romance: Bringing Up Baby,"** you'll learn how to polish your prose and to do your best at making a rejection-proof submission. At this stage, you're ready to find an agent and an editor.

In **Part 4, "The Writing Biz,"** you'll learn how to present yourself professionally to publishers and how to ensure that your first sale turns into a long-lasting career. You'll also find out how much money you can expect to earn and why promotion is so important to the health of your new career.

By the way, you won't feel intimidated by publishing terms because there's a glossary at the back of the book. That's also where you'll find a list of publishers who buy romance novels. In short, there's a wealth of knowledge that you'll need to launch your writing career, and here it is, all in one easy-to-read "how-to" book.

Extras

You'll find lots of advice, warnings, tips, and definitions scattered throughout the book in the form of sidebars. This is what they'll look like:

Speaking of Romance ...

These are words of advice from romance writers. You'll love these nuggets of wisdom from some of the most talented authors in the genre.

Write On!

These words of wisdom will keep you on the right course. Sometimes it's the little tidbits of advice that make all the difference.

Stop the Presses!

These warnings and anecdotes will help you avoid painful mistakes and enable you to learn from the problems other writers have experienced.

Love Letters

These definitions will help you feel like you're "in the know." They'll help you understand the romance industry lingo.

Acknowledgments

First and foremost, I'd like to thank my agent, Evan Fogelman. His faith in me, his friendship, and his wonderful wit have made my journey as a writer all the richer. Special thanks to Shirl Henke, who painstakingly read every word of this manuscript and generously shared her vast knowledge of the romance industry. Pat White and Martha Ambrose also read copiously and gave me excellent feedback. Thanks also to Karyn Witmer-Gow, Michelle Hoppe, Mary Micheff, and Dee Stauffer.

I owe a debt of gratitude to the board, staff, and membership of Romance Writers of America: Allison Kelley, Charis McEachern, Alicia Rasley, Jo Ann Ferguson, Libby Hall, Teresa Medeiros, and many others gave me their all-out support when I needed it the most. The organization also gave me permission to quote freely from its wonderful publication, *Romance Writers' Report*. Quotes taken from the RWR are identified throughout this book with an asterisk (*).

I'd like to thank my family for being so patient and helpful during the time I lived in front of my computer writing this book. Thanks to Nancy Brown, Doris and John Beard, Aiko Brown, and especially dear Connor and Dale.

Finally, I'd like to thank Alpha Books for the opportunity to write about such a great topic. My involvement in the romance industry, in the Chicago-North and Missouri chapters of RWA, has brought me great joy and deeply treasured friendships. And so it is with heartfelt love that I dedicate this book to all the wonderful women (and men!) who write romances. You're the best!

Trademarks

Part 1

Falling in Love with Love: Understanding the Magic of Romances

There will always be a place in the market for books that touch the heart. By reading a great romance novel, a reader can re-live the excitement and passion of falling in love, see the world for about $6, view famous historical figures naked, meet a man who is more disgraceful than her husband and watch him being reformed by the love of a good woman, and know without ever worrying that they're in for a happy ending.

—Susan Wiggs, author of more than 18 romances

Ask any romance writer what she likes best about her job and chances are she'll likely say, "Making people happy!" Why do romance novels bring so much joy to so many people? That's what you're going to find out in this part. I'll analyze the enduring popularity of romances. More important, you'll learn how to tap into some of the classic romance fantasies to pen your best-seller. So, get ready to fall in love with the romance genre.

Chapter 1

The Power of Love

> ## In This Chapter
>
> ➤ Are you ready for romance?
>
> ➤ The secret to romance writing success
>
> ➤ The real reason romance novels are hot, hot, hot
>
> ➤ Ways to make readers love your book from page one
>
> ➤ Writing all the way to the bank

Ain't love grand? Romance writers certainly think so. We get to make people happy. We assure our readers that no matter how bad things get, our heroines will always win in the end. We confirm what romance readers believe in their heart of hearts: Love will conquer all. Frankly, as a writer, I can think of no higher calling.

But wait a minute! You've just noticed a few other perks in the job description for romance writing. You can show up for work in your bunny slippers, take all the coffee breaks you want, and if you're lucky, you just might make a fortune in the process! (More on the money later.)

Now that I have your attention, read on. In this chapter, you'll find out why romance writing is so emotionally and financially rewarding. And I hope you'll decide it's time to get off your rusty-dusty and write those two magic words: Chapter One.

Love Letters

Romance novels focus primarily on the development of a love relationship between a man and a woman. By the end of the book, the hero and heroine should be ready to commit—the required happy ending readers expect. No cold feet allowed!

Love Letters

A **genre** is a category of fiction characterized by a particular style and content that readers come to count on. In the romance genre, readers expect a happy ending. Mystery buffs expect the cops to catch the bad guy. In the horror genre, readers anticipate being scared. Each genre has a dedicated following, so disappoint their expectations at your own risk!

Love Is in the Air

Most people desperately want and need love, even if they won't admit it. That's why 95 percent of the tunes jamming the airwaves are love songs. That's why people pay thousands of dollars to dating services to find Mr. or Ms. Right. That's also why 99 percent of the movies coming out of Hollywood have romance plots or subplots. I think it's safe to say that love is big business.

Love Sells

Notice I didn't say "sex sells." If you think you can dash off a *romance novel* by stringing together a series of mindless sex scenes, you'd better prepare yourself for a batch of painful rejection letters. Romances have to be extremely well written to satisfy today's sophisticated and dedicated readers. How dedicated are they? Look at the statistics:

➤ Romances generate about $1 billion a year in sales.

➤ Fifty-three percent of all mass-market paperback fiction sold is romance.

➤ A couple of thousand romances are released (and gobbled up) every year.

Sound like the kind of success story in which you'd like to play the role of the protagonist? You bet!

Why Are Those "Little Books" So Popular?

First of all, not all romances are little. The romance genre includes short novels that focus exclusively on one relationship, as well as larger books that have multiple subplots and characters. Second, they're popular because they're written by some of the most talented and innovative authors of popular fiction. Romance writers continually push the boundaries, looking for new settings and plots that will keep hungry readers satisfied. If you haven't taken a good look at the latest trends, your perceptions of the romance industry might be out of date.

How Much Do You Know About Romances?

Test your knowledge of the romance *genre* with this true or false pop quiz:

True	False	
_____	_____	All romances are about wimpy secretaries who fall in love with older, domineering bosses.
_____	_____	Romances are so simple even a monkey could sit down and crank one out.
_____	_____	Romances feature savvy women with spines and hip heroes who actually admit to their feelings—just like men today!
_____	_____	The hottest new trend in romances features heroes who are movie stars.
_____	_____	Editors love rape scenes.
_____	_____	Today's romance writers are among the most talented and highly educated writers working in genre fiction.

The answers: F, F, T, F, F, T.

Okay, I'll admit that last question was a bit self-serving, but you get the point:

➤ Wimpy heroines went out with the '70s.

➤ Those "simple" romance novels are a lot more complicated than you'd think—especially for the writer!

➤ Heroes and heroines are always changing with the times.

➤ Movie stars are generally pooh-poohed in traditional romances.

➤ Rape scenes, particularly involving the hero, are generally *verboten*.

So you didn't ace the pop quiz? Don't let that get you down. I, too, was green when I started in this business 15 years ago. If I can do it, so can you. First things first. Let's get to know the romance reader, since she's the one who will be plunking down her hard-earned money for your book.

Stop the Presses!

Don't model your story after a book written 10 years ago or you may find that your novel is hopelessly out-of-date. Romances are constantly evolving to reflect the changes in women's lives. When you research the market, definitely study the classics of the genre, but also buy books with recent copyright dates to check out the newer story lines.

Look Who's Reading!

Chances are your reader is in a committed relationship or would like to be. She works hard at her job as well as at home. She may face the stress of being a single mom, a high-powered career gal, or an over-achieving stay-at-home mother who valiantly tries to be all things to all people. Whoever she is, she enjoys escaping into a romantic world where good always triumphs over evil and a happy ending is assured.

Incidentally, *she* might be a *he!* Some men prefer to read about relationships instead of, say, nuclear submarines that threaten to destroy the world.

Here is what statistics tell us about romance readers:

➤ They range in age from 15 to 105 years of age.

➤ Sixty-eight percent attended or graduated from college.

➤ Fifty-five percent work outside the home.

➤ Women with full-time, executive-level jobs report reading an average of 14 romances a month.

That means your average reader is educated, industrious, and a voracious reader, so don't talk down to her. Write the best book you can, and if she loves it you'll have a fan for life.

Speaking of Romance ...

Who says real men don't read romances? Ted Johnson, the 6'3", 240-pound linebacker for the NFL's New England Patriots apparently has a romantic streak as well as biceps of steel. He has publicly admitted to relaxing with a good romance novel. With a defense like that, who cares what critics say about romance novels?

Scoping Out the Competition

All right, admit it. You still have this outdated image of romance writers. You know the one I mean—the frumpy, sexually frustrated housewife writing at the kitchen table in her robe and curlers. Or maybe you think we write in bathtubs while trying to keep our feather boas dry. If so, time for an upgrade on your perceptions!

Author! Author!

Today's romance writers come from all walks of life. Many juggle their writing careers with motherhood. And many had successful careers in other professions before turning to writing. Bet you didn't know that …

➤ Kathleen Korbel (a.k.a. Eileen Dreyer) was an E.R. nurse for 16 years before she started writing and has since been inducted into the Romance Writers of America's Hall of Fame.

➤ Merline Lovelace was an Air Force colonel before she started writing romances and military thrillers full-time.

➤ Superstar Sandra Brown was a television broadcaster before getting her start in series romances.

➤ *New York Times* Bestselling author Tess Gerritsen was a medical doctor before she started writing romantic suspense, and later medical thrillers.

By the way, you don't have to have a prior career or a special degree to write romances. Some of the genre's most enduring talents began their careers while bouncing children on their knees. To name a few …

➤ LaVyrle Spencer, a recently retired megastar, whose touching stories about simple people revolutionized the genre.

➤ Bobbi Smith, a western romance author who says she could only eke out two hours of writing a day when her kids were young.

➤ Nora Roberts, probably the genre's most prolific author, who says she began writing during a 1979 blizzard to keep herself sane when her children had endless "snow days" off from school.

➤ Debbie Macomber, who nearly gave up her dream of writing because of her family's financial strains. She hung in there and has since penned more than 100 romances with 45 million copies in print and has signed million-dollar contracts.

These women were all once like you. They had a dream that wouldn't die. They wanted to write a book. And the rest, as they say, is romance history.

Boys Will Be Girls and Girls Will Be Boys

You don't have to be a woman to write romances. There has been some gender-bending in the publishing industry ever since Mary Ann Evans wrote under the pen name George Eliot. It should come as no surprise, then, that some of your favorite romance writers may belong to clubs for men only.

Speaking of Romance ...

Publishers seem willing to give male romance authors a fair shake, as long as the writer is willing to take a female pseudonym. Still, male romance writers get their share of odd reactions. Ed Kolaczyk, a former engineer, has written more than 50 romances with his wife, Anne, under the pen name Andrea Edwards. He says, "Even other writers aren't quite sure what to make of me. Most of them figure that Anne does all the writing while I walk the dogs and clean the cat sand. The truth is that, although Anne develops the ideas, the outline, and does a re-write, I write the first draft of everything except the love scenes. (Hey, even engineers have their limits.)"

Bet you didn't know that ...

➤ Historical writer Leigh Greenwood is really Harold Lowry.

➤ Category author Jean Barrett is really Bob Rogers.

➤ Jennifer Wilde, author of sexy historicals such as *Love's Tender Fury,* was really the late Tom E. Huff.

So, don't let your testosterone levels scare you off.

I hope I've convinced you that there is absolutely no excuse to put off your dream of writing a romance. But before you start, you should be really clear on just what qualifies as a romance. Doing your homework just might save you a few rewrites later on.

First Things First: What Is a Romance Novel?

Quick! Picture a romance novel in your mind. What do you see? A thin book with a modern couple on the cover, gazing into each other's eyes? If so, you're picturing a category romance. That's one of two main types of romances. The other type is the single-title romance. It's important to understand the difference between the two because in many ways, they're very different animals.

Category Romances

Category romances are novels released to bookstores as part of a monthly package. They range in length from 40,000 to 100,000 words, and the publisher's identity is often more important to the reader than the author's name. For example, readers often buy Harlequin-Silhouette's entire publishing list every month regardless of who authored the books.

Category romances are numbered and are also called series romances. Harlequin-Silhouette is the biggest publisher of series romances.

Single-Title Romances

Single-title romances are bigger books, contemporary or historical, that usually exceed 100,000 words. They're not sold as part of a package, and the identity of the author is more prominent than that of the publisher. In fact, sometimes the author's name might be several inches tall on the cover. The kinds of romances published as single-title releases are so broad in scope that the market is often referred to as "Women's Fiction."

Where Do I Go from Here?

So, how do you decide which type of romance best suits you? Here are a few clues that might point you in the right direction.

You may be right for category romances if …

➤ You like a shorter word length.

➤ You think the tone and style of your writing will fit a specific romance line.

➤ You can adjust your plot to follow strict editorial guidelines.

➤ You can accept the fact that if the major romance publishers turn your book down you may not be able to sell it anywhere else because it has been written for a very specific market.

You may be right for single-title romances if …

➤ You think you can handle writing longer books.

➤ You think your plot will be more complex than those found in series romances.

➤ You don't like the idea of writing to specific editorial guidelines.

➤ You want to write about very controversial subjects.

So Many Romances to Write ... So Little Time

Although there are two main types of romances, there are a million variations on both of those themes. If you choose to write a series romance, for example, you can write one that's hot-hot-hot or one that's ultra sweet. You can write a medical romance or a romantic suspense. You might decide to write a spiritual love story or one that's designed to make the reader laugh hysterically. There are specific *lines* for each of these kinds of romances. The choice is yours.

As for the single titles, how about writing a big beach book, a multi-generational family saga, a pre-history love story, or a romance set a hundred years in the future? The possibilities are only as limited as your imagination.

Love Letters

A **line** is a specific category within the so-called "category romance" industry. Lines at Harlequin-Silhouette include Harlequin Temptation, Harlequin Historicals, Silhouette Desire, and Love Inspired, to name just a few. Each line has a different tone, word-length requirement, and intended audience. Some lines allow for sex, while others don't.

You Gotta Love It (to Write It)

Every beginning writer has heard the old adage, "Write what you know." I've always found that advice frustrating. Does that mean I can't write about astronauts because I haven't been to the moon? What's the point of having an imagination if I can't use it?

I have a better saying, and it's particularly appropriate for romance writers: "Write what you love."

Pour Your Heart Out

The best story to write is that special one you've been keeping safe in your heart. Readers can tell the difference between a writer who sweats blood onto the manuscript and one who is just phoning it in. Love your story and your reader will, too. For that matter, go ahead and fall in love with your hero. If you don't, why should anyone else? Besides, what your husband (or boyfriend) doesn't know won't hurt him!

R-E-S-P-E-C-T the Genre

You don't have to be a life-long reader of romances to write one, but it helps. I'd never read a romance before I sat down to write my first one, and I'm convinced that's why it took me 10 years to get it right. You have to know and respect the market. Reading this book will speed up that process for you. But I have two quick pieces of advice for those of you who aren't huge romance fans already:

➤ Read until it clicks. Devour as many different kinds of romance novels as you can sink your teeth into. Read until you find a book that truly excites you. Then, sit down and try to write your own book in a way that will excite someone else with equal intensity.

➤ Forget Frank Sinatra—Ol' blue eyes did it his way, but you have to do it the editor's way. You may as well accept the fact that if you're going to write a category romance, there are some rules you just can't break. For example, you can't kill off your heroine or have a hero who's a serial killer. If that's the kind of story you want to write, romance may not be your bag. Learn the rules of the road before you set off on your journey and you'll save yourself the heartache of an unnecessary flat tire (i.e., rejection) later on.

Speaking of Romance ...

Here's some good advice from the editors at Harlequin-Silhouette. "We expect you to enjoy reading romance fiction. If you are already a fan, your appreciation of this type of book will be apparent in the writing. If you have not done so already, we encourage you to read many, many books from each series available on the market. The series that emerges as your favorite is probably where you should submit your manuscript."

For Love or Money

One last point before you start the race. What kind of experience do you hope to have writing your romance? Perhaps I should be more blunt: Are you doing this just for the money? If so, you may have a problem.

In the Name of Love

The best reason to write any kind of novel is because you love to write. You have a story to tell. Of course you want to get published, but it may not happen for months or even years to come. In the meantime, you need to enjoy the process of writing for its own sake.

Stop the Presses!

In general, writing a novel is not a great way to get rich quick. It's a business of delayed gratification. Writing your book will probably take longer than you think. Even getting a rejection letter can take months! And once your book is accepted for publication, your publisher will have up to two years to actually print the darned thing, so be patient.

Am I Rich Yet?

If you're writing so that you can become rich and famous, we need to talk! The average advance for a first romance novel is generally $3,000 to $10,000. Since most first novels require a lot of rewriting, you may end up earning only about 10¢ an hour.

But What About Danielle Steel?

It's true Danielle Steel and Nora Roberts, to name two, sell millions of copies of their books and are doubtless millionaires many times over. That's what makes this business so exciting. It *is* possible for you to become a mega-best-selling author—just don't expect it to happen overnight. This is a business of delayed gratification. Work hard and be patient.

Speaking of Romance ...

Nora Roberts's first category romance was published in 1981. She toiled for another 10 years, writing nearly 60 books, before reaching the *New York Times* Bestseller list. Once she broke that barrier, there was no stopping her. In 1997 alone, six of her books appeared on the *New York Times* list. So far, she's written more than 130 novels and shows no signs of slowing down! Danielle Steel almost gave up writing after the publication of her first book. Her next several efforts were roundly rejected, and she spent years trying to come up with another winning plot. Needless to say, she finally succeeded. She now has more than 380 million copies of her books in print, and 21 Danielle Steel novels have been adapted for television.

Signs of Success

So, you've decided romances are pretty cool. You have a story, or the inkling of a story, and you're excited about getting started, but you still wonder if you have what it takes to succeed.

I've been studying the art of romance writing for 15 years. I've met dozens and dozens of successful, talented writers. I've noticed that the most successful ones have a few things in common. They are generally …

➤ Ambitious and dedicated.

➤ Professional about meeting deadlines and agreeing to rewrites.

➤ Astute observers of human nature.

➤ Willing to help other aspiring writers.

➤ Prepared to weather the ups and downs typical of a writing career.

➤ Feel they have something important to say.

Perhaps most important of all, successful writers simply won't take no for an answer.

Aspiring Romance Writer's Checklist

If you share any of these traits, chances are you're a good candidate for the job. In various chapters throughout the book I'll give you a checklist of important questions to ask yourself. Let's start with one that focuses on your suitability to the profession.

❑ You love happy endings.

❑ The thought of creating characters and stories excites you.

❑ You long to see your name in shiny, bold letters on the cover of a book.

❑ You want to leave a legacy that will live on.

❑ Great books thrill you.

❑ You long to create worlds in which readers can happily get lost.

❑ You are determined to finish your book.

I'll bet you checked off more than a few of these statements. If so, you've been bitten by the writing bug. You have no choice but to proceed to the next chapter with visions of best-seller lists dancing in your head!

The Least You Need to Know

➤ Romance is one of the most rewarding genres in publishing.

➤ You might get rich, but it could take years.

➤ Even published authors have books rejected.

➤ Read lots of romances before you try to write one.

Chapter 2

Love Is Here
to Stay

In This Chapter

➤ Tapping into the most dynamic romance themes

➤ Romance has come a long way, baby!

➤ Deciding what kind of story to write

➤ Riding romance trends in the new millennium

So, you've decided you've got what it takes to write a romance. Congratulations! Welcome to the club of creative and nurturing writers who treasure this fantastic genre. Before you learn the secret handshake, though, you must learn what makes romance novels so special.

Critics of the genre often belittle romances as "formulaic" simply because they all end "happily ever after." What these hard-bitten cynics don't understand is that romance writers use a great deal of creativity to make classic themes spring to life in unique and delightful ways. And it's those mythic fantasies that draw romance readers back to bookstores over and over again. So much so that one out of every two mass-market paperbacks sold is a romance!

In this chapter, you'll learn more about what touches readers' hearts, and understanding these basic human emotions and fantasies will take you one step closer to the best-seller lists.

Rules to Write By

If romances are written using a simple formula, I wish someone would give me the recipe. I'm the kind of writer who creates every story from scratch—and without a measuring cup! Fortunately, there's lots of room for creativity in a genre that has more flavors than a Baskin-Robbins ice-cream store. As its readership has grown, so have the genre's boundaries. As a writer you have lots of freedom and lots of exciting choices to make—and only a few limitations.

Your characters could be vampires, Civil War Confederates, alien life forms, or devoted Christians. When love blossoms, you can close the door just as the lights go out, or you can open the windows and let daylight shine in on a liberated sex scene. You can write a whimsical, contemporary romp or a brooding and tortured historical tale of love. In fact, you can do just about anything as long as you follow two basic rules.

Stop the Presses!

The romance genre is one that celebrates the virtues of faithful relationships. Romances are one-man/one-woman stories. If your heroine and hero sleep around after they've begun a significant relationship with each other, your readers will be disappointed and most likely offended. If your characters bed-hop, they do so at the risk of your writing career!

I Do, I Do!

You've probably noticed that all romances have a happy ending. That means the characters must make it to the altar, or at least set a date, before the end of the book.

Why such a traditional ending? Most romance readers are by their very nature relationship-oriented, and most have, or long for, a permanent mate. To them the only satisfying conclusion to a relationship novel is one that includes a commitment. Your readers have enough problems and unhappy endings during the day. When they curl up in bed at night with your novel, they want a money-back guarantee that all will end well.

Focus on the Relationship

Here's the second rule: The majority of your book should focus on the love between the hero and heroine. This requires getting the hero and heroine together quickly at the beginning and keeping them together throughout most of the book. Just about every scene should feature one of the following:

➤ The hero or heroine

➤ The hero and heroine together

➤ The hero thinking about the heroine, or vice versa

➤ The hero or heroine experiencing something that will affect the way that they regard their relationship

Speaking of Romance ...

There is a rash of new novels that are essentially romances, but with sad endings. They're written by men and are quasi-literary in tone. *The Bridges of Madison County* and *The Horse Whisperer* are two wildly successful examples. Both involved infidelity and both ended on a bittersweet note. If this is the kind of love story you want to write, have at it! Just be sure to pitch it to the right publisher. Traditional romance houses won't buy it unless there's a "happily ever after."

"Is that all I can write about?" you ask incredulously. Of course not! You can have subplots, fascinating secondary characters, and outside complications, especially in longer books. These secondary elements, however, simply can't dominate the story.

Empowering Message

Romances have been accused of many things over the years. In the 1800s, romantic fiction was blamed for instilling in British girls the ridiculous notion that one might actually marry for love! In the 1970s, the younger secretary/older boss romances and the so-called *bodice rippers* were accused of promoting a victim consciousness in contemporary women. Today's romances might well be accused of something very different. They promote the idea that a woman can love a man and still have her own goals and identity. So not only are today's romances entertaining, they're empowering to their readers.

Write On!

The development of the love story is so fundamental to romance novels that some authors chart it out scene by scene. They write a synopsis of the overall plot, then they write a second synopsis dealing only with the love relationship. This ensures that the love story won't get lost in the shuffle.

Love Letters

Bodice rippers is a term that critics of the romance genre used to describe the big, sexy historical romances popular in the 1970s at the peak of the sexual revolution. Often the heroine's bodice was ripped away, hence the term.

Aw, come on! How can a simple happily-ever-after story empower readers? Listen closely, because the answer to this question is central to the incredible popularity of the genre. Romances tell the female reader that …

➤ Like the heroine, she'll solve all of her problems and win in the end.

➤ Like the heroine, she may sometimes feel lost and confused, but deep down she's strong and ultimately will survive.

➤ Love conquers all—including the most surly, hardened hero ever to strut across the pages of a romance novel!

Speaking of Romance …

"I believe that what we write can be a healing influence for some reader out there somewhere. We will never know what words of ours may help someone else get through a hard patch, to reach inside themselves for that extra dollop of fortitude to carry on, but it's there. When I receive a letter in which the reader speaks of an act of kindness by a heroine or hero, it makes me feel good. I know that story had impact on that person's life, maybe not a large impact and maybe only for that moment, but it happens."

—Libby Hall (a.k.a. Laurie Page), past President of Romance Writers of America*

New Spin on Classic Characters

One of the most exciting developments in the romance genre has been the evolution of the characters. The hero and heroines of today's romances are people readers can relate to. The situations the protagonists find themselves in may be larger than life, but their emotions are real and felt deeply by readers. It might do well to examine a couple issues regarding characterization that have led to some misunderstandings about the genre by nonromance readers.

A Rogues' Gallery

Frequently, the most exciting romance heroes are men who are devilish, embittered, and cynical. You know the type—the dangerous, dark-haired, sardonic hero who has broken not only all the rules, but a few women's hearts as well. In early romantic fiction he appeared as Heathcliff, Mr. Rochester, and Rhett Butler. In today's romances, he frequently appears as a renegade pirate, an embittered medieval knight, a charming highwayman, or a rebel motorcycle biker.

The rogue-hero is exciting because he has the power to make the reader wonder if there really will be a happy ending. After all, how on earth will the heroine tame him? That doubt keeps the reader turning the pages.

Though this rogue-hero is misunderstood by critics of the genre, he has propelled many a writer to the top of the best-seller lists. He is also a good match for today's strong heroines.

There are certainly heroes who exhibit more consideration and subtlety than the rogue, but he is probably the one character that the public at large identifies most with the genre. We'll talk about more great heroes in Chapter 7, "Characterization: Heroes to Die for and Heroines to Cry For."

Damsel in Distress? Not!

Today's readers tend to like strong and resourceful heroines. However, your heroine doesn't have to wear her strength on her sleeve. She doesn't have to be, let's say, a corporate raider or a shrew waiting to be tamed. But if she's outwardly timid or demur, we'd better see glimpses of her inner strength early in the book. She may be reluctant to sail the world on a pirate ship, for example, but she'll have enough smarts and courage to lower the sails in a storm after the crew has jumped ship. She offers quite a contrast to the delicate romance heroine of years gone by.

We'll analyze what makes memorable heroines later in the book.

Enduring Romance Fantasies

There is a reason that fairy tales have survived through the centuries. They speak to certain core human desires and fantasies. Romance novels that tap into these enduring fantasies do especially well at the cash register. Cha-ching! Let's take a look at some of the most popular and obvious romance fantasies. These are not formulas to be followed, but mythic stories to inspire you.

Speaking of Romance ...

Some of the genre's best and brightest authors have contributed to a fabulous book titled *Dangerous Men, Adventurous Women: Romance Writers on the Appeal of Romance.* This 1992 collection of essays was edited by Jayne Ann Krentz and published by University of Pennsylvania Press. In it Doreen Owens Malek makes some astute observations about the rogue-hero: "We may want a caring, sensitive, modern man in our lives, but we want a swaggering, rough-hewn, mythic man in our books. He provides the best foil; the more obdurate the hero, the sweeter the triumph when the heroine brings him to his knees."

Beauty and the Beast

If there's any doubt about the popularity of this classic love story, you need look no further than Hollywood. Recent television and film renditions of the "Beauty and the Beast" fairy tale were wildly successful. Here's the gist of it:

➤ The hero is wild, outwardly cruel and unattractive, uneducated, or socially unacceptable.

➤ The heroine is classically beautiful but nevertheless prepared to risk all to love the seemingly unlovable beast.

➤ Her ability to see his inner beauty transforms him.

➤ For her insight and faith in the hero, the heroine gets to marry a prince (the hero transformed).

Cinderella

There is nothing quite as satisfying as watching a character climb her way to the top in spite of the odds stacked against her, especially a nice person like Cinderella. This fantasy works equally well in contemporary and historical settings:

➤ Cinderella is the dutiful, hardworking girl who can't go to the ball.

➤ Even though she's picked on mercilessly by her stepsisters, she never gives up on her dream of being loved.

➤ With the help of a fairy and a tenacious prince, love prevails.

In historical romances, the heroine often rises out of poverty by marrying a rich nobleman. What a fun fantasy! It's like winning the lottery. But your reader probably won't be thoroughly satisfied unless your heroine realizes at some point that love is more important than moolah.

The Rake and the Virgin

These two classic characters can make for a delightful romance. Let's look at them both in turn.

The virgin is an oft-used and oft-misunderstood character. In this post-sexual revolution era, critics see the virgin as a throwback to a time when women were sexually repressed. But to the romance reader, the virgin's significance has little to do with sexuality. She usually symbolizes …

Stop the Presses!

If you base your plot on a classic fairy tale, be sure to update the characters, even if they're in a historical setting. While Cinderella is sympathetic, you can't use a romance heroine who acts like a character in a Disney movie. She has to stand up for herself now and then; otherwise she'll be too one-dimensional and wimpy for modern readers.

➤ A woman who is pure-hearted.

➤ A woman who knows her worth and is waiting for a worthy man.

➤ A woman who is so endearingly unaware of her own charms that she hasn't had the confidence to snag a man.

Ironically, this sweet character ends up snagging her polar opposite—the rake. He's the cad, the reprobate, the one who drinks too much and sleeps with too many women. Sound like a mismatch? Not when you throw in the redeeming power of love. Here's a typical scenario:

➤ The virginal heroine has been protected by her parents, doesn't fit into society and therefore hasn't found a mate, or she's holding out for something better—an education, culture, or her principles.

➤ She's thrust into intimacy with the rake, the one man in all of society who couldn't possibly deserve her less.

➤ His *joie de vivre* loosens her up, and her high principles make him a better man.

➤ These two opposites—both charming in their own way—find true love by bringing out the best in each other.

In historical novels, these characters fit well into the Georgian and regency eras, periods when manners were paramount. In contemporary books, the rake might be a millionaire playboy or a bad-boy outcast. The virginal heroine might be a bookworm type or an innocent with Victorian sensibilities who feels she doesn't quite fit into modern society.

Speaking of Romance ...

As a writer, Debbie Macomber went from obscurity to the top of the best-seller lists by analyzing romance fantasies. "I noticed titles played an important role," Debbie says. "Titles that had the word wife, bridegroom, rancher, cowboy, anything that had to do with the military. Then I noticed that they were falling into the key romantic fantasies." Armed with this knowledge, Debbie based her next books on the "Cinderella," "Beauty and the Beast," and "Snow White" fairy tales. They sold very well. "The next one I did, I played on the title. I took two words that I knew were popular—playboy and widow. I named my book *The Playboy and the Widow*. That was the first time I made the Waldenbooks Romance Best-Seller list."

The Prince and the Frog

Ribbet. Need I say more? This story is a classic and pretty straightforward:

➤ The heroine longs for a prince but can only find a frog.

➤ She relents to his wooing, sees his worth, and kisses him.

➤ She's rewarded for her new-found depth of character with the transformation of the frog into the prince she's hoped for all along.

My editor frequently reminds me that my heroines must learn to love the frog before they get the prince. Loving someone when he still looks like a frog shows character. This story has some similarities to "Beauty and the Beast," but it incorporates another fantasy—the transforming power of a kiss.

The Healing Power of Love

Modern studies show that people who are loved heal faster and live longer. This scientific data reinforces one of the most popular romance themes: Love has the magical power to heal and transform. After all, love can turn a wounded beast or a misunderstood frog into a cherished lover!

Wounded heroines, and especially wounded heroes, are perennial favorites. Here are some possible takes on this theme:

➤ A hero scarred by war learns to feel again through the love of a good woman.

➤ A heroine abused as a child overcomes her past when she meets a patient man who loves her through thick and thin.

➤ A hero burned by a bitter divorce forgives and forgets with the nurturing help of the heroine.

The wounds can be external or internal. The important thing is to show the healing process as the relationship develops. Love can be a giant Band-Aid.

Stop the Presses!

There's a fine line between the healing power of love and co-dependence. Your characters' problems shouldn't disappear overnight just because they've fallen in love. Love is the catalyst that leads to life-changing realizations. With greater insight, your hero and heroine can then resolve their own personal dilemmas. It's the old "two-hearts-are-better-than-one" cure.

You've Come a Long Way, Baby

Empowering messages. Classic fantasies. Sound complicated? It definitely adds layers to the old "Boy-Meets-Girl" plot. As well it should. Romances today are as sophisticated as the women who read them. But don't worry. You're going to be writing from your heart. Follow your instincts and you'll write a beautiful and successful novel.

Just remember that romances constantly evolve. In the 1970s, books usually featured young women with little or no independence who were rescued by an older, richer hero. In the 1980s, many stories focused on women struggling to break into the career world. In today's romances, there is no question that the heroine will set her own agendas and goals. Instead of marrying a millionaire, she may be a millionaire herself. And she's just as likely to save the hero as he is to save her. That's what I call progress!

Speaking of Romance ...

Leslie Wainger, executive senior editor at Silhouette Books, says she can't predict trends in the new millennium, but she says good writing will always be in style. "What always gives me hope and what always makes me feel very good about how discerning the readers can be is how they respond to authors who just take their own tack, whatever it is," says Leslie. "Whether it's a new trend or an old trend, I think what we'll continue to see is room for those people because I think the readers are really looking not just for themes that resonate for them but for authors whose voices and whose story-telling approaches resonate for them."

The New Millennium

Romantic stories have been around since the dawn of society. So what trend will they follow over the next hundred years? More to the point, how can you tap into the next wave of popular romantic fiction?

Trends are impossible to predict. But I'd bet a royalty check that romances will be just as popular in the year 2100 as they are now and as they were a hundred years ago. To help you prepare for the future, I'll share a few time-honored tips for creating a great romance, no matter what the century:

➤ **Tap into your own emotions.** Explore your feelings about love. Remember your first kiss. Your desires and yearnings are universal. The more you use your own experiences, the more real and vivid your romance will be.

➤ **Keep your eye on popular culture.** Read newspapers, magazines, and listen to the radio. Watch trendy shows like *Party of Five* to find out how the newest generation deals with dating. If you want to write about hip characters, you don't have to walk the walk, but you should be able to talk the talk. You can even tap into current issues in a historical novel as long as you don't violate the sensibilities of the era. Readers love issues they can relate to.

➤ **Avoid clichés like the plague.** (Oops! Sorry. That was a cliché.) Stay away from clichéd plots, characters, and phrases. If you choose a classic fantasy, do it with a new twist. Give tried-and-true characters a unique quirk. Perhaps your bad-boy motorcycling hero knits in his spare time. Perhaps your Amazon warrior princess is afraid of mice. As for words, if you use the emotion-laden language that works so well in romances, try creating metaphors you've never read before. Try setting a tone that is unique.

➤ **Write the book *you* want to write.** Editors want you to feel passionately about your story. If you merely try to imitate one of the genre's best-selling authors, guess what? You'll spend hours of blood, sweat, and tears writing a story that's already been told and may end up boring you to tears (not to mention the reader!).

You have a unique story to tell. I can't wait to see it in print. To increase the chances of that happening, keep reading. In the next chapter we'll examine the various categories that most romances fall into. If you can pick a mark before you start, you'll have a much better chance of hitting the bull's-eye with your first effort.

The Least You Need to Know

➤ Your novel must have a happy ending.

➤ Don't let your subplots get in the way of the romance.

➤ The most popular romances often tap into classic fantasies.

➤ Write the story that excites you the most.

➤ Avoid clichés and over-used plots and settings.

Love Is a Many Splendored Thing

Once upon a time, there was a college professor who decided to write a novel. She didn't know and didn't care about the rules of romance writing. She didn't even have a particular story in mind. She just wanted to see if she really wanted to write. She ended up combining an epic love story, the eighteenth-century Scottish Highlands, time travel, homosexuality, and witch burnings in a sweeping 850-page romantic novel that broke all the rules. This book, called *Outlander,* which the author calls a "historical fantasia," was a stunning success. With its publication, Diana Gabaldon rocketed to stardom.

And once upon a time there was a housewife who struggled for five years to get her first category romance published. She could barely scrape together the money for postage for her submissions. Her perseverance paid off with the publication of her first series romance in 1982. She now has more than 45 million copies of her books in print, earns million-dollar contracts, has had one of her books turned into a made-for-TV movie, and has taken her upbeat romance themes into the realm of women's fiction. Debbie Macomber also climbed the best-seller lists. She did so, in fact, long before Diana Gabaldon burst on the scene.

What's the point of this tale of two authors? Simply that you, too, can be wildly successful, by taking either the beaten path or the road less traveled. But first you must learn the difference between the two. This chapter will serve as your road map for both routes.

Periscope Down: Plumbing the Depths of Subgenres

In the old days, there were two kinds of romances: historical and contemporary. The historicals usually involved pirates and medieval knights, or a gothic hero who sulked around the family castle. The heroines were demur Maid Marian types who waited for Robin Hood to save the day.

In contemporary settings, the hero was rich and never talked about his feelings. In fact, the story was told exclusively from the female point of view. As for the heroine, she was just as stoic as her historical counterpart, except she wore slacks and a sweater. Boy, have things changed!

Stop the Presses!

Think long and hard before you decide to place your historical romance in an obscure location such as Turkey or Zimbabwe. It might be the greatest story every told, but if you're shooting for the traditional romance market it probably will be rejected anyway. Romance editors are reluctant to try nontraditional locales.

Pirates and medieval knights are still favorites, but the demur damsel in distress is history. New trends have pulled the genre's limitations out by the roots, leaving a fertile field of creativity wide open. You say you like modern heroes, but you want to write a historical romance? Why not put them together in a time-travel romance? Or consider putting a Native American hero in a Western romance, or a Western hero in a Native American romance, which is sometimes referred to by readers as an Indian romance. You can write in the future, the present, the past, or in prehistory. In other words, just about anything goes! So go for it!

Historical Romances

How do I love thee? Let me count the *subgenres*. The popularity of historical romances waxes and wanes every decade or so. But there always remains a core group of avid fans who read nothing but historicals. What's the appeal?

➤ Historical settings allow readers to escape to a completely different time and place.

➤ Historical settings seem more romantic, more dangerous, and more exciting than today's oftentimes routine world.

➤ Historical characters, at least in fiction, live larger than life. Knights and cowboys, for example, settle conflicts by fighting to the death. That makes for high drama, and drama is the essence of a darned good book.

Most editors prefer historicals set in America or the British Isles, but more exotic locales occasionally find their way into print. (A listing of publishers that accept historicals can be found in Appendix B, "Romance Publishers.") Let's take a look at the kinds of historical settings you might choose from.

Knights in Shining Armor

Medieval romances are a perennial favorite. Everyone has romantic notions of chivalrous knights who fight for love and honor. Medieval romances are generally set from 700 to 1400 A.D., though anything up through the Elizabethan age is included in the subgenre. Anything before the year 700 is considered the Dark Ages. Choose the year and then research carefully. Medieval readers tend to be history buffs and will know if you make an error.

FYI:

➤ **Story lines.** They tend to revolve around feudal society. Everybody answered to a liege lord, and ultimately to the crown. We think of knights fighting for the honor of a lady, but more frequently they fought for property and survival.

➤ **Tone.** Many medieval novels are dark in tone and rich in texture. But some writers, like Teresa Medeiros, have successfully taken a lighter approach to the era.

➤ **Authors to read.** Roberta Gellis, Denise Domning, Elizabeth Stewart, Anita Mills, Rexanne Becnel, Suzanne Barclay, and (dare I say?) Moi.

Love Letters

A **subgenre** is a recognizable type of fiction within a particular genre. It's a subcategory. The romance genre has expanded so much that the number of subgenres seems to grow every year. That's good news for you!

Write On!

You should research marriage laws before writing a historical. In the Middle Ages, marriage ceremonies were conducted in front of the church door, rather than at the altar. A priest had to "cry the banns" (announce the upcoming marriage) on three consecutive Sundays before the ceremony. And people couldn't marry relatives, a former brother-in-law, for example, or even a godparent.

Write On

Penguin/Putnam's Signet imprint and Kensington's Zebra imprint are the only lines that currently publish traditional short regency romances. They generally pay low ($3,000 to $5,000) and with print runs sometimes as low as 25,000 copies, there's little chance to earn more in royalties. For many authors, the regency romance is a labor of love.

Write On!

Movies can be an excellent way to get a feel for a particular time period. For a sense of the manners and dialogue of the Georgian/regency era, for example, watch any of the movies based on Jane Austen's novels. Films such as *Braveheart* and *Rob Roy* can give you an excellent feel for the Middle Ages. Just don't rely on the movies for your research—the details are often inaccurate!

Regency Romances

This time period has been very popular since the success of the beloved Georgette Heyer and Jane Austin. The regency subgenre is named after the nine-year period between 1811 and 1820 when King George III was declared mad and his son ruled as prince regent. However, much of the regency manners and culture stretched through the Georgian period from 1795 to 1825.

The traditional regency romances that have been around forever are short and sweet. The books run up to 75,000 words and contain no sex scenes. A new hybrid of long regencies has been met with great success. These books run 90,000 words or more and can include explicit lovemaking, longer scenes, and more subplots.

FYI:

➤ **Story lines.** They tend to revolve around whether the hero or heroine will make a socially acceptable match. Regency England was politically stable and the wealthy didn't have to worry about survival, so everyone obsessed over his social status. The *ton* (high society) used amusing phrases peculiar to the era, so familiarize yourself with the lingo. The backdrop of the Napoleonic Wars offers the opportunity for spy and intrigue subplots.

➤ **Tone.** Most regencies are light, witty, and charming.

➤ **Authors to read.** Edith Layton, Mary Balogh, Amanda Quick, Jo Beverley, and Joan Wolf.

Gothic Romances

If it's a dark and stormy night, it must be a gothic!

Gothic romances are brooding stories of *women in jeopardy* who must battle some unknown evil. In the 1960s, these book covers showed a woman fleeing from a house, and not because she hated housework! This subgenre owes much to Emily Brontë's brooding tales. Victoria Holt, Daphne DuMaurier, Mary Stewart, and Phyllis Whitney made the gothic uniquely their own, moving into the realm of romantic suspense. This subgenre tends to die and revive itself every few years, so check out the market before you start one if you're intent on getting published.

FYI:

➤ **Story lines.** Gothic romances are told in first person from the female point of view. ("I arrived at the estate ….") Typically, the plot involves an orphaned heroine who is hired as a governess by a dark and handsome hero who lives in a spooky mansion.

➤ **Tone.** Brooding and a little scary. The heroines are often financially or emotionally vulnerable. And until the end, the reader wonders if the hero is perhaps also the villain.

➤ **Authors to read.** Mary Stewart, Victoria Holt, and Phyllis Whitney.

The Wild West

Western romances are among the most popular of the American historicals. The potential for story lines is as broad and wide as the Grand Canyon: the Gold Rush, cattle barons and cowboys, sheriffs and outlaws, to name a few.

FYI:

➤ **Story lines.** Lots of Western romances focus on land—either taming it, acquiring it, or keeping it, not unlike stories in the medieval time period.

➤ **Tone.** There's plenty of room for humor in Westerns since the Wild West attracted some outlandish characters. The tone of these romances ranges from very funny and light to very dark and gritty.

➤ **Authors to read.** Shirl Henke, Elizabeth Grayson, Rosanne Bittner, Jodi Thomas, and Georgina Gentry.

Love Letters

Women in jeopardy is yet another romance subgenre. The term can be used to describe a variety of types of romance novels—from a Harlequin Intrigue to a big romantic suspense. The basic idea is that the main protagonist is a female who faces danger throughout most of the book.

Native American Romances

Native American romances, sometimes referred to by readers as Indian romances, are popular enough to qualify as a subgenre of their own. Janelle Taylor can be credited with the first interracial romances with her Gray Eagle series. Many Native American romances feature a Native American or biracial hero, who falls in love with a white heroine. Kensington's Zebra imprint and Leisure Books are big publishers of this subgenre.

FYI:

➤ **Story lines.** Many Native American romances deal with the cultural conflicts that arise between the Native American and white cultures. In romances where the woman is abducted and taken into Native American culture, for example, she's forced to examine her values and issues of social acceptance, which creates internal conflict. In many Native American tribes, women had more value and rights than they did in European-based cultures.

➤ **Tone.** Though the love relationship in these novels has a happy ending, the stories tend to be darker in tone because of the cultural and racial conflicts.

➤ **Authors to read.** Janelle Taylor, Rosanne Bittner, Georgina Gentry, Elizabeth MacDonald, Cassie Edwards, and Bobbi Smith.

Speaking of Romance ...

The beauty of the American West is that it offers so much variety to writers. "I can do so much," says veteran Western romance writer Shirl Henke. "From the Native Americans to the Spanish to the mountain men to English noblemen, Chilean tin miners, the Irish, the Cornish, the Chinese—absolutely everybody was there. So you have a fascinating international assembly of people and you can turn your story in any direction. At no other time or place do you have that many different kinds of people coming together."

As American as Apple Pie

The West isn't the only American historical setting to consider. Don't forget the Revolutionary War, the Civil War, and the conquest of the Frontier. There are also homespun romances that feature simple folk who lived in the 1800s and early 1900s. LaVyrle Spencer and Pamela Morsi are two extraordinarily talented authors who created this niche.

FYI:

➤ **Story lines.** Lots of American romances involve people who are taming new frontiers, coping with political struggles, or grappling with the elements. Stories about American high society are usually set along the East Coast, where civilization was first established.

➤ **Tone.** American romances tend to be more down-to-earth than those set in England, but not always. America is so vast it can't be defined by one attitude or writing style.

➤ **Authors to read.** Heather Graham, Jill Marie Landis, Pamela Morsi, LaVyrle Spencer, and Susan Wiggs.

Kilts and Heather

There's something irresistible about men in skirts who speak with charming brrrrrrogues. (Ach, mon! We'll talk more about dialects in Chapter 9, "Voice: Yours and Your Characters'.") To get in the mood for this popular subgenre, think *Braveheart,* but with a happy ending!

FYI:

> **Stop the Presses!**
>
> Don't try to start your historical romance without doing research. Your plot and characterization will be affected by historical events. If you plunge ahead without understanding those events, you'll find that your story lacks authenticity and relevance.

➤ **Story lines.** You'll want to research this country carefully. Scotland was ruled by family clans, which had their own unique systems of justice and honor. A number of Scottish romances deal to some extent with clan politics.

➤ **Tone.** The misty moors of Scotland seem to beg for a haunting and beautiful tone. But some authors have dealt humorously with this setting.

➤ **Authors to read.** Lois Grieman, Jude Deveraux, Bertrice Small, Julie Garwood, and Diana Gabaldon.

In a Category of Their Own

There are lots of other time periods to consider that don't fit into a well-defined subgenre. The Victorian era has its own unique charm, for example. Pick a year ... any year ... and make it work for you. Authors such as Jean Auel and Joan Wolf went so far as to write romantic stories about cave people, creating a small but popular category of fiction called "prehistory."

There are also many talented authors who don't confine themselves to the previously mentioned subgenres, such as Laura Kinsale, Penelope Williamson, Kat Martin, and Kimberly Cates, to name a few. Their readers follow them from time period to time period.

Contemporary Romances

Moving from the Ice Age to El Niño, what's hot in contemporary romances? I'm glad you asked! This is an exciting segment of the genre because it keeps growing and changing. In contemporary fiction you have series romances as well as the bigger so-called women's fiction books. Let's start first with the tried-and-true series romance lines.

Write On!

One of the advantages of category fiction is its dedicated audience. "Category is here to stay," says Jennifer Greene, author of more than 50 category romances. "If you successfully build up a readership, this field is both lucrative and likely as secure as any you can find in writing."*

Ah, Sweet Mystery of Life!

Sweet romances are just right for writers and readers who don't enjoy graphic sex scenes. Love scenes usually begin and end with the closing of the bedroom door, though the sexual tension is frequently high throughout the book. Lines include Harlequin Romance, Silhouette Romance, and Avalon Books.

FYI:

➤ **Story lines.** They're written for the "G" or "PG" audience. They revolve around everyday relationship issues and courtship but steer clear of the details of sexual intimacy.

➤ **Tone.** They tend to be clean-cut and nice, but they can also have a dark tone and deal with serious issues.

➤ **Authors to read.** Lindsay Longford, Myrna MacKenzie, Debbie Macomber, Bethany Campbell, and Maria Ferrarella.

Short but Not Necessarily Sweet

The temperature is rising here! There are many lines that publish short, sensuous romances—how sensuous depends on the line. Silhouette Desire and Harlequin Temptation are hot, hot, hot. Then again, Harlequin Presents and Kensington Precious Gems aren't exactly cool to the touch!

FYI:

- ➤ **Story lines.** Rated "R," the plots allow plenty of room for the development of strong emotions and physical attraction.
- ➤ **Tone.** Readers should be able to cut the sexual tension with a knife. Graphic descriptions of sex scenes are expected by readers.
- ➤ **Authors to read.** Jennifer Greene, Anne McAllister, Diana Palmer, Anne Marie Winston, and Beverly Barton.

Longer Category Novels

There are a number of lines that publish books that look, feel, and read like single-title books. The added length gives you a chance to do more with subplots and secondary characters. Harlequin's Superromance and American lines fit this niche, as do Silhouette's Special Edition and Intimate Moments lines. Kensington has the Bouquet Romance line. The Harlequin Intrigue line is longer as well, but sets itself apart by focusing on romantic suspense plots.

FYI:

- ➤ **Story lines.** The stories are aimed at readers who want a complete reading experience, including an array of emotion, intricate action, and in-depth characters.
- ➤ **Tone.** It varies depending on the author.
- ➤ **Authors to read.** Margaret Watson and Patricia Rosemoor for romantic suspense, Kathleen Korbel and Linda Howard for moving characters, Nora Roberts and Sharon Sala for deft plotting and shear enjoyment.

Young Love

Teens today probably know more about young-adult romances than they do about *Romeo and Juliet*. There's always a market for stories about chaste kisses and disastrous first dates. Unless you come up with the next hit "club" series, though, don't plan on retiring soon. It's tough to get rich writing in this competitive and volatile market. Lines include Bethany House, Bantam Sweet Dreams, Sweet Valley High, Harper, Parachute Press, and Willowisp.

FYI:

- ➤ **Story lines.** Some are geared toward high school readers, and some are aimed at kids in middle school. The level of sensuality, obviously, will vary based on the targeted readers, but in either case there should be no explicit sex. Veterans of this market say your story shouldn't be preachy and should definitely be fast-paced.

➤ **Tone.** Hip, as far as kids are concerned. You should study not only the tone of these books, but understand the way kids think.

➤ **Authors to read.** Sherry Garland, Lurlene McDaniel, Arlynn Presser, Wendy Corsi Staub, and Arlene Erlbach.

Inspirational Romances

There is a growing market for romances aimed at Christians. Even Harlequin/Silhouette has jumped on the bandwagon with its Steeple Hill subsidiary. The line is called Love Inspired. Inspirationals are squeaky clean and highlight family values and morals. If you're not a Christian, this is probably not the market for you. By the way, some of the *Christian publishers* will not even consider an author who also writes secular romances. Publishers include Baker Books, Barbour, Bethany House, Harvest House, Thomas Nelson, and Tyndale House.

FYI:

➤ **Story lines.** They should integrate the development of romance and faith in the main characters' lives.

➤ **Tone.** Definitely romantic, but wholesome. Any physical contact like hugging should show emotional intimacy rather than sexual longing.

➤ **Authors to read.** Robin Lee Hatcher, Francine Rivers, Lori Copeland, Cheryl Wolverton, and Lynn Bullock.

Love Letters

Christian publishers are publishing houses that print religious fiction and nonfiction books exclusively. The books are typically sold in Christian bookstores and through other religious outlets. Zondervan, Bethany House Publishers, and Tyndale House are a few of the more than half-dozen members of the Christian Booksellers Association (CBA) who publish romances.

Women's Fiction ... Bigger and Better Than Ever

Women's fiction is a broad term (so to speak) for books written by and for women. So if you think you might want to write something bigger than a category novel, listen up! You may have found your niche.

In the old days, "women's fiction" consisted mainly of Glitz 'n' Glamor books (like Judith Krantz's *Scruples*) or family sagas (like Colleen McCullough's *The Thorn Birds*). Today, those two niches are passé. The newest kid on the block is Romantic Suspense. Authors like Nora Roberts, Linda Howard, Catherine Coulter, and Tami Hoag are making a killing (pun intended) off of this new hybrid genre that combines romance with danger.

Women's fiction encompasses a lot more than suspense and women-in-jeopardy stories, though. You can write a broad multi-layered story and include distinctive elements like fantasy, adventure, angels, and friendships. Publishers run the gamut from A (Avon) to Z (Zebra). Here are a few authors with their own take on women's fiction:

➤ Susan Elizabeth Phillips writes lighthearted books with quirky characters.

➤ Kathleen Eagle writes resonant stories about the modern-day struggles of Native Americans.

➤ Barbara Delinsky, Diane Chamberlain, Deborah Smith, and Mary Alice Monroe create in-depth characters and plots revolving around women's issues and friendships.

➤ Jennifer Crusie and Susan Andersen go all out for humor.

Other authors to read: Donna Julian, Kristin Hannah, Tess Gerritsen, Eileen Dreyer, Merline Lovelace, Meryl Sawyer, Stella Cameron, Carla Neggers, and Katherine Stone.

Stop the Presses!

If you decide to write a multicultural romance, make sure you don't let the multicultural aspect overwhelm the love story. Publishers aren't looking for a social treatise. They're looking for stories that exhibit strong emotion and good storytelling.

Characters of Color

One of the most exciting new developments in the romance genre is the birth of ethnic and *multicultural romances*. In plain English, that means that romance readers of Latino, Asian, and African-American descent can finally read about lovers who look like them. And it's not just a color thing. When appropriate, the characters should be rooted in their culture. Beverly Jenkins says her African-American historical romances have been so well received that she's been swamped by thousands of fan letters from readers who say they've hungered for this kind of fiction.

Love Letters

Multicultural romances are love stories that include the flavor and culture of ethnic experiences. The culture might be African-American, Hispanic, Asian, or otherwise.

Kensington Publishing Corp. led the charge with Arabesque Books, which has since been sold to Black Entertainment Television (BET). Kensington also launched the Encanto line of Hispanic contemporary romances. Genesis Press is another multicultural publisher with several imprints: Tango2 for Latin romances, Indigo for African-American romances, and Love Spectrum for interracial romances. Some traditional houses like Avon include ethnic romances in their regular lines as well.

Authors to read include Shirley Hailstock, Eboni Snoe, Sandra Kitt, and Beverly Jenkins.

Beyond Reality (and Other Nifty New Trends)

Nothing strike your fancy yet? Then how about a little unreality? In the old days, there were romance novels and science-fiction novels and never the twain did meet. Now you can feel free to include sci-fi and fantasy elements in your romance.

And what the heck! While you're at it, why not throw in a vampire, too? Penguin-Putnam's Berkley/Jove imprints have cultivated this market with lines devoted to the paranormal.

Time Travel (or What Century Is This Anyway?)

This popular niche can thank H. G. Wells for its birth. He was the first writer to introduce the time machine. June Lund Shiplett carried the torch into the romance genre with *Journey to Yesterday*. And Constance O'Day-Flannery followed with a number of successful time-travel romances.

In these fun novels, romance heroines and heroes hurtle backward and forward through time, often with hilarious results. You must juggle three main elements: the romance, the method of time travel, and the traveling character's decision whether to go or to stay. Balancing these can be tricky, but you rarely run out of things to write about.

Authors to read include Linda Lael Miller, Eugenia Riley, Dara Joy, and Lynn Kurland.

Futuristic and Fantasy

These two subgenres are fairly small in comparison to the others, but doubtless have a core of devoted fans. Futuristic romances combine romance and science fiction. Fantasy romances include typical fantasy novel elements such as magic kingdoms and characters with special powers, for example the *second sight* and the ability to heal with touch. You might consider "friendly and trendy" new elements such as angels and fairies.

Stop the Presses!

Before you pitch a paranormal romance to an editor, find out what she's looking for. Many editors won't consider magical elements at all. And those who will are very particular about what they want. Berkley/Jove, for example, has a line called Haunting Hearts dedicated to light ghost stories. Another Berkley/Jove line is called Magical Love, which can include elements of magic ... but no ghosts! So investigate the market.

Love Letters

Second sight is the ability to see events before they happen, or to see events happening far away. Sometimes called "the sight," precognition is sometimes used in medieval or fantasy romances.

Authors to read include Jayne Castle (a.k.a. Jayne Ann Krentz), Justine Davis, Kathleen Morgan, J. D. Robb (a.k.a. Nora Roberts), and Mary Alice Kruesi (a.k.a. Mary Alice Monroe).

Ghosties and Ghoulies

The paranormal romance has definitely arrived in a big way. Romances featuring ghosts, vampires, empaths, and clairvoyants have found an enthusiastic audience. However, there are only so many paranormal elements to choose from. To make your story unique, you'll need a distinctive voice (or writing style).

Authors to read include Anne Stuart, Linda Lael Miller, Susan Carroll, Modean Moon, and Angie Ray.

Phew!!!!

That's a lot of romance. You now have an excellent overview of the genre. The next step is figuring out what's right for you. I'll tell you how to do that in the next chapter, so stick around!

The Least You Need to Know

➤ The tone of your book should fit the subgenre you choose.

➤ Romantic suspense is one of the hottest trends in women's fiction.

➤ You can pick a traditional romance category or subgenre or you can create your own.

➤ The popularity of certain subgenres rises and falls, so research the market before you invest a lot of time in a subgenre that's hibernating.

➤ You should take the time to read the best authors in the subgenre of your choice.

Match Made in Heaven

You look across the crowded room. Suddenly, you know it's love at first sight. Your heart begins to hammer. Your cheeks flush with warmth and you beam with an ecstatic smile. This is it—the passion you've been waiting for! You push your way through the crowded room and reach out with open arms. You grab the book from the shelf and rush to the cash register. Now that you've found the kind of romance you feel passionately about, you're not going to let it get away!

What did you think I was talking about? Not every happy ending has to include a man, you know! Finding a subgenre or a style of romance writing that truly excites you is one of the happiest endings of all for an aspiring writer. In this chapter, I'll show you ways to find your own niche so you can write happily ever after.

Read, Read, Read!

After reading Chapter 3, "Love Is a Many Splendored Thing," you know how much variety there is in the romance genre. But it's not enough to know it intellectually. You have to experience it as a reader. You have to get excited by a romance before you try to write one. There are many reasons to read as much as possible before you start your book. Reasons other than keeping published authors in business, that is!

I Loved That Book!

Have you ever read a romance you loved so much you couldn't wait to tell someone about it? If so, you may have found the kind of romance you want to write. If not, keep reading. Chances are, there is an author or a niche out there that will really turn you on. Once you find it, you'll feel like a ship that's finally found a harbor. Reading is the best way to find out what you like and what you want to write.

Read Between the Lines

It's hard to predict what kind of books publishers will be looking for in the future, but you can certainly figure out what they've bought recently. Just look at what's being published. Of course, what you see on the shelves now was purchased more than a year ago—for readers, that's as current as it gets.

To make sure you're reading the latest releases, look at the copyright page. It's usually located in the front of the novel. You'll see the copyright symbol, ©, followed by the author's name and the year the book was published. Try to read books that have been published in the last year or two so you know what's most current. That's not to say that you can't learn from older romances. Many of the genre's best remain in print for years. But reader's preferences evolve over time. You want to know what today's readers are looking for.

The Latest Styles

The romance genre is like the fashion industry. Styles change. Fifteen years ago, long, wordy historicals were all the rage. Authors often put the action on hold so they could spend paragraphs, or even pages, describing costumes and scenery. The longer and more flowery the sentences, the better. Now the opposite is true. In romances today …

➤ *Narration* is kept to a minimum.

➤ Costume descriptions are brief and usually just long enough to set the scene.

➤ There is a lot of *dialogue,* which is often used instead of narration to pass along exposition (information) to the reader.

➤ The story frequently starts in the middle of a scene to make sure the pace gets off to a roaring start.

Love Letters

Narration is the storytelling, the words spoken by the narrator, who is usually an invisible observer. **Dialogue** is what the characters say, the words in between the quotation marks. A good book balances both narration and dialogue. However, many of today's romances effectively use much more dialogue than narration.

These are all style changes. Only by reading recent books—and lots of them—will you get a sense of the current trends in style.

Appearing in a Bookstore Near You

Where's the best place to find good romances? They can be found anywhere, including your local gas station. If you can't find what you want, put on your Sherlock Holmes hat and investigate the options.

The Virtues of Mom and Pop

If you have a local bookstore that's not part of a chain, it's probably run by a bookseller who will bend over backward to find what you want. If it's a romance-friendly store, you'll also get good tips on what romances are selling well and why. You can learn a lot from the independent bookseller, and, at the same time, help him compete against the superstore chains that are dominating the market.

A Link in the Chain

The smaller stores operated by chains such as B. Dalton, Waldenbooks, and Crown Books usually have a great supply of romance novels. They often have at least one staff member who knows the romance market and can make book recommendations. Waldenbooks and B. Dalton publish monthly newsletters highlighting current romance novels. Reading these free publications is a good way to determine trends and identify authors who are on the rise because of publisher support.

Superstore Mania

The super-size bookstores (you know, the ones that contain coffee shops) are the newest trend in the book-selling biz. These chains are forcing many smaller stores out of business. On the upside, the big stores like Barnes and Noble and Borders often have not only new books, but authors' back lists as well. So, if you liked one book by an author, you can easily pick up the author's previous titles, too. Unfortunately, superstores usually shelve novels spine out, which makes browsing difficult.

Write On!

A number of independent bookstores have closed in recent years, but the "indies" are starting to fight back against the superstore chains. The American Booksellers Association is launching an e-commerce site that would allow readers to buy books through independent stores over the Internet. The Web site, www.booksense.com, will debut in early 2000.

New and Used

New and used stores are usually small storefront operations that sell a few new titles and lots of used books. Hopefully, for the authors' sakes, you will buy very few books secondhand since authors don't earn any royalties on books sold a second time. However, the owners of used bookstores often know the market backward and forward and are a great source for recommendations. And sometimes a used store is the only place to find an older book that's no longer in print. Most authors hope that if you enjoy one of their books bought in the "used" section, you'll look for their next novel in the "new titles" area of the store.

A Brave New Book-Selling World

The Internet has turned out to be a convenient way to buy books. Sites such as Amazon.com and Barnesandnoble.com offer a wide variety of titles at discounted rates. How do you use this service? Just type in the online store's URL (Web site address), such as www.amazon.com, and when the site appears, enter the title or author you want to find in the search box.

If you put in the author's name, all of his or her available titles will appear. If you open up a screen on a particular title, you can find a list of other similar books. For example, on the listing for my medieval novel, *Falcon and the Sword,*

Amazon.com says readers who bought that book also tended to buy books by Suzanne Robinson. So that's a good way to find authors who may write in a similar vein.

Narrowing the Choices

What do you read when there are so many books to chose from? Go to a bookstore and do the following:

1. Browse for titles and covers that appeal to you.

2. Turn the book over and read the *blurb* on the back cover to see if the story sounds appealing to you.

3. Read the first page and see if you like the author's writing style.

4. If the book gets a thumbs up after steps one through three, buy the book. You'll probably like it. If you like it, you may want to write something similar.

This isn't a scientific process. Go with what appeals to you. After all, these are the same steps readers will be making when trying to decide whether to buy your book!

Love Letters

The **blurb** is the text found on the back cover of the book. It's usually a two- or three-paragraph description of the story. The whole point of the blurb is to entice you into buying the book. It's so important to the sale that some authors actually get to be involved in writing the blurb. However, the blurbs are usually written by freelance writers.

Making a Decision

Now it's time to narrow your focus. To do this, you have to make some broad decisions by answering some questions. Namely ...

➤ Do I like the contemporaries or historicals best?

➤ If I want to write contemporaries, do I want to write the bigger single-title books or the category romances?

➤ If I want to write historicals, what period and what level of sensuality do I want to use?

After you answer these questions, you should start reading books that fit the niche you've identified. Let's say you're considering writing a category romance. Read a few books from all the categories—try a Harlequin Romance *and* a Silhouette Romance. Note the differences or similarities. Read a Harlequin Temptation *and* a Silhouette Desire. And don't forget Kensington's Precious Gems line (available in

Wal-Mart) and Avalon romances (available in libraries). Read the longer category books, too.

Now step back and decide which category line appealed to you most. That's probably the line you should be writing for. To see if your taste in stories will fit in, read as many authors and titles in that line as you can. And now congratulate yourself. You've done far more homework than most of the people who sit down to write a novel.

Have Some Spine!

The process of sifting through a stack of single-title romances is a little different. Once you find books that you really like, look at the imprint, which is located on the spine of the book.

The imprint, by the way, is not the same as the publisher. For example, Penguin-Putnam publishes paperback romances under several imprints, including Berkley, Jove, NAL, and Signet. Penguin-Putnam's name is listed on the copyright page inside the books, but the spines will say Berkley, Jove, NAL or Signet. If you start to see the same imprint on the spines of the novels you like, you've found a publisher who might be interested in your work.

Write On!

If a favorite author mentions an editor in her acknowledgments, write down the editor's name. When it's time to submit your book, query that editor. Tell her you've been following her work, and mention your love of her author's work. It will indicate you've studied the market, and it just might make the editor more inclined to look at your manuscript!

Ten Signs of a Great Romance

As a reader, you already know everything you need to know about good books. Basically, you know a good one when you read one! But since you also want to be a writer, you have to be a little more analytical than that. You need to know why books are good and how they affect readers. That knowledge will come in handy when you start to write your own novel.

How do you know when you've found a fabulous romance? Here are a few clues:

1. You buy into the premise and hang with it until the end.

2. You fall in love with the hero and/or heroine.

3. You think of the characters as people, not characters.

4. You read faster during the climactic scenes because you want to know what happens next.

5. You start reading slower near the end because you don't want to say goodbye to the characters.

6. You truly wonder if the hero and heroine will work out their problems.

7. You get turned on by the *sexual tension.*

8. You hope for a sequel.

9. You can either relate to the way the hero and heroine express their love, or you wish you could experience love as they do.

10. You tingle all over when you close the book for the last time because it was so good!

Creating a World of Your Own

Not every great book will affect you in the same way. Some books will move you to tears and make you appreciate the poignancy and fragility of love. Others will make you laugh and root for the characters and reinforce your faith in the decency of the human race. A book's effect on the reader is a result of the attitudes and outlook of the writer.

So what effect do you want to have on readers? What message or theme will your books communicate? What emotions do you want your readers feel after reading your love story?

You need to decide what kind of experience you want your readers to have. You also need to decide what kind of romance suits your personal outlook and attitudes. Following is a worksheet to help you evaluate what kind of story would suit you best:

Love Letters

Sexual tension is the attraction between the hero and heroine. They're both aware of it, but often it goes unacknowledged. The reader can see it, too, and wonders with anticipation when the attraction will lead to satisfaction. That's how sexual tension can help make a romance a "page turner."

Evaluation Worksheet

1. As a writer, I want to …

    a) Move my readers to tears.

    b) Make them laugh.

    c) Amuse them with charming characters and a cozy world.

    d) Take them on a wild, adventurous journey.

    e) Or _____

2. I feel best when I'm writing scenes that are …

    a) Fast-paced and snappy.

    b) Rich in detail and multilayered.

    c) Full of innuendoes and sexual tension.

    d) Sweet and focused on the goodness of my characters.

    e) Or _____

3. I believe my greatest strength as a writer will be …

    a) Developing real characters the reader feels she truly knows.

    b) Creating clever plots with lots of twists and turns.

    c) Creating a unique and rich world the reader wants to inhabit.

    d) Showing the psychology and inner motivations of characters.

    e) Or _____

4. I sense that I'm best suited to a book that …

    a) Has one main plot focusing mostly on the hero and heroine.

    b) Has lots of subplots and many secondary characters.

    c) Or _____

5. My personality is best suited to a book that is full of …

    a) Angst and looming danger.

    b) Humor and whimsical characters.

    c) Hip dialogue and trendy accessories.

    d) Insights and touching realizations.

    e) Or _____

Now examine your answers. Jot them down, and add anything else to the list you'd like to include. Compare your list to the descriptions in Chapter 3. Find the subgenre or category line that seems to best fit your style.

Picture This ...

As you start making general choices, there's a good possibility that something very specific and very significant will happen as a result. A scene will pop into your head out of nowhere. When that happens, write it down it in a notebook. This is the beginning of your novel! When you start seeing scenes, you know that your imagination has begun building a story. This is truly an exciting moment!

You may see a scene between your hero and heroine, kissing or arguing, picking flowers or meeting for the first time. You may see a fight scene or an amusing incident at the ballpark. Remember these events because you will probably use them in your novel. The scene may start your book, end it, or land somewhere in between. But this is how your characters are created. They take on a life of their own in your head, doing and saying things unique to their personalities.

Putting It All Together

Now that you know what kinds of romances are being published, you have a general idea what direction you want to go in, and you have characters coming to life in your head. How do you mix them all together? Very carefully! Or rather, very respectfully. You can't force characters into a plot or setting that doesn't suit them, so try to get to know your hero and heroine before you lock them into an ill-fitting plot.

Testing the Creative Waters

Trying to mix characters, plot, and setting takes some finesse on your part. Be patient. You have to feel your way through this process. That's what I did when finding a time period for my novel *Romance of the Rose*.

Write On!

Very few writers are strong in all areas of the creative process. Some authors have fabulous writing styles, some are masterful at plotting, some have an uncanny ability to heighten emotion, while others are simply good at creating a world that readers want to spend time in. Recognize your strengths and work on your weaker skills, but don't obsess about them. Leave that to the critics!

Stop the Presses!

Characters are at the heart of every romance. If you're the kind of writer who starts with a plot, be sure to take the time to develop your hero and heroine as you go. Great action scenes won't be exciting if you haven't created living, breathing characters to inhabit them. Romances aren't about events; they're about people and feelings.

The hero and heroine appeared in my head late one night when I was driving. They were having a terrible fight! I quickly realized that my heroine, Lady Rosalind Carbery, had almost as much personal freedom as my hero, so she probably wouldn't fit into the Middle Ages—the period I'd focused on up to that point. Then, I remembered that women in Shakespeare's time had a lot of freedom. Suddenly, it clicked. The Elizabethan era was perfect for my tempestuous heroine. Once I had the right setting, everything else fell into place.

If the Shoe Doesn't Fit

What happens if you go through this process only to discover that your story just doesn't fit into any of the categories or subgenres I've talked about? What if your characters start to gel, you find the perfect plot, and your setting couldn't be better … but none of it fits a niche? Don't panic! We can work this out.

Sizing Up the Problem

If the shoe doesn't fit, you may need a new size, or you may need a new store. It's possible that your story simply doesn't fit the romance genre. If your hero and heroine are headed for divorce court, for example, with no reconciliation in sight, you definitely will have to find a different genre! But that's the last solution to consider. As my mother always said, moderation in all things … including writing.

Write On!

Just in case you're wondering, you can throw the baby out with the bath water. I give you permission. Sometimes a fledgling story has so many problems it's best to trash it and start over. It doesn't mean your creative process is broken. It simply means that you're smart enough to know when to give up and try something better.

Redesigning the Shoe

If the shoe still doesn't fit, stretch it. If your plot is causing problems, rework it. Oh, sure, you have these great characters with melodramatic tendencies. The hero is telling you he wants to kiss the heroine goodbye and walk off into the sunset in a poignant scene that will leave the reader sobbing. Tell him to get with the program! He can be melodramatic throughout the book, but he'd better get his act together by the end and say "I do" with a smile on his face.

I've found from many a revision (requested by my editor) that my stories can go a hundred different ways, and all of them will work as long as I'm true to my characters. I can even nudge my characters into doing things differently for a change as long as I don't change the essence of who they are. See if you can make a few changes in your plot to fit the niche you're aiming for.

Try a Boot!

If the shoe still doesn't fit .... Oh, forget this silly serial simile (and forget the alliteration, too!). If your story won't fit into a niche or category, no matter how hard you try to stuff it in, it could be you are destined for something bigger or newer.

If your story won't fit a category, maybe it's a big book waiting to be born. If it doesn't fit the tone or form of any of the subgenres, maybe you are destined to create a new one. Maybe you're a trend-setter! While that might seem a little scary, remember that if you march to a different drummer, you just might end up leading the band.

Be a Trend-Setter

Being a trend-setter is sort of like being Austin Powers, the big-screen international man of mystery. You don't realize you're trendy until you're already passé. (Okay, so I stretched a metaphor!) Here's my point: Few writers set out to write a novel with the intention of setting a trend. They usually sit down to write either a great book or a best-seller.

Here's a quick peek at some trend-setting romance authors and what they did for the genre:

➤ Kathleen Woodiwiss put love and sex into the big historical book.

➤ Janet Daily transported the British category romance to American soil.

➤ LaVyrle Spencer took historical romances from glittering ballrooms to dilapidated shacks, creating fabulous characters who were plain on the outside but beautiful inside.

➤ Constance O'Day-Flannery wrote time-travel novels before it was the cool thing to do.

➤ Susan Elizabeth Phillips fine-tuned the light, humorous read with skillfully drawn and quirky characters.

How did these women succeed in setting trends, or in at least expanding the genre? Let's look at what they have in common:

1. They all took a familiar fiction form and reshaped it to fit the needs of their own inner vision.

2. They all have strong voices (or writing styles).

3. They all took a chance and wrote the kind of book *they* wanted to write.

By the way, you don't have to be a trend-setter. Writing a darned good book is a great accomplishment in itself. In fact, some veteran writers advise beginners to get a book or two under their belts before attempting something radically new.

LaVyrle Spencer and Rosamunde Pilcher both wrote short categories before breaking out into broader romantic fiction.

Speaking of Romance ...

Only you can decide if you're ready to break all the rules in the book. But a word of advice from RITA award–winner Kasey Michaels, author of over 50 books: "The romance genre starts nearly every new trend, pushes more envelopes than Publishers Clearing House sends through the mail, is more innovative than any other genre, has more editors willing to try new ideas. The trick is to establish yourself in print first, become solid in your writing, learn how to do your job well, and then jump off the creative bridge into new territory, because by then you'll have your professional parachute of experience."*

Stop the Presses!

Don't try to ride the latest trends in fiction. By the time you recognize the trend, it will probably already be several years old. It will take you time to write your trendy novel, and it will take your publisher another year to bring it out. By then the trend might be a glut in the marketplace.

Oops! There Goes Another Trend

If you're not a trend-setter, that doesn't mean you have to be a trend-follower. You should write the book from your heart. If it fits a current trend, great! Just don't waste your time chasing that rainbow.

Trying to ride a trend in fiction is like trying to surf the big kahuna. Once you finally reach the crest of the wave, you might discover it has already peaked and you're about to crash into the shore. Most agents recommend that you forget about trends and simply write the book that *you* want to write.

Probably the most recognizable trend in the publishing industry is the lawyer book. It's been going strong for years, undoubtedly making John Grisham and Scott Turrow very rich in the process.

The biggest trend right now (meaning at the time I'm writing this book) in the category romance industry is the cowboy-rancher-baby-bride books. Here are a few titles:

➤ *The Cowboy, the Baby and the Runaway Bride,* by Lindsay Longford

➤ *The Rancher and the Amnesiac Bride,* by Joan Elliot Pickart

➤ *The Rancher and the Runaway Bride,* by Joan Johnston

➤ *The Cowboy, the Baby and the Bride-To-Be,* by Cara Colter

These books often feature independent cowboys or ranchers who need to be coaxed into settling down, and single mothers who need a good father for their children as well as a loving husband.

Category publishers are pretty explicit about what they're looking for. They actively seek out plots and subjects they think readers want. Sometimes that doesn't leave much wiggle room if your stories deviate from the editor's expectations. On the upside, when editors are specific about what they want, you have a clear goal to shoot for. If you want to write category romances, here's some good advice:

➤ Look closely at publisher guidelines *before* you start.

➤ Network with other writers about what editors are looking for. (More on networking in Chapter 24, "Romancing the Industry.")

Single-title publishers tend to be less explicit about the kinds of stories they want. That gives you more freedom—but it also gives you less structure and guidance.

Write On!

Silhouette executive Senior Editor Leslie Wainger says cowboys and babies are elements that should continue to sell well in the new millennium. As she explains it, the cowboy is a classic American archetype that will always be a favorite. And since Baby Boomers approach parenting and grandparenting with an almost professional zeal, romances involving children will continue to draw readers.

Hardcover, Here I Come!

"But wait a minute! Hold the phone! Forget paperbacks. I want my book to come out in hardcover!"

If these thoughts have crossed your mind, let me gently put them in perspective for you. Being published in hardcover is definitely a possibility—now more than ever. Romance authors are regularly published in hardcover and regularly appear on the *New York Times* Bestseller list. However, very few of these authors started with hardcover books. Many wrote dozens of romances before they saw their first hardcover edition.

Authors such as Catherine Coulter, Nora Roberts, Johanna Lindsey, Julie Garwood, Kathleen Eagle, and Sandra Brown broke into the hardcover market because of one of two reasons: 1) they started writing broader fiction, 2) they had such a huge following their publishers knew loyal fans would fork over the money for a hardbound edition.

Here are two good reasons to hope your book comes out in a hardcover edition:

➤ Your book won't be picked up by the mail book clubs unless it is a hardcover.

➤ Some readers won't touch your book with a 10-foot pole if it's a paperback. So a hardcover edition exposes you to a wider audience.

The only downside of hardcover editions is that they are often too expensive for traditional romance readers, who tend to buy dozens of books every month. I've never seen an author turn down a hardcover offer for that reason, though. So if Dutton offers you a contract … say yes! Your cost-conscious fans can just wait until the paperback edition follows.

Love Letters

A **hard-soft deal** is one in which a publisher buys the rights to print your book in hardcover and paperback. Typically, the hardcover version will come out first, and the paperback issue will be released a year later, often in conjunction with the release of your next hardcover novel.

Cinderella … and the Rest of Us

You may be one of the lucky ones. You may live out one of the classic romance fantasies and be Cinderella. A fairy godmother (a publisher) may appear at your door with a golden carriage (a three-book *hard-soft deal*) ready to transport you to the ball (New York). You'll meet Prince Charming (a powerful critic) who declares you a princess (the hot new author) and throngs of townspeople (adoring readers) hail your virtues (run out and buy your book).

Or … you may be like the rest of us. You start with one book, then hopefully publish another and another until you have a following. And *then* you go hardcover. I hope you turn out to be Cinderella, but if not, you'll be in good company!

The Least You Need to Know

➤ Reading is the best way to prepare to write a novel of your own.

➤ Start to analyze why you enjoy certain books.

➤ Figure out what kind of writing style best suits your attitudes and outlook on life.

➤ Following trends is often an exercise in futility.

➤ You can analyze what's selling, but remember that editors are always looking for books written from the heart.

Chapter 5

Lover's Leap

In This Chapter

➤ Ideas are all around you—just grab one!

➤ Two things that every published writer does

➤ When, how, and where to write

➤ How to overcome doubts and fears

➤ A sure-fire way to get started

Pssst! I have a secret for you. Most professional writers aren't as confident as you think. They may know from past experience that they'll have a book finished by deadline, but often they aren't sure if the book is any good until it's done. So here's the deal: If even the pros feel insecure now and then, why shouldn't you? It's okay to doubt yourself, and your book, as long as you keep writing!

In this chapter, I'll show you some steps you can use to overcome first-time jitters. I'll give you tips on how to come up with ideas and how to get yourself to page one. Most important, I hope to convince you that the time to start your novel is now!

Got Ideas?

If there is one question that *every* author has probably heard, it's "Where do you get your ideas?" I usually just shrug. Ideas come from your imagination and most people who want to write have that in spades. You do! If you're not convinced of that, then it's time for another pop quiz.

Do You Have Imagination?

Yes	No	
_____	_____	Do you ever remember your nighttime dreams?
_____	_____	Do you ever guess how a movie will end before it's over?
_____	_____	Do you wince when you read a news account of a gruesome crime?
_____	_____	Do you ever embellish details when you repeat an anecdote?
_____	_____	Do you ever mentally fill in the details of narrative radio hits—songs such as John Cougar's "Jack and Diane," or Harry Chapin's "Cat's in the Cradle," or Aerosmith's "Janie's Gotta Gun"?
_____	_____	Do you ever buy a lottery ticket and fantasize so much about winning that you nearly have yourself moved into the Vanderbilt Mansion before the winning ticket is drawn?

If you answered yes to any of these, you have imagination. Imagination isn't a secret form of alchemy that only professional writers are privy to. Everybody has it. That means you can definitely come up with an idea for a novel. If you don't already have one eating away inside of you, waiting to be written, fear not. There are lots of places and ways to find story ideas.

Music, Music, Music!

I used music to come up with the idea for my Elizabethan novel *Romance of the Rose*. Remember that I said the characters popped into my head in the car? I was driving home from my job as a TV news writer, listening to the radio, when a pop rock song (I don't even remember what it was) triggered an image. I started seeing Michael Douglas and Kathleen Turner in the movie *War of the Roses* throwing objects at each other. I hadn't even seen the movie, but I'd seen the scene in the previews. Suddenly it occurred to me: Why not have that kind of extreme battle of wills in a historical setting? Thus, my idea and my characters were born. I started with the fighting lovers and built my "Taming of the Shrew" romance from there.

Music has a unique and universal way of stirring the soul and arousing feelings. What kinds of music can you use to inspire ideas? Any kind. Try classical, pop rock, jazz, New Age, Irish, African, or Scottish music, to name just a few. Different kinds might inspire different ideas. For example, you might ...

➤ Listen to a jazzy torch song and get in touch with your character's sense of lost love.

➤ Listen to an upbeat show tune and decide to write a romantic comedy.

➤ Listen to Mozart's *Requiem* and come up with a tortured historical hero whose angst is as deep as the ocean.

➤ Listen to Irish pub music and come up with a whimsical comedy-of-errors plot involving Irish immigrants in New York.

Take time from your writing to listen and be inspired.

Reel Romantic

A great movie is like a great novel. Both have the power to transport you to a different world. So when the well of your imagination seems to be running dry, go see a flick. You might see an actor, a plotline, a mood, or a setting that works for you. I'm not suggesting you steal plots scene by scene from movies—hopefully you have more imagination than that! But at the very least, movies can inspire you. They can also key you into new cultural trends.

Write On!

Dream analysts say a great way to increase your ability to remember dreams is to jot them down first thing in the morning. Likewise, if you jot down story ideas in a journal, you're telling your creative imagination that you're paying attention. The simple act of writing down an idea can motivate your imagination to come up with even more ideas.

Stop the Presses!

Story ideas are contagious. Everybody seems to catch the same ones around the same time. You may think you have a unique plot, but then you go to the movies a month later and see it on the big screen. It's almost as if ideas rise from your brain into the ozone layer and then scatter into the wind. So, if you have a hot plot idea, start writing now before someone else comes out with the book!

If It's Good Enough for Shakespeare ...

We all know that William Shakespeare was brilliant. But did you know that he was the Elizabethan equivalent of a pop-fiction writer? It was his job to make sure the seats were filled at the Globe Theatre in England. Fortunately for us, the plays he dashed off for this mercenary purpose also just happened to be timeless classics.

If you feel like you're on shaky ground when it comes to plotting, consider falling back on stories that worked for the greats like the Bard. He took ideas from other sources; why can't you borrow from him? Here are a few possibilities:

➤ A romance featuring star-crossed lovers with bickering families—without the tragic ending, of course! (*Romeo and Juliet*)

➤ A comedy of errors involving mistaken identities and a girl who dresses up like a boy. (*Twelfth Night*)

➤ A romance highlighting the hero's journey from youth to manhood set against the backdrop of a war. (*Henry V*)

You can blow the dust off a few other classics as well. You contemporary folks should check out the movie remake of *Great Expectations* starring Ethan Hawke and Gwyneth Paltrow. That was a great romance based on Charles Dickens' classic tale. My nineteenth-century romance titled *My Fair Lord* used the plot from *Pygmalion* courtesy of George Bernard Shaw. You probably remember the movie titled *My Fair Lady*. However, I added a twist. Instead of having a lower-class heroine, I had a rogue—a hero who had to be transformed into a gentleman. There are always ways to make old stories new and fresh.

Brainstorm Predicted

When all else fails, you can sit down and brainstorm. Come to think of it, brainstorming may be the best place to start. What is brainstorming? Well, picture it literally—a storm of ideas swirling around in your head. There are three ways to go about this—alone, with a friend, or with a group of friends.

Harvesting Your Creativity

The simplest way to brainstorm is to ask yourself the short but profound question, "What if?" Here's an example off the top of my head:

What if my heroine had become pregnant by the hero when she was a teenager, but he didn't know about the pregnancy? What if he returns home for a 25-year high school reunion? What if he doesn't even remember her? (Oh, no!) What if he unwittingly starts flirting with his own daughter? (Ugh!)

Okay, okay, that's a terrible idea. But at least it's an idea. The "What if?" question can lead you in many directions. Go with the flow, and then separate the good ideas from the bad.

Speaking of Romance ...

Best-selling historical romance author Jill Marie Landis belongs to a plotting group made up of five published writers who work in different subgenres. Jill says: "You get five different points of view on how your book could go, and you can take them or leave them. It fills in a lot of holes. Somebody will ask a key question like, 'What's his motivation?' or 'What's the key conflict?' Somebody else might notice you don't have any conflict. It helps you validate whether your story is working or not. Somebody will say 'That's a great idea' or 'Gee, I just read a book like that.' You always think your own baby is pretty. But you put it out there and discover it might not be."

Take a Hike!

A great way to come up with ideas is to get away from it all. Take a long walk and force yourself to think only about story ideas. Or take a long drive in the car. I do my best plotting on the 5½-hour trip from Chicago to St. Louis. You can't get distracted in a car and walk away. Or try programming your subconscious: Before you go to bed, tell yourself you want to come up with an idea and let your mind work it out in your dreams. Asking for ideas really works. My brain usually delivers within a week or so.

Group Brainstorming

At some point you may find a critiquing partner or a group of writer friends you value and trust. If so, you can try a group brainstorming session. Your conversation might go something like this:

You: I have this idea about a corporate raider who wakes up one day and realizes he doesn't like himself very much. The heroine sings in an Irish pub and has 10 brothers and sisters, and she's never been able to fall in love. She wants a big family but is worried about money, since her parents were so poor. She has fantasies about rich men but thinks they're all selfish. That's all I have so far.

Karen: I can really see her living someplace like Chicago, because you have the big corporations and all the ethnic groups, too.

Rose: I've got a great idea. What if he quits his job and decides he's going to run for mayor to give something back to the community. They meet when he's campaigning on Irish alley and ….

Pam: Oh, oh, I've got it! He finds out that politics are even more soul-numbing than the corporate world.

You: Yeah, but what's the internal conflict that keeps them apart until the end?

Karen: Maybe he wants all her attention and she's not willing to devote herself to him. She feels obligated to care for her family.

You: Naw, I don't see her that way. What if …

See how it works? It's an amazing process when you work with the right people. Just be careful not to lose your own vision. Some writers would never dream of involving others in this way, for fear they'll end up writing someone else's story. Others feel it's a great way to fine-tune characters.

Write On!

Do you ever sit in front of your computer and stare at a blank screen, waiting for words to come, the longer you sit, the more stuck you feel? If so, try something different. Sit in an easy chair with a notepad and write by hand, or dig out your old manual typewriter. Once the story starts to flow, you can ease yourself back in front of the computer.

The First Date (with Your Computer)

"Do I look okay? My idea's not too fat, is it? Are my characters wearing the right outfits? Oh! There he is: My Muse. He's knocking at my door. He's early! Wow, is he good-looking. Oh, but I'm not ready. Tell him to go away and come back another time. I have to wash my hair!"

—Excerpt from a conversation you don't want to have

Sometimes sitting down to start a new book feels like a first date. Naturally, you're nervous. But it's exciting, too, isn't it? Just think—you may create an award-winning, bestselling novel! But you'll never know until you sit down and open your first computer file or slip your first sheet of paper into the typewriter.

A Professional Rewriter

You can count on rewriting your book once, twice, maybe even a dozen times. I'd say 99.9 percent of the books you see in bookstores have been rewritten. Hemingway reportedly rewrote *For Whom the Bell Tolls* more than two dozen times! Instead of calling yourself a writer, just start calling yourself a rewriter.

So if a *rewrite* is a given, guess what? It doesn't have to be perfect the first time! To make starting your book easier, I want you to type the following sentence, cut it out, and tape it to your computer:

No Perfectionists Allowed—Writer At Work Here!

Perfectionists make lousy writers. They write one sentence, sit back, and judge it. It can't possibly measure up, so they replace it with another sentence, which also doesn't measure up. By the end of the day, they're lucky if they have even one paragraph written. A word of advice: Don't go there. Life is too short.

Two Things You Must Do

I can absolutely, positively, unquestionably guarantee that you must accomplish two things before you get published:

➤ You must start your book.

➤ You must finish your book.

Duh, Julie, tell me something I didn't know! Okay. You know it on an intellectual level, but you won't *really* know it until you do it. There are probably 10 million people in this world who want to write a book and get it published. Only a fraction of those people will ever sit down and start one. An even tinier fraction will ever finish one. Why not be one of the few?

Here are some incentives. If you actually complete a book …

➤ You'll be waaaaaay ahead of the game.

➤ You'll rightly feel an incredible sense of satisfaction.

➤ You'll garner much more interest from editors.

Editors rarely buy unfinished books from beginning authors.

Love Letters

Rewriting is something you do after you have a first draft of your entire book, or you might rewrite each chapter as you go along. A **revision,** on the other hand, is requested by your editor. She asks you to revise your story based on her comments and suggestions.

A Closet of One's Own

You can see it now—a quaint cabin in the woods, a dog sleeping before the fire, the perfect cup of tea steaming at your desk, and absolutely no interruptions. Sounds like the ideal place to write a book, doesn't it? Yes, and for most people it is and always will be nothing more than a fantasy.

It would be nice to have the perfect writing space, but I've been looking for one for 15 years and I still haven't found it. My husband complains that I've put a desk in every room in the house. I once even rented a room from a neighbor just to get some peace and quiet! But I still managed to write books.

Speaking of Romance ...

African-American historical romance author Beverly Jenkins wrote her first book sitting on the floor of a closet with her typewriter propped on a box. "I was able to close the door and didn't have to worry about cleaning it," says Beverly. "So when people tell me they don't have a place to write, that's bull****." Her next four books were written at a desk under the stairs in an unfinished basement. "My daughter used to call the spiders my pets," Beverly says, laughing. "It was so cold down there! I tell people that's why I wrote such heated love scenes—to keep me warm during the Michigan winters." With her fifth book, Beverly graduated to a real office. Yeah! Let's hear it for perseverance.

Just because this is a fantasy does not mean that you should settle for less! Go ahead and try to find the perfect space. Just know that you can still write even if you end up in an oversized closet. Here are a few tips for creating a comfy, workable space (and then using it!):

➤ Buy a computer—the ultimate room decoration. Unless you're allergic to technology, this one investment alone will make your life much easier.

➤ Find a desk and chair that will give you back support. Bad backs are occupational hazards for writers.

➤ Try to find a space with a door. Then shut it. Ignore knocking sounds. Tell children not to disturb you unless blood is involved.

➤ Buy a chair lined with Velcro. Sit in it. Do not get up to check the mail, the hummingbird feeder, the dog's food bowl, the rise on the carpet pile, or any other critical factor in your writing space.

➤ If you can afford it, consider renting an office outside the home. Some mega-rich romance writers (who shall remain nameless) swear by it. Hmmm ... Something to consider!

➤ If you can't afford an office, buy an answering machine and screen your calls. You have important work to do!

These suggestions not withstanding, don't wait for the perfect space or the perfect equipment. A computer won't make your sentences sound any better, and not even the perfect room can induce you to put your rear-end into your writing chair.

Romancing Your Calendar

The second most frequent question professional writers get is about time: "When do you write?" or "How much do you write a day?" and "How do you find the time?"

Here's the simple truth about scheduling writing time. There are no rules. There is no right way or wrong way. Just do what works for you.

What Schedule Works for You?

Here are few sample writing schedules I've heard about from professional writers in the romance industry. As you can see, no two are alike.

➤ Put the kids to bed by 10:00 P.M. Write until 4:00 A.M. Let hubby get the kids off to school, and sleep until noon.

➤ Write from 9:00 A.M. to 5:00 P.M. and go out to eat with husband every night. (Sounds good to me!)

➤ Write from 7:00 A.M. until noon, then do publicity work until dinner.

➤ Write from 4:00 A.M. until 7:00 A.M., then go to a nine-to-five job.

➤ Write for a couple of hours in the morning, a couple of hours in the afternoon, and a couple of hours after dinner.

➤ Write for a couple of hours in the morning. Period.

➤ Write from 6:00 A.M. to noon, take a nap and putter around, then go back to the computer after dinner and work until midnight.

Write On!

Many authors wrote their first best-sellers around a full-time job. Scott Turrow reportedly wrote when commuting to and from his law firm. P. D. James wrote for an hour or so in the early morning hours before she went to work. You can dream about quitting your job and writing full-time, but it's not a requirement for success in this business. Unfortunately, that takes away one more excuse not to write!

Here was my schedule after I sold my first book. I'd just had a baby and was putting my husband through graduate school:

Wake up at 6:00 A.M. with the baby, play with him until 1:00 P.M. Drive downtown to the TV station and do news writing until 10:00 P.M. Listen to music on the way home to switch from left brain to right brain. Write romances from 11:00 P.M. to 1:00 A.M. Go to bed. Get up with baby at 6:00 A.M., etc.

I wrote two books on that schedule and lived to tell the tale, which leads me to the other big time-related question:

Question: How do you find the time?

Answer: You don't find the time. You make the time.

That one, I hope, is self-explanatory. You simply have to make writing a priority. And you have to make writing a priority *before* you're published or you never will be published. It often requires courage to tell family and friends you're going to set aside precious spare time to pursue your dream of writing.

Don't Wait for Your Muse

I've never met a professional romance writer who waits for inspiration to strike. The muse (inspiration) is too unpredictable. Publisher deadlines, on the other hand, are as predictable as death and taxes. If you want to make a living at this, you must be prepared to write even when you don't feel like it.

A lot of writers say: "I don't like to write. I like having written." In other words, they enjoy the end product, but the process itself isn't exactly fun. Even so, they write. It's a matter of discipline and willpower.

Regularity: Metamucil for the Mind

There are three excellent reasons to write regularly:

➤ It's the fastest way to get a book completed.

➤ You flex your writing muscles often and your technique gets stronger.

➤ It's easier to create living, breathing characters when you work with them every day.

Regular writing primes the pump. Starting and stopping a project slows momentum.

One-a-Day

How many pages do you have to write a day to end up with a book by the end of the year? One. That's right! One page × 365 = a 365-page book. That's a formula that even the most mathematically challenged creative writer can understand. So, every day you should take a vitamin and write at least one page.

A writer friend, whose pen name is Laurel Collins, writes two pages every day. She polishes them at the end of the day. Then she never touches them again! Before the end of the year, she has a completed, cohesive book. I say that's amazing. She says it's all in a day's work.

Speaking of Romance ...

Catherine Coulter reportedly writes three hours in the morning five days a week. To make sure her creative engine stays revved up, she edits a little over the weekend. That doesn't mean she's not thinking about her books the rest of the time, though. "A writer's brain is always plotting," says Coulter, "like reels of film going back and forth, winding, rewinding all the time, refining what's already written, discarding dreck, coming up with new angles. It's a 24-hour process, no doubt about it. This is called real full-time work."*

Gone with the Wind

Scarlett O'Hara was nothing if not determined. So when things didn't go her way, she bravely announced: "Tomorrow is another day." That's a line you should borrow when (if) your writing schedule goes kablooey.

I'll be honest, I've never, ever, written as much as I'd like to or as much as I think I should. And yet I still write at least one book every year. Try to set a schedule, keep track of your progress, then forgive yourself if you can't keep up. Schedules shouldn't be used as a club to beat yourself up with. They're simply a tool to remind you to get to work. In fact, some writers prefer an irregular schedule. Sometimes you just can't write until you've worked out a scene in your head.

Can the Critic

Writing a book is hard. Criticizing a book is easy. That's why you have to be very careful about sharing your unpublished work with other people. Criticism can hurt. Sometimes it can hurt so badly that you stop writing for months, even years. Don't let this happen to you!

Opinions Are Like ... Hearts

Everybody has opinions, and they'll be all too happy to share their opinions of your writing, so be careful about exposing your work and your writing dreams to others. If you get stung by cruel feedback, make yourself feel better with the ultimate truth:

Writing is subjective.

Say that three times and click your heels together. If one person hates your story, chances are the next person will love it. If one editor rejects your story, it's possible the next editor will offer you a six-figure deal. So, take criticism with a grain of salt.

Speaking of Romance ...

Jennifer Greene, a multipublished, award-winning author, has wonderful advice for dealing with self-doubt: "Doubts and worries are dangerous enemies for a writer. They distract you from what matters, and trick you into focusing on things that don't. I have a mental exercise that works for me to get rid of those distractions. In the back of my closet, I keep an imaginary box. That's where I put all my professional doubts and fears. I can get that box down and look at it any time I want—and I do. Sometimes I get so busy that I have to make an appointment—like from 9:00 to 10:00 on Tuesday, I get to worry to my heart's content. But ... when I sit down at the keyboard, that box is put away and out of sight."

Your Own Worst Enemy

Unfortunately, your toughest critic might be you. That's certainly true for many published authors. As we sit at our computers, that crow called self-judgment perches on our shoulders and squawks, "No good! No good! You're not a real writer. No good!"

What's a writer to do? Open the window and shoo self-doubt away! Here are some tips on overcoming self-criticism and doubt:

➤ Start writing and don't quit, no matter how certain you are that your writing stinks.

➤ Put some affirmations on your computer and read them every day (i.e., "My best is good enough," "My writing gets better every day," "I am a prolific author," etc.).

➤ Listen to other writers' war stories. Listen to tapes from writing conferences. You'll feel better when you hear how much best-selling authors struggled when they were first starting.

➤ Don't look for signs of talent in your work. Look for signs of progress.

You shouldn't concern yourself with talent. We all have some and we all could use more. Concern yourself with doing your best to write a darned good book.

Make a Commitment—I Dare You!

It's up to you. You can put this off, or you can jump in and get started. I strongly vote for the latter. Repeat after me, "I think I can, I think I can, I know I can!"

In the next chapter, we'll get down to the nitty-gritty of how to build a great romance. You're ready. You can do this. See you on the next page!

The Least You Need to Know

➤ You have enough imagination to create a great novel.

➤ Music, movies, and classic books are great sources for ideas.

➤ When your story feels like it's at a dead end, try brainstorming ideas.

➤ Set a schedule that works for you, then try to stick with it.

➤ Don't judge your first draft—just keep writing!

Part 2

Seven Aspects of Highly Affecting Romances

Now that you have a better idea of the kind of romance you'd like to write, it's time to start writing. Fortunately, you already possess the most important qualification necessary to begin: the desire to write.

Great books aren't created by sleight-of-hand. They're crafted piece by piece, so skillfully that they appear seamless.

Take heart, novelist-in-the-making! These skills can be learned. In this very important part, you will learn seven critical components used in virtually every romance. These seven tools can transform your dream of writing into reality ... one aspect at a time.

Chapter 6

Plotting: Fresh Take on an Age-Old Story

In This Chapter

➤ Going beyond "boy meets girl"

➤ What to write between "Chapter One" and "The End"

➤ Learning from the pros how to plot a great relationship

➤ Plots to avoid if you want to avoid rejection letters

➤ The perils of writing without a plot

If you think you need talent to *plot* a great romance, you're wrong. What you need is knowledge. You need to know how to get your characters together and when to tear them apart. You need to know how to build to the big crisis scene and just how long to drag it out. You need to know how to weave in *subplots*, and how to let inner conflict drive your main plot.

These are the things you need to know. And—good news, people—these are the things that can be learned. So, let's start right now. I'm going to give you something I didn't have when I was starting out—a parachute. You don't have to jump out of the plane unprepared. The parachute is structure—a simple plan on which to build your plot. Then it's up to you—and your talent—to let your story soar from there.

Boy Meets Girl

Romance plots are deceptive. To the outsider, the critic, and even the reader, they seem simple. Here's the basic premise (and I do mean basic!):

> Boy meets girl. Boy loses girl. Boy gets girl in the end.

How hard can it be to write a story that simple? Well, I don't mean to be discouraging, but coming up with fresh settings, characters, dialogue, and conflicts within the confines of such an age-old storyline is truly challenging! Readers know how your romance will end. The trick is getting them to forget the end *until* the end. The readers have to get caught up in the plot's twists and turns or they'll be bored.

It's easy to find romances that leap to life and make you forget how they'll end. They're the books …

➤ That keep you turning the pages.

➤ That make you weep with the heroine.

➤ That make you angry at the hero.

➤ That make you sigh with satisfaction when the hero and heroine finally work out their problems.

Hmmm …. How can the simple "Boy-Meets-Girl" formula do all that?

The Plot Thickens

The plot always thickens in a well-crafted romance. The so-called simple formula then looks a little more complicated:

> Boy meets girl. Boy sort of gets girl. Boy really gets girl! Boy loses girl. Boy and girl are convinced the relationship is doomed. Boy and girl must overcome some outward obstacle. As a result, boy and girl learn something important about themselves. This realization enables boy to recognize that he can't live without girl, and vice versa. Boy gets girl at last! They live happily ever after.

Ah, now there's a story! At least it will be when you flesh it out a little.

Between the First Kiss and "I Do!"

So how am I going to flesh out some 300 pages? you ask with a note of panic in your voice. Relax. There's a lot to write about. Let's start with a very general overview of the big picture. We'll look at the major things that need to happen in your book.

1. **Meeting: Hero and heroine meet**

   ➤ Sparks fly

   ➤ Seeds of future conflict are sown or revealed

   ➤ Subplots and minor characters are introduced

2. **Intimacy: The first kiss/growth of emotional intimacy**

   ➤ Conflicts arise between hero and heroine

   ➤ Subplots further develop

   ➤ Main love relationship develops

3. **Conflict: Obstacles to love lead to confrontation**

   ➤ Hero and/or heroine make difficult choices

   ➤ Subplots also peak

   ➤ Love relationship seems doomed

4. **Resolution: Crisis in love leads to mutual sacrifices**

   ➤ Hero and heroine act heroically and choose love

   ➤ Subplots are resolved

   ➤ Conflicts are resolved

   ➤ Everyone lives happily ever after

Write On!

Writing a book for the first time is a lot like swimming—you can start with a toe in the water, but at some point you're going to have to jump in. If plotting seems so overwhelming that you can't even put your toe in, just begin writing. Over-analyzing can sometimes kill your creativity. So jump in and start splashing around.

Love Letters

A **synopsis** is a summary of the novel's events and a cataloguing of character development in narrative form. Writers can use a synopsis to pitch an unfinished manuscript. They can also use it as a guide during the writing process. Some authors write synopses that are four pages long, and others write 75-page synopses. It's a tool, not a test to be graded.

Now let's put some skin on that skeleton and see what it looks like in the flesh with an extremely abbreviated *synopsis:*

Jake and Dee's Story

Part 1: Jake and Dee are introduced by a co-worker at a company party. They talk about the joys of parasailing and sparks fly. However, Dee can't let herself get involved, and Jake has a reputation for getting around. After being burned by a handsome philandering husband, Dee is determined to find a not-so-handsome guy who is short on charm and long on character—a family man. Jake wants to ask Dee out, but she's obviously a lady with integrity. She'll want someone who can settle down, and he's not the type. He has trouble making commitments. Meanwhile, their mutual friend is trying to get them both involved in a charity fundraiser for Big Brothers/Big Sisters. Jake sees this as a chance to find out if he really can make a commitment to somebody else and follow through, and maybe impress Dee in the process.

Part 2: Jake and Dee go parasailing together. On the beach, they kiss. Dee sees scars on his back, and he reveals to her that he was beaten by his father as a child. Dee feels compassion for him and begins to understand why family life isn't so appealing to him. She lets down her guard and intimacy grows. The next day, though, they have a fight when Jake doesn't show up on time for the theater. He won't admit it, but their growing love is making him itchy for freedom. Meanwhile, he's faithfully visiting the little brother assigned to him. But Dee, angry over his unreliability with her, stubbornly refuses to acknowledge he's being a model father figure to the boy.

Part 3: After a reconciliation, the relationship heats up. Dee and Jake make love. There are a series of happy scenes when everything is going right, but Jake realizes he's in way over his head emotionally. Dee starts to sense his withdrawal and panics. Meanwhile, Jake is unavoidably detained and can't make it to a meeting with his little brother. The boy, adoring Jake and feeling abandoned, runs away from home. A big crisis scene is played out when Jake and Dee help look for the boy. When it seems as if the child may never be found, Dee angrily accuses Jake of letting the kid down. Jake, in turn, accuses her of blowing one mistake out of proportion. At least he tried to do something for the boy, even if he failed, he argues. He wonders if she's the one who is really looking for an excuse to get out of the relationship. The child is eventually found, but Dee and Jake realize they're polar opposites when it comes to commitment. They decide to break up.

Part 4: Dee and Jake are miserable without each other, but neither wants to budge and find a compromise. Jake works things out with his little brother. In an emotional reunion with the child, he realizes how threatened Dee must feel by his unwillingness to commit. He realizes that he would never have had the satisfaction of being a big brother if he hadn't wanted to impress Dee. Knowing her has made him a better person. He loves her, and he's ready to commit. Dee, in turn, realizes that she hasn't really given Jake a chance. She's been judging him based on her ex-husband's behavior. Except for the one no-show date, he's been very dependable, and in many ways more willing to share his emotions than she has. Dee realizes she has to learn to trust men again. She loves Jake. She just hasn't been willing to admit it to herself. They each confess their love and live happily ever after.

This is admittedly a simplistic example. But see how the relationship, the subplot with the child, and the characters' growth are all intertwined? This multiple layering will give you plenty to write about to fill those 300 pages!

Analyzing Your Favorite Plots

Jane Austen's novels are good ones to analyze for plotting and character development. So are many of the books written by the romance genre's best and brightest. When you find a great romance, sit down with a pad of paper and plot out the major events or devices that worked well. Understanding the structure of a novel that moved you emotionally will help you learn to use plot to move your own readers.

I was so impressed with one of Laura Kinsale's romances that I identified the things she did to make her story superb. These were my notes on what Laura's story included:

> ➤ Escalating danger to hero/heroine, which lessens only through their actions. At one point, the heroine nearly made the danger worse by following her convictions.

> ➤ An enemy character who turns out to be an ally.

> ➤ Expansive circumstances—a huge estate and royalty.

> ➤ Narrative that reflects the characters' thought patterns and rhythms.

> ➤ Idiosyncrasies—pet names and inside jokes.

> ➤ A surprise follow-up at the end with heavy symbolism.

Stop the Presses!

Subplots can be fun to write, but they don't belong in every romance. Some of the shorter category romances simply aren't long enough for in-depth secondary plotlines. So be sure to study the guidelines of the category of your choice. That way, you'll know whether to include subplots before you start writing.

After identifying these clever devices, I tried to use some of them in my books. I won't tell you which of Laura's novels I analyzed so I don't ruin it for you. All of her books are outstandingly superb, by the way.

Speaking of Romance ...

Author Mary Alice Kruesi (a.k.a. Monroe) says an important aspect of plotting involves identifying the high points of your novel. "As you're plotting," she says, "always keep in mind what the key scenes of the story are. Not necessarily the climax, but the turning points, those scenes packed with decision making and emotions. If you know where those are in the early plotting stages, you can build to those moments as you write, and that helps give your story clarity and strength."

A Plotting Lesson from Jane Austen

Jane Austen might well be considered the great-grandmother of the romance genre. She was one of the first writers to develop the novel of manners and to put a romantic focus on marriage and family.

So, how did Grandmother Jane plot her stories? Here is a plot breakdown of *Pride and Prejudice* as analyzed by novelist Mary Alice Kruesi. First, Mary offers a general description of Austen's techniques that can be applied to any relationship novel; she then illustrates each step by pointing out the manner in which *Pride and Prejudice* exemplifies these techniques. These 10 steps work for any relationship-based story. Read on and learn:

1. **Setting the scene.** Location and time period are established. Characters are introduced, as well as a problem to be solved. In *Pride and Prejudice,* we meet the Bennet family and their five unmarried daughters, all of whom are in need of a spouse.

2. **The meeting.** Hero and heroine meet, attraction is established, but a problem arises. In this case, Elizabeth Bennet finds Darcy attractive, but soon intensely dislikes his proud demeanor. She overhears him remark on her lack of beauty and her mother's lack of modesty.

3. & **Development.** The relationship between hero and heroine is further explored.

4. The seeds of conflict sprout, as well as sexual tension. Elizabeth sees further evidence of Darcy's arrogance, and he doesn't show much evidence of appreciating her virtues.

5. **Conflict arises.** There is a reason why the hero and heroine cannot marry. Both recognize the differences in their family's stations. Darcy comes from rich gentry stock.

6. & **Periods of happiness.** Hero and heroine get along wonderfully, in spite of the

7. problems between them. They may recognize feelings of love, though not admit to them. Elizabeth realizes she was wrong about Darcy and sees his goodness. It appears as if their differences may be resolved.

8. **Conflict explodes.** The main lovers are boxed into corners. Problems reemerge and seem unsolvable. One, or both, decides there is no hope. Elizabeth's sister falls for a disreputable man and disgraces the family. Elizabeth knows this is an obstacle that a man of Darcy's social stature cannot overcome.

9. **Period of misery.** The characters see no way out. This is also called the *Black Moment*.

10. **Resolution.** New information is introduced that alters the landscape—either an outside event or an internal realization. Darcy secretly saves the day by helping Elizabeth's sister arrange a hasty marriage, thereby salvaging her family's reputation. Elizabeth, unaware of this heroism, nevertheless stands by Darcy in the face of criticism. His heroics are revealed, their love is declared, and they live happily ever after.

A Romance's Greatest Challenge

Are you feeling more confident about the prospect of plotting your story? I hope so, because you don't have to fly by the seat of your pants. The structures shown previously will give you some direction. By the way, if you look at them closely you'll notice something that 99 percent of all successful relationship novels have in common:

Love Letters

The **Black Moment** is the point at which the characters—and the reader—think the relationship is doomed. The higher you raise the stakes beforehand, the bleaker that moment will be. Likewise, the higher the emotional stakes, the more satisfying the resolution to the crisis will be. The big resolution is the five-hanky pay-off the reader has been waiting for.

The hero and heroine don't get together permanently or declare their love until the end of the book!

Why? There's a simple reason. If your characters declare their love halfway through your story, the reader will put your book down and never pick it up again. When the love-relationship is resolved, the story is over. End of story!

Holy moly. So how do you have two characters fall in love but a) not realize it, b) not admit it, or c) run away from it? The key is conflict. I'll devote a whole chapter to that important subject. Right now, though, I want to point out a few plot techniques to be avoided.

Flimsy as a Negligee

Whatever you do, don't base your entire plot on flimsy issues that could easily be cleared up by a simple conversation. The obstacles must be solid to make it worth the reader's while to keep reading.

Circumstantial Evidence

Many beginning writers mistakenly use overblown misunderstandings to keep their lovers from declaring their love too early in the book. This technique never works! Here's an example:

> Your heroine overhears a conversation and mistakenly assumes your hero cheated on her. Her injured pride and anger prevent her from asking him about the alleged infidelity. The misunderstanding (which is their only conflict) drags on and on, when the problem could be resolved with a direct confrontation.

Readers don't like circumstantial evidence any more than juries do. Misunderstandings can add fuel to the fire of other, bigger conflicts, but circumstantial problems should be resolved in a reasonable amount of time and through direct dialogue. Your hero and heroine must, after all, be reasonable people or your readers won't like them.

The "Other Woman"

Gone are the days when romance writers could rely on the "other woman" (or man) to provide the major obstacles between the hero and heroine. Here's a scenario you shouldn't bother to write:

> Things are hunky-dory between handsome Blake and homespun Janet until Blake's old girlfriend, Sybil the corporate witch, shows up. With red lipstick and cat-claw fingernails, Sybil flirts with Blake and glares at Janet. She threatens

Janet, saying she'll win Blake back. Janet, feeling insecure, never talks to Blake about his ex. Only in the end does Blake reassure Janet that she has nothing to worry about. He never loved Sybil to start with.

Flimsy, flimsy, flimsy! Forget this weak ploy and give your characters real issues to deal with.

No Can Do

There are certain premises you simply can't use because editors consider them forbidden. I talked earlier about the obvious ones: no ax-murderer heroes or psychotic heroines. Your plots should be appropriate for heroes and heroines who are well-adjusted, likable people. Sure, they can have problems and should have room to grow during the course of the book, but a romance novel is not the place to explore the extremes of human behavior. The obstacles that arise during the course of the plot should be ones that readers can relate to.

Plotting No-No's

No matter how talented you are and no matter how spectacularly written your novel may be, it will be rejected by 99 percent of the romance editors if it contains unacceptable elements. Here are a few examples of elements to avoid:

Stop the Presses!

If you're writing a sex scene in a contemporary novel, you're going to have to decide whether or not your characters will be having "safe sex." Some writers subtly make reference to condoms during lovemaking scenes, and some authors reference them explicitly. Other writers don't think readers should have to deal with the threat of sexually transmitted diseases in a novel designed for enjoyment.

➤ **Rape scenes.** They went out with the 1970s. Villains might get away with a rape, but it's a definite no-no for the hero.

➤ **Sadomasochism.** If you want to write super-kinky sex scenes, you should probably explore the erotica market.

➤ **Infidelity.** Today's readers want characters who reflect our post-AIDS sexual mores. Generally speaking, readers want heroines to be faithful to the hero. And heroes shouldn't be exposing themselves to every sexually transmitted disease known to humankind.

In historical romances, the hero often is sexually experienced. The heroine can be as well, but once they get together, you should think twice about having them sleep with anyone else.

Some writers want to delve into the darker side of human nature. If that's your goal, read the market thoroughly. Then at least you'll have a better idea of when you're pushing the envelope and when you're ripping it to shreds.

Hard Sells

Some story lines aren't forbidden, but they're just hard to sell to certain lines. Category editors tend to have lists of situations they won't buy, for various reasons. Here, for example, is a list of subjects Silhouette Desire editors shy away from, which was printed in *Romance Writers' Report*:

➤ **Art settings.** Heroes/heroines who are artists, musicians, actors, sculptors, painters, etc.—these books tend to be written more with the head than the heart.

➤ **Fighting City Hall.** This includes intellectualized issues that lack emotion, such as land-developers and environmentalists.

➤ **Sports figures/public figures.** Glamorous professions, such as professional athletes, politicians, rock stars, TV show settings/radio settings, don't often seem romantic and may not "translate" well to our overseas market.

➤ **"Stalker" stories.** These also aren't popular with our readers, who want to be moved, not disturbed.

While Silhouette Desire doesn't want stalker stories, stalking is an acceptable plot element in a Harlequin Intrigue. Publisher guidelines delineate these distinctions very clearly.

Write On!

Your plot can turn on a dime when you throw in the element of surprise. Bring in an unexpected event. Let your characters plan something without letting the reader know exactly what. When the surprise comes, the reader is thrilled and excited. She'll keep turning the pages to see if other surprises are in store.

Classic Romance Plotlines

Enough of what you *can't* do! Now let's look at what you *can* write about. There are so many exciting possibilities. We talked a little about classic romance fantasies: kissing the frog, beauty and the beast, the healing kiss, Cinderella (fella). Now let's look at how these concepts play out in classic romance plots. Readers respond positively to tried-and-true storylines—especially after you get done making them special in your unique way.

Perennial Plotlines

Let's take a look at some of the romance genre's most popular premises.

Marriage of Convenience

Basic premise: The hero and heroine are forced into a marriage they may not want. They marry for any reason but love—to secure an inheritance, to seal a contract, to secure some sort of pretense, to help some greater cause, etc.

Characteristics: These stories allow for plenty of conflict, since the characters don't even have to pretend they love each other. This set-up is easier to pull off in a historical than it is in a contemporary romance.

Secret Baby

Basic premise: Hero finds out the heroine is pregnant with his baby or has already had his baby.

Characteristics: These stories allow for plenty of emotion and sympathy on the reader's part.

Stop the Presses!

A good way to spice up a familiar plotline is to raise questions in the reader's mind, and then take your time answering them. Let us know the heroine has a dark secret, for example, but don't tell us what it is. Keep us guessing for a while. However, make sure that you answer all the questions by the end of the book, or you'll leave your readers frustrated and perhaps even reluctant to buy your next book!

Rags to Riches

Basic premise: The heroine (or hero) goes from being down-and-out to rich as Midas. The climb to the top is usually emotional as well as financial.

Characteristics: This plot reassures the reader that good gals really do win in the end, and it touches on a core fantasy just about everybody has had—instant riches.

Amnesia

Basic premise: The heroine (or hero) has an accident and can't remember who she or he is.

Characteristics: The heroine frequently finds herself in a marriage or a love relationship with someone she doesn't know or remember. This plot touches on fantasies everyone has probably had at some point or another—having a really good excuse to escape day-to-day responsibilities and fall in love without commitment. (How can you be committed if you don't even know who you are?)

Kidnapped!

Basic premise: The hero kidnaps the heroine (or vice versa) and they fall in love while she's in captivity.

Characteristics: These stories are usually rife with intimacy, since the kidnapper/kidnapped are often together in a remote place. The power/control issues are also prominent and make for strong conflict.

Other Popular Setups

Here are a few other situations, plots, or premises to consider when blocking out your story:

➤ Taming of the shrew

➤ Taming the savage beast (or conqueror)

➤ Mistaken identities/masquerading as another

➤ Reunion of former lovers

➤ Divorced couple rekindles love

➤ Hero as bodyguard, protective cop, or secret benefactor

➤ Guy from the wrong side of the tracks falls for the patriarch's daughter

➤ Heroine plays nanny to hero's motherless child (or children)

➤ Loner hero becomes father figure to heroine's fatherless children

➤ Social fixture falls for social outcast (rake and virgin, lord and governess, rich woman and poor man, or vice versa)

These are just a few possibilities. As you read up on the genre, you'll notice many, many more.

Write On!

Most writers don't sit down and say, "What classic plot am I going to use this time?" Most are inspired by an intriguing idea and go from there. Romance writers have identified these perennial plots because they're popular. It doesn't mean you have to use them. They're there for you if you need a structure to hang your story on. If you already have a structure, go for it. Tell your story, and tell it well!

Writer's Road Map Versus Spontaneous Construction

A final word on plotting: At some point you'll need to figure out whether you're going to wing it or plot your story out before you begin writing. Susan Elizabeth Phillips is reportedly one who plots as she goes, and with great success. Others prefer to plan ahead. A case can be made on the merits of each method.

Speaking of Romance ...

Connie Bennett is an oft-published contemporary and historical romance writer who has studied plotting extensively. She says writers who don't plot ahead often write their way into a dead-end. "You get an idea that you're very excited about and you can't wait to get it on paper," says Connie. "You get three or four chapters and where did it go? The enthusiasm dies because you don't know where you're going. It's suicide. That's where the book takes a dive and goes into the drawer, and a new idea surfaces that's much more exciting. And so you start again." Connie says plotting ahead will increase your chances of finishing your book. "If you never get a book done it will never get sold."

Plotting Ahead of Time

Advantages: You'll catch plot problems before you write yourself into a corner, and you can foreshadow later events because you know they're coming.

Disadvantages: You'll lose some spontaneity and may feel confined by the direction you had planned.

Plotting as You Go

Advantages: You'll definitely feel free to write the story as it unfolds and you won't be tempted to force your characters into a pre-ordained plot.

Disadvantages: Writers who build as they go sometimes end up with a mish-mash of subplots and loose ends that are hard to tie up at the end of the book.

I start with a plot, then allow myself to change course as I go. Do what works for you! This is an art, after all, not a science.

Next we tackle characterization. What fun! Move over Tom Hanks and Meg Ryan. We're going to create some chemistry that will set the pages on fire.

The Least You Need to Know

➤ "Boy Meets Girl" is just the beginning of a great romance plot.

➤ Subplots should be entwined with the main plot and help move the story forward.

➤ Sow the seeds of conflict early and don't resolve them until the end of the book.

➤ Don't rely on flimsy misunderstandings as your major obstacles.

➤ Marriages of convenience, secret babies, and amnesia are popular plot devices.

➤ Plot before you write if you want to avoid a dead end.

Chapter 7

Characterization: Heroes to Die for and Heroines to Cry For

In This Chapter

➤ How to make readers fall in love with your characters

➤ The importance of being heroic

➤ Creating dynamic and vibrant lovers

➤ Using characterization to kick your story into high gear

➤ Things your characters should never do

Now we're getting to the good stuff! Characterization is probably the most important element of your story. After all, romances are about relationships, and relationships are about people. Your mission, Ms. Phelps, should you choose to accept it, is to create great characters that are so vivid they seem like real people.

The Heart of a Romance

I know you have a lot to think about—plots, conflicts, the Black Moment, and now characterization. But before you start to feel overwhelmed, let's make this piece of the puzzle really simple. You have one major and overriding goal when it comes to characterization:

Make the reader fall in love with your hero and heroine.

If you succeed at this, your romance will be a success. To put it another way, no matter how great your plot, or how dazzling your style, or how mind-blowing your metaphors, the reader won't give a damn if she doesn't fall in love with your characters.

Tea and Sympathy

Creating enticing, dynamic lovers doesn't mean they have to be overly dramatic. Your heroes don't have to be as strong as John Wayne, as dashing as Errol Flynn, or as mysterious as Bela Lugosi. Nor do your heroines have to be as beautiful as Scarlett O'Hara, as adventurous as Amelia Earhart, or as sexy as Marilyn Monroe.

Basically, readers enjoy heroines they'd like to have as a friend. Sometimes they like heroines who are the way they'd like to be. I always feel like a bull in a china shop, so I enjoy reading about heroines who are delicate and graceful and patient.

As for heroes, readers typically like men who are strong and attractive, yet still sympathetic. It's really quite simple.

Just Like You and Me

If you're not sure how your characters would react in any given situation, just put yourself in their shoes. If they're well-drawn, they will respond to events like real people. So ask yourself—how would I react in this situation?

Sometimes beginning writers make their characters do weird things in an effort to make them seem dramatic. If you want drama, give your characters clear strengths and weaknesses and then throw them into a dramatic situation. No matter how wild or bizarre the circumstances, though, your lead characters should respond intelligently and sensibly.

Speaking of Romance ...

Writers who start their careers in romance and then branch out to other fiction often have a leg up on their competition. That's because the romance genre requires such a strong focus on characterization. Just ask Tess Gerritsen, the *New York Times* Bestselling author of medical thrillers. Tess started her career writing romantic suspense. She says, "I believe that my career would never have gotten this far if I hadn't started writing romantic fiction, which is the absolute best place for any author to learn the craft. Romance novels focus on character and conflict and relationships, in other words, the people in the story."*

Respect Your Characters

A character is more than a device on which to hang your plot. By the time you're done with your book, your characters will seem like old friends. So treat them with the respect they deserve! Don't make them do dumb things just to please you.

You wouldn't run into a burning building just to make love to somebody, for example. That would be dumb, not to mention suicidal. So don't make your characters do dumb things in the name of love (or for the sake of a rigid plot).

Here are three simple tips to follow when creating your lead actors:

1. Start with a hero and heroine *you* like and find really attractive.
2. Put them in a story and setting that fits their personalities.
3. Don't force them to do anything they, or any other intelligent person, wouldn't do.

If your protagonists do silly things, or behave out of character, you risk having your novel thrown across the room by a frustrated reader. That's a terrible way for a paperback novel to become dog-eared!

Heroes We Love

There are so many wonderful romance heroes. Remember Raine, the Black Dragon, the embittered and powerful medieval knight in Penelope Williamson's *Keeper of the Dream*? And Will Parker, the skinny ex-convict whose hunger for love and a home endeared us in LaVyrle Spencer's classic *Morning Glory*? And don't forget Remington Carr in Betina Krahn's *The Last Bachelor* and Zachary Benedict in Judith McNaught's *Perfect*.

What do these great heroes have in common? In terms of personalities, not much. But ...

➤ They were all clearly defined by the authors.

➤ They were all strong, though sometimes in quiet ways.

➤ They ultimately acted with integrity (honest, caring, sacrificing).

➤ And if they acted badly, it was for a darned good reason.

These strong male characters all moved the plot forward; they weren't swept along by the course of events.

The Alpha Male

Get a few romance writers together in the same room and sooner or later the phrase "alpha male" will pop into the conversation. This is an industry code word for the tough-guy hero. Think John Wayne. Think Sean Connery. Think macho with a heart of gold.

Typically alpha heroes …

➤ Are take-charge kind of guys.

➤ Are handsome in a natural, manly way.

➤ Are not about to throw their coat down over a puddle, but they will swing you up in their arms and carry you across the street.

➤ Are the kind of hero you either love or hate (or love to hate).

> **Stop the Presses!**
>
> The hero or heroine you have in your mind might not be the character the reader sees. You may have a strong heroine, but if she cries a lot, no matter how good the reason, the reader will see her as weak. Try to see your characters from the reader's point of view, then adjust your characters' actions accordingly.

Some editors and writers claim that this is the only true romance hero. They argue that the alpha male's softer counterpart is simply a 1990's invention designed to make the macho hero politically correct. I'll let you be the judge of that. As an editor writing a rejection letter would put it, "editorial tastes vary."

Beta Man

For those of you who don't like machismo, there's a kinder, gentler hero popping up in romances today. Romance writers call him the beta hero.

Typically beta heroes …

➤ Consider their lover's opinions and feelings before acting.

➤ Aren't afraid to say that they're sorry or wrong.

➤ Talk about their feelings, but can be stoic, too.

➤ Make up for a lack of he-man charisma with extreme charm.

A beta man is the kind of hero you know the heroine will actually be able to live with once the honeymoon is over!

By the way, you can create any type of hero you want. Many writers use a blend of the alpha and beta types. Who knows, maybe you'll create the sigma hero!

Speaking of Romance ...

Even big-name *New York Times* Bestselling romance author Iris Johansen says introducing her characters is a challenge. "The first three chapters are always the hardest for me," says Johansen. "A plot has to be established, characters introduced to me as well as the reader, and I have to make sure I have a hook that will keep the pages turning. That's when writing can be a real headache for me as I seldom succeed in doing all three on the first try."*

Heroines We Relate To

Think about some of your favorite heroines. Who are they? What do they have in common? Here are a few of my favorites: Hattie Colfax, the homely old maid in Pamela Morsi's beautiful classic *Courting Miss Hattie;* Antonia Paxton, the tender yet efficient blue-stocking in Betina Krahn's wonderful Victorian romance *The Last Bachelor;* and Brianna Concannon in Nora Roberts' *Born in Ice*.

Let's look at what these heroines have in common:

➤ They are intelligent women with well-defined opinions and values.

➤ They have a vast well of love inside them and ultimately make love a priority.

➤ They're resilient and would be a great friend in a time of need.

➤ They're passionate, though sometimes in a tempered way.

In other words, the most popular heroines are those who are sensible, self-sufficient, though still in need of love. They're women much like the women who read (and write) romances today.

Does that mean you have to write yourself into every book? No, of course not. It does mean, however, that if you create a heroine with more extreme qualities you may be at risk of losing the reader's empathy.

A Case Study: Scarlett O'Hara Versus Melanie Wilkes

You've probably read and/or seen *Gone With the Wind*. So let's use it as an example. Scarlett O'Hara is a wonderful *protagonist* with many great strengths, but she'd be troublesome as the heroine in a romance novel because of her glaring weaknesses. Likewise, her competition and polar opposite, Melanie Wilkes, would be a tough sell in a romance. Let's look at the personality traits that make these characters problematic as heroines in a traditional romance novel.

Scarlett: Selfish and conniving; a liar and a lousy friend who can't admit when she's wrong.

Melanie: Pliable and too giving; your basic doormat.

The ideal romance heroine would be someone who falls in between these two extremes—someone who is strong-minded, even willful, but also giving, loving, and able to recognize her mistakes enough to grow as a character.

Love Letters

A **protagonist** is the principle character in a story or novel. It has a more neutral connotation than the terms hero or heroine, which imply a certain amount of heroism. A protagonist may be the main character, but that doesn't mean he or she is sympathetic.

Nobody's Perfect (at Least They Shouldn't Be!)

Don't you just hate perfect people? Readers certainly do! Perfect people are boring and predictable. They're also a reminder that we are *not* perfect. Who needs that?

Typically, readers don't like a heroine who has a perfect figure, who never has a bad hair day, who has a charming personality, a high IQ, and a freshly polished, already-paid-for Porche sitting in the garage. (Did I just describe a Barbie doll?)

As for heroes, the flawlessly handsome Tom Selleck is nice, but isn't the slightly balding Bruce Willis more interesting and fun?

Remember, nobody's perfect. If your characters are, go back to the drawing board and come up with some new traits. This is one of the most important things you can do to avoid cookie-cutter characters.

Every Story Needs a Hero

Your hero and heroine should have flaws, but they shouldn't be broken beyond repair. They may make a few wrong choices, but when push comes to shove they should act heroic. This goes for the heroine as well as the hero.

There is a place in the publishing world for novels about people who wallow in the mire. It's just not in the romance department. In a romance, the main characters must strive to make their lives better, and ultimately they must succeed. So if your main characters seem destined for the psychiatrist's couch, you may want to reduce their flaws or pick new characters.

When Bad Things Are Done by Good Heroes

Readers are pretty forgiving. They're capable of overlooking a so-so plot, uninspired prose, even an occasional factual error if your book has other redeeming qualities. But they will never forgive a hero who unjustifiably acts like a cad.

Unforgiven heroes are those who ...

➤ Intentionally lie or deceive without just cause.

➤ Sleep around.

➤ Wimp out or side-step tough choices.

➤ Leave the heroine to fend for herself.

➤ Think with their you-know-what. (Remember, your characters have to be intelligent!)

Write On!

Often in life a person's greatest strength is also, in certain circumstances, his weakness. That's an interesting way to create balance in your characters. For example, if your hero is successful because he's ambitious, perhaps his ambition blinds him to his need for love. If your heroine has a heart of gold, maybe she cares so much for others she's neglected her own welfare.

Heroic Qualities

Sure, you know your hero has the right stuff. You know that in the end the heroine, and the reader, will see his sterling character. Unfortunately, you can't wait until the end of the book to show signs of his inner fortitude. The reader needs to see evidence of a strong hero early on, or she'll lose interest in your book and stop reading. And if your hero is behaving badly, the reader must know why—or she'll throw your book across the room!

A forgivable hero might be someone who ...

➤ Works hard and never gives up.

➤ Has faith in the heroine even when she doesn't.

➤ Does good deeds without announcing them.

➤ Is honest, even to a fault.

➤ Helps children, animals, and little old ladies. (Go, Beta Man!)

➤ Avenges loved ones and rights wrongs. (Go, Alpha Male!)

➤ Is willing to fight to the death for justice and the good of others.

Lest you think I'm neglecting your heroine, the same qualities can be considered heroic in a woman as well.

Speaking of Romance ...

Romantic suspense superstar Tami Hoag has some good advice about creating heroic heroines: "Would you ever put your hero in dangerous circumstances and have him do nothing but hope that someone will come and get him out of that? No, you wouldn't. That wouldn't be considered heroic. Would you ever have him portrayed as meekly enduring an abusive relationship? No, you wouldn't. You'd say the guy's not a hero, he's a wimp. Why would you treat a heroine any differently? A heroine is a woman who exhibits heroic qualities."

Motivation: The Saving Grace

Wait a minute! If I include all those good qualities in one character I'll end up with an Eagle Scout or a Miss Goody-Two-Shoes, you argue. You're right, if those are the only traits you give your characters. But don't forget you will have character flaws to add balance to your leading lovers. And character flaws often lead to bad behavior—temper tantrums, running away, clamming up, being heartless.

Without these unhappy moments, your romance would be hopelessly boring. The trick is to make sure bad behavior on the part of your hero and/or heroine is motivated by noble intentions. A few examples:

➤ **Bad behavior.** Medieval hero takes over heroine's castle and imprisons her.

 Good intentions. He's trying to restore his family honor by reclaiming the castle her father stole from his father.

➤ **Bad behavior.** FBI hero lies to computer-whiz heroine about his real reason for taking a job at Microsoft.

 Good intentions. Her life would be endangered by a psychotic computer hacker if he told her about his covert operations within the computer company.

➤ **Bad behavior.** The hero takes a hike whenever he starts to feel close to the heroine.

 Good intentions. He thinks he's bad company and doesn't want to hurt the heroine by letting her get too involved with him.

In some of the most exciting and emotionally powerful romances, the writer pushes the characters' behaviors to the edge of the cliff—then rescues the situation by coming up with a fantastic motivation.

Consistently Consistent

Have you ever read a book that had characters that somehow just didn't seem believable? It wasn't that you didn't like them, you just didn't understand them. They didn't seem … real. Chances are the writer wasn't being consistent in her characterization. Once you decide who your characters are, their actions should be consistent with their beliefs and personalities.

For Example

The best way to understand inconsistency is to see it in action. Here are some simple examples:

➤ A cop heralded for his bravery stands by and watches a building burn down without making any effort to help the victims escape.

➤ The vice president of a company specializing in conflict management makes no effort to talk about her problems with the hero.

➤ A heroine who is the soul of patience breaks off an engagement because the hero is five minutes late for a date.

➤ A hero who is a shy, stoic Amish farmer incessantly psychoanalyzes his feelings and is the life of every party.

Stop the Presses!

Even with an ostensibly good motivation, your hero should never abuse the heroine, physically or emotionally. You can't have your hero mistreat the heroine throughout the book and expect the reader to believe that in the last two chapters he's truly been reformed by love. A hero who mistreats the woman he supposedly loves is, in a word, unheroic.

Now all of these examples of inconsistent behavior could be explained away by a good extenuating circumstance. In the first example, perhaps the day before the fire the cop accidentally caused the death of someone he was trying to help. He thinks if he tries to save the fire victims, he might make things worse. Without knowing that motivating factor, though, his behavior just doesn't make sense.

Sometimes it's hard to recognize our own characters' inconsistencies. But it's important to try. It took me five years to get my first book published. It finally happened only after someone pointed out that my characters were inconsistent. I fixed the problem, and the book was accepted for publication soon after.

Cause and Effect

If your characters' actions aren't consistent with their personalities, the reader will become confused. She'll start to distrust your judgement. She won't be able to suspend disbelief enough to enjoy your story. Fear not! There are ways to avoid this subtle, but significant problem.

Speaking of Romance ...

A wonderful book called *Goal, Motivation and Conflict,* by Debra Dixon offers good advice about goals. Debra writes: "Characters should want what they don't have yet. Characters who simply want more of what they *already* have are not strong characters. In fact, story people should desperately *need* what they don't have. Dangle a carrot just out of their reach and make sure they haven't had a bite to eat in weeks. Then that carrot becomes important. The carrot becomes something your character desperately needs." That need, Dixon says, inspires your characters to take action. "Active characters make your life much easier because action creates plot."

Ready, Set, Goal!

Give your characters goals—and figure them out before you start writing your story. That way you'll be less likely to put your characters into situations where they don't belong. Goals will keep you and your characters on track.

Here are a few things goals can do for your story:

➤ They give your characters a clear direction and motivation.

➤ They give the reader something to root for.

➤ They provide a source of conflict when the hero's and heroine's goals clash.

Goals don't have to be complicated. They can be as simple as wanting to buy a new house or wanting to mend a broken friendship. Or they can be as complex as wanting to take over the world. The underlying goal of most romance heroes and heroines is the desire to be loved.

Interview with a Character

The other way to avoid inconsistent actions is to get to know your characters better. If you do that before you write your book, you may save yourself a few rewrites later on.

The most common way to get to know your characters in advance is through a character interview or survey. Various writers have come up with lists of questions to ask or answer regarding each main character. Here are a few examples:

Character Profile

➤ Color of hair, eyes, skin?

➤ Appearance (skin texture? teeth? good-looking? flaws?)?

➤ Posture?

➤ Defects (health problems? deformities?)?

➤ Occupation (income? job title? hours?)?

➤ Education (grades? favorite subjects? friends?)?

➤ Religion (attends church? beliefs about God?)?

➤ Sex life (history? favorite positions? morality rules?)?

➤ Dreams and goals?

➤ Strengths and weaknesses?

➤ Attitude toward life?

➤ Most guarded secret?

➤ Most memorable trait, physical and internal?

Often the answers you come up with will change as you begin writing and get to know your characters better. The key is to remain flexible. If you think your heroine is a six-foot-tall redhead with a sunny disposition and half-way through your book you realize she's instead a 5'2", raven-haired spitfire, go with the flow!

Write On!

Doing a character profile before you start your book is a good idea. But you may not know your characters well enough to answer all the questions until after you've written a completed first draft of your novel. After you finish the first draft, update your character profiles, and they will help you hone your characterization as you rewrite.

Second Fiddles

Unless your lovers are stranded on a deserted island, your book will probably have secondary characters. These roles might be walk-on parts by bit players who are never seen again. Or they might be fully developed characters who add charm, depth, or danger to the plot. Here are a couple of tips regarding these second fiddles:

➤ Secondary characters should never overshadow or outshine your hero and heroine.

➤ Second bananas should generally serve a purpose—to move the plot forward, to provide an important opinion or information, or to act as a foil to the main characters.

Type Out Stereotypes

There is a good reason certain characters become stereotypes. They strike a common chord and therefore become perennial favorites. If you're going to use a classic character that verges on a stereotype, be sure to add your own personal touch.

Here are a few class character types:

➤ The taciturn and principled sheriff at high noon

➤ The warm "I've seen it all" Miss Kitty saloon madam

➤ The savage but noble knight

➤ The debonair, womanizing regency rake

➤ The homespun school marm

➤ The millionaire playboy

➤ The ice princess and rich man's daughter

All these might be considered stereotypes, but that doesn't mean you have to avoid them. You just have to make them your own by delving beneath the surface. Do a thorough character profile and see what makes your characters tick. This kind of homework will add depth to your characters.

Write On!

Sometimes you can give depth to stereotype characters by adding the unexpected. If your villain is a completely evil Snidely Whiplash, give him a redeeming quality that surprises the reader. If your hero is a squeaky-clean Dudley Do-Right, give him a dark side. Making your characters multifaceted will make them seem more real, and definitely more interesting.

Character Checklist

Now you understand the basics of characterization. You've figured out how to make readers love your hero and heroine. In the next chapter you'll learn how to keep readers turning the pages until "The End." First, here's a checklist to bear in mind when you start your novel:

❏ I am in love with my own hero and heroine.

❏ They react sensibly to external events.

❏ I've avoided the wimp factor in my hero and heroine.

❑ They act with integrity.

❑ They have flaws as well as strengths.

❑ I've given their good and bad deeds strong motivations.

❑ My characters are consistent.

❑ I've given my leads specific goals to achieve.

❑ I've made my secondary characters interesting without letting them steal the spotlight.

❑ I've added depth to stereotypical characters.

The Least You Need to Know

➤ The best plot in the world will go nowhere without strong and likable characters.

➤ Don't force your characters into situations where they don't belong.

➤ Real heroes don't abuse women, and real heroines don't stand for abuse.

➤ Your book won't be complete until you make sure your characters act consistently with their personalities.

Chapter 8

Pacing: Timing Is Everything

In This Chapter

➤ The most important line you'll ever write

➤ Creating a heart-pounding page-turner

➤ Using time and danger to speed up your story

➤ Five signs that your pacing is too slow

➤ Putting your prose on a diet

As a novelist, you're going to have some tough competition—and I'm not talking about other writers! I'm talking about movies, the Internet, and all of the cable channels and magazines that compete for the reader's attention. What's the key to making sure she reaches for your book instead of the remote control? Pacing!

In this chapter, you'll learn a potpourri of techniques to make your story exciting and fast-paced. So rev up that plot and put the pedal to the metal!

Pacing at the Speed of Light

We live in a world of instant gratification. People want information now, if not yesterday, and thanks to fax machines, modems, and cell phones, they get what they want when they want it.

Love Letters

A **word count** is the number of words in a novel. The shorter category romances run around 55,000 words. Bigger contemporary and historical novels generally run 90,000 to 120,000 words. Ten or 15 years ago, historical romances were twice that size, but paper costs and shorter attention spans among readers have made that kind of book length a thing of the past.

What does that have to do with the pacing of a novel? It means you have to tell your story more quickly than writers did 10 years ago. Once upon a time, big fat family sagas were all the rage. The more subplots the merrier. A 200,000-*word count* was a drop in the bucket! But this is not the case any more. Sagas aren't big sellers today, perhaps because they take too long to read.

So what is the moral of this story? As a writer you must cut to the chase. To appeal to today's busy readers you should …

➤ Start with a bang.

➤ Move the story along at a crisp pace.

➤ Keep your subplots to a minimum.

The Big-Bang Theory

Some scientists believe that the world was created when a bunch of combustible gases converged and exploded with a terrific bang. Actually, that's not a bad way to create your novel. Combine some hot elements (a hero and heroine with great chemistry) in a volatile environment (a sexually charged romantic setting) and start with an explosion (action). The key here is to start with a bang, not a whimper.

Find the Hook

A hook is a great way to fish for readers—drop the lure in the water and wait for them to bite. The lure, of course, is the exciting opening scene. To hook the reader, the scene should start with one of the following:

➤ An action

➤ A problem

➤ A surprise

➤ A change

In other words, open with anything other than a static scene. Something must be happening in the first scene, the first paragraph—even the first line!

In the Mood

Some books are more mood-oriented than plot-driven. If that's the kind of book you want to write, your hook will be the mood. Make sure the atmosphere you begin with sets the right tone; also make sure the first scene matches the mood of your whole book.

First Lines First

The most important line in your entire book is the very first line of your story. If it's really good, it just might make the difference between a reader taking your book to the cash register or putting it back on the shelf.

Here are a few catchy first lines:

Write On!

Dialogue is easy to read and moves a story along quickly. That's why writers today increasingly use dialogue to communicate plot points or exposition. Some writers even start the first scene of their books in the middle of dialogue. For the reader, it's like jumping on a carousel that's in motion. It leaves no doubt that the plot is moving along at a fast pace.

> "He had maybe a minute to live."
> —*Night Magic,* by Karen Robards

> "She should have known better than to trust a man whose brawn was bigger than his brain."
> —*Sherlock's Home,* by Sharon De Vita

> "Catch them two whoreson actors!"
> —*The Greatest Lover in All England,* by Christina Dodd

What do these opening lines all have in common?

➤ They catch your interest with humor, action, or danger.

➤ They get right to the point.

➤ They raise a question: Why is this so? Or, what is happening? If you raise a question, you increase the odds that the reader will keep reading to find the answer.

Cut to the Chase

Once you hook the reader, keep the action going. Get to the best part of the story. Don't save it for a rainy day. Think about the pacing of best-selling, blockbuster novels. In stories like *Jurassic Park* and *Hannibal,* the plots unfold cleanly, escalate persistently, and reach incredible climaxes, taking readers on a gripping and exhilarating ride.

Does a romance novel have to be as fast-paced as a Michael Crichton or Thomas Harris thriller? No, but it doesn't hurt! Especially if you're writing broader "women's fiction" or a romantic suspense novel.

Whatever you're writing, don't start your book with the mundane details of everyday life. Don't begin a scene when the alarm clock goes off and your heroine gets out of bed, brushes her teeth, reads the paper, gets dressed, yada, yada, yada. Start the scene when she's dressed and the phone rings and she learns her boyfriend has just fled the country after embezzling three million dollars. In other words, start with the most exciting action.

It Can (Should) Only Get Worse from Here

Conflict drives a romance forward, so introduce problems and challenges early on—the earlier the better. In some of the most compelling novels, the reader learns on page one exactly what conflict the main characters are facing. The reader immediately wonders whether the problem will be overcome. Throw your characters into hot water, then turn up the heat to high.

Back Story on the Back Burner

One of the most common mistakes that beginners make is putting all kinds of history, or *back story,* in chapter one. You won't make that mistake, will you? (Shake your head no.) Sure, you know your characters' entire history, and it's fascinating, but you also know that if you tell it all right away, it will bog down your story.

Here's a very brief synopsis of a romance that starts with too much back story:

> Rafe Bouchet was born next to a swamp in Cajun country. His mother only spoke French, so Rafe didn't learn English until he reached school and consequently made poor grades. He was picked on by the kids and became a loner. During his high school years, he only dated girls who spoke French. It made him feel like he was in an exclusive, though outcast, club. When he became a politician, he had a strong affinity for the Cajun fishermen in his district. When the story opens, Rafe is fighting for their rights, which are being threatened by a real-estate developer, Cindy Sullivan, the heroine of the story.

Oh, my gosh! We didn't even meet the heroine until after we heard Rafe's entire life story! If this were a real romance, we'd have to wade through four or five chapters before we even get a glimpse of Cindy Sullivan. Granted, Rafe has an interesting childhood, and one that provides insights into his motivations. It just doesn't belong in chapter one. To keep your novel's pace moving, intersperse bits and pieces of your background as you go.

A synopsis of a more balanced story would go like this:

> Rafe Bouchet storms down the hall of the capitol building until he finds real-estate developer Cindy Sullivan. He confronts her about her lobbying efforts. It's clear to him she won't give up until the legislature passes a law allowing her company to develop condos on formerly secluded fishing harbors. Rafe and Cindy have a loud argument and sparks fly. He can't understand why he finds her attractive. She's nothing like the women he dated in high school. She probably doesn't even speak French …

Write On!

Beginners often want to spill their guts in chapter one, but withholding critical information is a good way to build suspense. Raise questions, drop hints, but hold out on a few juicy tidbits until later in the book. It gives the reader one more reason to keep turning the pages.

Notice that his high school history is briefly mentioned, and only after the action is established and flowing. It's all a matter of timing.

The Time Bomb

Whenever I hear the tick, tick, tick, tick sound effect at the beginning of *60 Minutes* I always feel a sense of anticipation—who will Mike Wallace grill this time? It's the same feeling I get when I hear the sizzling sound of the fuse at the beginning of the movie *Mission Impossible*. It's just a matter of time before a bomb explodes—unless the situation can be diffused.

That's the feeling you want your readers to have. You want them to know that there isn't much time before all hell breaks loose. Associating time with danger will spur your reader on.

To create a time bomb, you need to introduce a problem with a deadline. For example …

➤ Your heroine's daughter will be killed by kidnappers if your heroine doesn't come up with a million dollars in cash within 24 hours.

➤ Your medieval hero has three weeks to overtake a castle before the king comes to inspect his progress. If your hero succeeds, he will be named lord of the

castle. If he fails, he'll be sent off to a foreign country to fight for mere booty.

➤ Your heroine wants to love again, and she's falling for your hero. But the second anniversary of her husband's death is a month away. With each passing day, she senses her loss of equilibrium and fears her lingering grief will destroy her chance to love again.

That last example is subtle, but once the reader knows about the anniversary, she won't forget it. It will be a tiny time bomb ticking away in the back of her mind. You want to make your readers hear the sizzle of the fuse. They won't hear it unless they know when the bomb is scheduled to go off.

Warning! Warning!

Danger, danger, Will Robinson, there is a giant asteroid heading our way! Did you ever notice that movies set in space always have the coolest, most terrifying dangers imaginable?

It's easy for writers to create danger in outer space because readers have no point of reference. Therefore, they're completely willing to suspend disbelief. In fact, when I saw *Alien,* I accepted the monster without question. What I had a hard time swallowing was the fact that Ripley, the character played by Sigourney Weaver, actually went back into the monster-infested ship alone to find her lost cat! (I questioned her motivation.)

Your job as a contemporary romance writer is harder than that of a science-fiction writer. To create a page-turner, you have to create believable and heart-pounding threats in ordinary settings. For example, you need to make your readers *really* care …

➤ Whether your heroine is able to pay rent or ends up on the streets.

➤ Whether your hero is shot by Mafia thugs who have been following him throughout the story or gets away.

➤ Whether your heroine regains custody of her children or not.

➤ Whether your hero proves, before he lands in jail, that he was framed by his ex-partner or spends the rest of the book in the big house.

Danger doesn't have to be extreme or dramatic. It just has to be real to your characters in order to seem real and pressing to your readers.

The Mary Higgins Clark Chapter

Danger is just one way to keep the pace going. Chapter length is another. If you write a 40-page chapter, your reader has to commit a lot of time to finishing it in one sitting. If she has to put your book down to take her kids to the soccer game, she may have trouble getting back into the book in the middle of the chapter. She might have to start the chapter again. That means she's less likely to finish your book.

Short chapters make it easy for the reader to keep turning the pages. Just ask Mary Higgins Clark. She's made a successful career out of writing incredibly short, incredibly tight chapters that end with *cliffhangers*. In fact, some of Clark's chapters are only one or two pages long!

What are the advantages of short chapters?

➤ They force you to write tightly since there's not a lot of room to waste.

➤ They lure the reader from chapter to chapter with the promise of a short and easy read.

➤ They make it easy for busy people to pick up and put down the book without losing momentum.

Write On!

Some romances require more danger than others. If you want to write a sweet, charming, homespun romance, mood might be more important than pacing. Creating a wonderful, cozy mood might be all the enticement you need to get readers to step into your fictional world. However, even the coziest of romances must have some crisis point, and an element of danger can help make matters worse.

Scenes Within a Chapter

If you aren't as succinct as Mary Higgins Clark, you might have more than one scene in each chapter—two or three or even more depending on their length. In order to be able to write a successful scene, there are a few things you need to understand.

Arc of the Scene

Each scene has it's own arc, or shape. Sometimes the shape looks like a bell curve and the action peaks in the middle. Sometimes it looks like a loading ramp and the action peaks in the last paragraph. Whatever its shape, each scene should …

➤ Have a beginning, middle, and end.

➤ Have some drama, or at least a purpose.

➤ Move the story forward.

Let's say your first scene in chapter five is a chase scene on horseback. It begins with a blaze of gunfire; the villain gallops away, and the hero decides to give chase. In the middle of the scene, the hero is nearly shot. He falls off his horse and is dragged by a stirrup for more than a mile. The scene ends when the villain negotiates his way through a narrow valley and an avalanche of rocks keeps the hero from following. The hero vows revenge.

This scene had a beginning, middle, and end. It had a point of drama (when the hero falls off his horse), and it had a purpose: It showed the hero's decision to seek revenge (character development). If the reader learns early on that all your scenes add something important to the story, she'll keep turning the pages.

The Cutting Room Floor

After you finish your first draft, you may decide to cut out entire scenes. It can be painful to do, but sometimes it's necessary. When should you take this drastic measure?

Stop the Presses!

Sometimes beginners fail to clearly identify their scenes. They narrate event after event in a rambling style for 20 pages or more with no peaks or valleys and little dialogue. Use narration sparingly as an introduction or as a conclusion to dialogue and action scenes. That will keep your story moving!

The answer: when the scene slows the overall pacing of the book to an unacceptable degree or when the scene doesn't move the story forward. A story is like a shark. If it's not moving forward, it dies.

To move the story forward, a scene should accomplish one of the following:

1. Show character or plot development.
2. Deliver new information.
3. Significantly engage the reader's emotions.
4. Generally enlighten the reader in a new and important way.

The Long and Short of Sentences

You probably remember getting a lecture from your high school English teacher about run-on sentences—the ones that seem to go on forever. There is a time and a place for long, complex sentences, but you should use them sparingly. The point of all writing, fiction included, is communication. If you confuse the reader with a convoluted sentence, you're not communicating, no matter how inspired your prose!

Speaking of Romance ...

Advice on pacing from Jennifer Enderlin, executive editor at St. Martin's Press: "In editorial meetings, we sometimes say, 'That book practically read itself,' meaning it had a fast pace. Pacing is crucial to a good story. I think the best pacing comes when each chapter is constructed to bring the readers to a new emotional level in the story: The stakes are higher with each chapter. I don't think it's necessarily the 'cliffhanger' at the end of each chapter; in fact, a cliffhanger at the end of every chapter gets tiresome. But I do believe that each chapter should accomplish something—whether it's to shed a new, sympathetic light on a character, to unveil a secret, or to plummet a character into a sticky situation."*

Variety Is the Spice of Paragraphs

If all your sentences are long, or if all your sentences are short, you need variety. Scan through the pages of your manuscript and note the length of your sentences. If they're all the same, the rhythm of your otherwise sparkling writing will seem monotonous. It's an easy problem to fix. Just make sure each paragraph has an even mix of long and short sentences.

The Rhythm of Emotions

Think about the emotions your characters are feeling. Then, let your sentence length reflect those emotions. When you describe a relaxed character, your sentences might be long and languid. When describing an anxious, neurotic character, your sentences might be short and terse.

For example, if your heroine is walking into a haunted house and she's frightened, you can tighten your pacing by shortening your sentences to communicate her fear:

> She opened the door and a plume of dust littered her eyes. She blinked and coughed. Rallying her courage, she took a step forward. Then another. And another. She forced herself to let go of the doorknob, and the door slammed shut behind her. Black. Pitch black. That was all she could see.

You can see in this example that some sentences are long and some are short. The short ones, however, are the ones that help build the tension of the scene. Size does matter, at least when it comes to sentences!

Tightening Your Prose

So, you're doing everything right, but your pacing still seems slow. Your scenes are laid out in a logical, fast-paced manner. The action is tight as a drum. Every scene moves the story forward. But still, something isn't quite right. What's the problem?

It could be that your *prose* is a little flabby. If that's the case, you need to trim the fat. You need to say what you mean and mean what you say. Here are some ways to tighten your prose:

➤ Cut out unnecessary words.

➤ Cut repetitive thoughts, ideas, and phrases.

➤ Keep descriptions to a minimum.

Let's look at a paragraph that needs a good diet:

> She walked along the wharf, walking to soothe her nerves. She was nervous about Billy. Would he commit suicide as he had threatened, or was he bluffing? She was afraid to the core of her being. Would he really do it? She could sense that he was afraid, too.

After editing:

> She walked along the wharf to soothe her nerves. Would Billy commit suicide as he had threatened, or was he bluffing? She was afraid and sensed he was afraid, too.

You see how much you can cut? The paragraph is a few pounds lighter after much-needed editing. Sometimes that's all it takes to turn a sluggish story into an exciting page-turner.

Be Your Own Guinea Pig

Pacing is an art. If your story seems slow at first, don't despair. Polishing and editing will help a lot. One of the best ways to detect poor pacing is to read your story out loud. If you start getting bored, so will your reader. Here are some signs that your pacing may be a little slow:

Write On!

An easy way to avoid run-on sentences is to write like you talk. Most people don't use huge words and lots of clauses in everyday conversations. If you want to make sure your sentences are a manageable length, read them aloud. If you run out of breath in the middle, your sentence is too long!

Love Letters

Prose is a word used to describe natural writing—fiction that reflects regular speech and rhythms. The word is often used in contrast to **poetry,** which is a formalized style of fiction. When someone comments on your prose, they're basically commenting on your writing style.

➤ Your story doesn't become interesting to you until chapter two.

➤ You find yourself skipping paragraphs, or even pages, to get to the "good parts."

➤ Several scenes seem redundant.

➤ After an exciting start, you become antsy because the middle of your story is sagging.

➤ You start to feel irritated that the characters aren't evolving fast enough.

Stop the Presses!

If your book doesn't get interesting until chapter 15, you'd better go back to the drawing board. A reader won't hang in there that long, and neither will an editor. When you send in a manuscript for submission, you're expected to send in the first three chapters, so those had better be among your best.

If you have any of these reactions to your novel, you must cut out the extraneous fluff. It's hard to do, but it will make your story much better—you'll be glad you did it.

By the way, it's possible to write a book that's too fast-paced. Your book has to have some downtime to give your readers a chance to breathe. And you shouldn't rush love scenes and mood-setting moments. Your story is not a sprint. It's more like a marathon that builds to an exhilarating finish.

Pacing Checklist

Test yourself on your knowledge of pacing:

❑ I started my first chapter with a bang, or at least set the proper tone.

❑ The first line and/or paragraph makes the reader want to buy my book.

❑ I avoided overloading the beginning with too much history.

❑ I have more dialogue than narration.

❑ It's possible to shorten the length of my chapters.

❑ They're already just the right length.

❑ I varied the length of my sentences.

❑ There are extraneous or repetitive words, ideas, and actions that can be cut without taking anything away from the story.

❑ If possible, I have included a time bomb or a lurking danger.

❑ I've included some downtime so my characters and readers can relax.

❑ I've been careful to make sure the romance remains paramount, regardless of pacing issues.

The Least You Need to Know

➤ Pacing is one of the most important ways to keep your readers turning the pages.

➤ Many beginners overload chapter one with too much history.

➤ Avoid flashbacks until you're sure you can handle them.

➤ If you find yourself skipping to "the good parts" you know your story needs editing.

➤ Your characters' emotions can affect your story's pacing.

Chapter 9

A-HEM

Voice: Yours and Your Characters'

In This Chapter

➤ What editors are really looking for

➤ How to find your own style

➤ Making each character a unique individual

➤ The key to effective dialects

➤ One thing all best–selling authors have in common

Have you ever found yourself completely absorbed in a book that really doesn't have much of a plot? Is there an author whose books are on your "automatic purchase" list regardless of the cover, title, or subject matter? If so, you have fallen under the spell of that hard-to-understand but worth-its-weight-in-gold thing we call the "author's voice."

In this chapter, you'll learn how to recognize and develop your own voice. We'll also look at ways to bring out your characters' unique voices. By the time I'm through with you, you'll be so spellbound by your own writing that you'll read it and weep … with joy, that is!

The Alchemy of "Voice"

You've probably heard about alchemy. It was the so-called art of turning common metals into gold. The techniques were developed in the Middle East in medieval times and were practiced for hundreds of years in the West as well. Here's the catch—there is not a single verified and recorded incident of anyone ever turning metal into gold. It seems no one ever discovered the true secret of alchemy.

This search for an alchemy formula reminds me of the writer's search for "voice." You can study all the "how-to" books in the world (including this one), but there is no single method of finding the hidden gold in your writing. Like alchemy, a writer's voice is impossible to define, but nevertheless worth its weight in gold.

What Is Voice?

Now that I've just said the author's voice is impossible to define, I will attempt to do that very thing. (I don't want to leave you hanging here!) So here goes …

A writer's voice is the style that reflects her personal rhythm, attitudes, and outlook. It's the way sentences are put together and how they feel and sound; it's how the paragraphs gel to form a unique mood or vision of life. In other words, a writer's voice is her own distinctive personality translated onto paper.

The best and most successful writers have voices that are fully developed. In fact, they became successful because their voices or writing styles are so distinctive. Think about the words you would use to describe the style of some of your favorite writers:

➤ Nora Roberts: direct, fluid, and sassy

➤ Loretta Chase: cutting, off-beat, and powerful

➤ Eileen Dreyer: ironic, snappy, and frank

➤ Laura Kinsale: poetic, true, and poignant

➤ Betina Krahn: gracious, funny, and wise

Novels are as unique as the authors who write them. That's voice.

Stop the Presses!

Some writers start to unconsciously pick up the voice of other writers when they read fiction, so they refuse to read other novels while writing their own. If you start to sound like the writer whose current novel you're reading, you might want to put your pleasure-reading material on hold until you get a better handle on your own voice.

Editor's Radar

Editors and critics are always quick to sing the praises of authors who have an outstanding voice or style. If you go to a writers' conference, you will undoubtedly hear an editor say she's looking for an author with a "fresh new voice." This is good news. That fresh new voice could be yours!

So, what steps can you take to make sure your voice is fresh and new?

1. Don't imitate another author just because she's wildly popular. She already has a following. You need to create one of your own.

2. Practice writing until you feel a rhythm develop in your work. Read it out loud, then polish your prose until it flows in a way that sounds natural to you. If you're writing the way you think, the words will feel right.

3. Dare to be different. Don't worry if it seems like your writing is quirky or odd. Different is good. It will set you apart from the crowd. Just don't assume a style that's quirky unless it's really you, or your writing will seem affected and unnatural.

4. Get feedback. Ask your friends to read your work and give you their impressions. What words would they use to describe your style or approach? What themes do they see coming through in the stories you write? You'll probably start hearing the same reactions. Make a mental note of what others perceive as your strengths, and then play on those strengths as you develop your next book. Just be aware that friends may have a hard time understanding or articulating what they like about your work. They may not even appreciate your strengths! Don't despair. Just remember, writing is subjective.

A Natural Storyteller

You shouldn't confuse the author's voice or style with the ability to tell a good story. Some people are born storytellers. (They make me so jealous!) They magically create seamless worlds that are so real you never want to leave them. A natural storyteller may not have a particularly dazzling style or an unusual voice, but something about their books sweeps us along into another world.

Maeve Binchy is certainly a natural storyteller. So are Victoria Holt and Mary Stewart. In the romance genre, there is LaVyrle Spencer, Heather Graham, and Jude Deveraux, to name a few. Their ability to tell absorbing yarns has touched millions of readers.

Write On!

Voice comes from deep inside. If someone criticizes your voice as too different or unappealing, ignore her. Everyone's style is unique. For every reader who doesn't like your style, you'll find one who does. So just keep writing!

If you are a natural storyteller, congratulations! If not, you'll have to work at it like the rest of us. Either way, accept your gifts for what they are and don't covet those of another writer. Your style doesn't have to win a Pulitzer Prize. This is popular fiction. Your goal is to entertain your readers with a darned good story.

Are You Sure I Have a Unique Voice?

Yes, I'm sure! When I was a kid, some other kids told me that my epidermis was showing. I didn't know that was the technical word for skin, so I hid in the house for a few hours until my so-called friends enlightened me. So what does that anecdote have to do with the price of a paperback? Worrying about your voice is like worrying about your epidermis. It's there. Even if you don't know what it is and even if you can't see it, it's still there.

If your style isn't unique now, it will be if you keep writing. Write until you develop a style that seems right for you. It will sound natural—you'll know it when you hear it.

Writing on the Wall

Sometimes finding your own voice is like reading a big message scrawled on a wall. If you're standing too close, you can't read the whole sentence. You have to step back to get some perspective.

When you finish your book, put it away for a few weeks, then read it from cover to cover. See how it strikes you, what mood it creates. If you've been writing for a while, dig out your first, second, and third attempts. What do you notice about your writing style? Do you see any patterns? If so, you're probably getting a glimpse of your own writer's voice. If you don't see any patterns, or if you've never written before, relax. Ve have vays of finding your voice!

Speaking of Romance ...

Megan Chance is a RITA–award-winning author of historical romances who makes an interesting point about writing. She says a book's theme comes from the writer's voice. Chance says, "Voice manifests itself in theme. Each of us has a central theme, something we want to explore, our own 'hot button,' if you will. Look at the writers you know, and see if you can find the central theme that runs through their work. Kristin Hannah writes about rebirth in some form or another in every one of her books, Laura Kinsale about redemption. Susan Elizabeth Phillips explores finding and empowering yourself. These themes come from your own life, they are the demons that haunt you, your angels. They are your personal vision, and they give you your voice."

Find Your Niche

If your writing seems awkward and stilted, it may be that you aren't writing the right kind of romance. Try something different and see how it feels. When you find your niche, you'll know it. The words will start to flow, and you'll have fun!

My first hideous attempt at writing was a wretched novel whose name has mercifully escaped my memory. It was a short, contemporary romance. I studied the market and did my best to follow the guidelines. But it was ... well, bad. Enough said. On a whim, I decided to try a medieval romance. I had always loved Mary Stewart's *Merlin Trilogy*. Suddenly, I was writing in a firestorm of excitement. The words flowed, and my characters leapt to life. When I read the chapter to my critique group, they literally applauded and told me that I had found my niche.

Go with the Flow

I can't emphasize enough the importance of writing naturally. Don't sit down and try to analyze your voice. Just tell your story and let it flow naturally.

If there is no flow and you feel stuck, then go ahead and try to imitate your favorite authors if it helps you get the words out of your head and onto paper. Frankly, when I began my first medieval, I tried to write with the same velvety richness that marks Mary Stewart's books. Soon, my imitation turned into inspiration, and I was off on my own unique tangent. Imitation can be a good way to jump-start the writing process, but soon you should find your own style and take it from there.

Distinctive Dialogue

But enough about you! What about your characters? They have, or should have, their own voice as well. Each person in your novel will speak with different ...

➤ Tones and qualities.

➤ Rhythms and speeds.

➤ Words and levels of sophistication.

➤ Degrees of formality.

A working stiff from the Bronx will use lots of contractions (I can't, shouldn't, won't, etc.). If he's from Chicago he may be a "dem and doze" kind of guy. (Give me dem bricks there, Charlie! Doze ain't for you.) In contrast, a member of the British Parliament in the 1800s probably wouldn't use any contractions at all (I cannot, should not, will not, etc.).

Write On!

If your dialogue seems to be lacking, you might consider taking an acting class or trying out for a play. A number of romance writers have had experience in the theater. Actors learn how to give characters different speech patterns and qualities, and they quickly learn when an audience is getting bored.

Naturally Speaking

If you're writing a contemporary romance, your characters should talk like people you know. In other words, they should talk naturally. They may use trendy words like "dis" or "awesome," or they may be more formal. But a character should never talk like she stepped out of a college textbook. (Unless she's a college professor!) There are a couple easy ways to make dialogue natural:

1. **Don't use dollar words when a nickel word will do ya.** Instead of saying, "I anticipate the prevaricator will expostulate on his desire and hope that his associates and acquaintances will embrace the concept of redemption," say "I think the liar is going to say he wants his friends to forgive him."

2. **Study real conversations.** Frequently, people will interrupt each other, stop in the middle of a sentence, or mumble. To portray a realistic conversation, remember these tendencies. Here's an example of realistic dialogue:

"Hey! There you are! I thought I …."

"Well, what do ya know! I haven't seen you since, oh, what was it? The …"

"Since the college reunion."

"Uhuh. Boy, that was …."

"Oh, man! Do you remember when you started swinging from the chandelier?"

Stop the Presses!

If you want your dialogue to sound natural, don't use your characters' names in every other line. "What are you doing, Joe?" "Joe, can you help me?" "Joe, I love you." In real life, people don't use names that often. So read your scenes out loud. If you've used names excessively, you'll notice right away.

A Word About Dialects

Dialects can be fun, but they can also be confusing and hard work for the reader. Let's look at an example of a sentence with too much Scottish dialect:

"Och mon, I dinna noo ye were aboot to git the wee bonnie lass oot o' the inn. Ye shouldna be 'errrrr."

Hard to read, isn't it? Now here's the same sentence with too little of a dialect:

"Ah, man, I did not know you were about to get the little pretty girl out of the inn. You shouldn't be here."

How about a compromise between the two?

"Och, mon, I didna know ye were about to get the wee bonnie lass out o' the inn. Ye shouldna be here."

Use common sense when it comes to dialects. You want to give a flavor of an accent, but you don't want your reader to have to work too hard. It's like subtitles in movies. Some people simply won't see foreign films because they don't want to go to the trouble of reading every line.

The Narrator's Voice

Geez, everybody has a voice—you, the characters, and even the narrator! In general, the narrator's tone or style of communicating will be similar to your own. This is your story, after all. In most romances, the narrator is a generic storyteller who relays events without drawing attention to himself (or herself). You can have fun with narration, though. The richer it is, the better your story will be.

Objectively Speaking

A narrator who is not a character in the book should not spout opinions, make predictions, or otherwise step out of line. You would not, for example, want your narrator to say things like:

> "Little did Richard know, dear reader, that his life was about to change entirely. Oh, poor doomed Richard! If only he hadn't missed his plane, he wouldn't be in this predicament. What he doesn't know is that just around the corner, he will meet his death in a most unexpected way."

This kind of narration went out with … I dunno, the dinosaurs? In this example, the narrator is excessively foreshadowing events, casting unnecessary opinions, and pulling the reader out of the story for a very loud side conversation. Not a good idea!

The narrator should tell the reader what is happening, or what has happened in the past, not what is about to happen in the future. And unless he's a character in the book, he should describe the action without a running commentary. Like a news reporter, he should paint a thorough picture of the scene, yet remain objective.

The Mood-Ring Approach

You want your narrator to be reasonably objective, but that doesn't mean the narration has to be boring or dispassionate. In some of the best romances, the narration reflects the moods of the characters—specifically, the character whose point of view dominates the scene.

Take a look at this passage from Laura Kinsale's *Flowers from the Storm*. In this English historical romance, the hero suffered a stroke. He cannot speak and, after being misdiagnosed, was locked up in an insane asylum. In this passage, he's angry at the heroine, a visiting Quaker, for not setting him free. The Ape he refers to is his guard.

"He'd thought they were going. Where, how, why; none of that mattered. Only to go. Only his freedom. Out of the cage with her for assurance that he could manage in the outside.

He hated her.

Hated her.

Hate hate hate hurt cold blood faithless bitch.

Mixed up with it was the pain, a different rancor from the pure and honest malice he had for the Ape. To the Ape, he was a moving piece of meat, an ox to be trussed and prodded like all the other mad and dangerous dumb beasts in this place."

See how the rhythm and length of the sentences reflect the thoughts and mindset of the character? He's obviously frustrated, angry, and impatient. The narration reflects these moods, without interfering with the story. In fact, by being so grounded in the mood of one character, the narrator fades into the woodwork where he/she belongs. The character rightfully becomes the most important person in the scene.

Write On!

If your voice or style seems lackluster, it's time to focus on details. Go through each line and make sure they're not overwritten or underwritten. Cut excessive words and use punchy verbs and appropriate adjectives. Read out loud and make sure each paragraph is easy to read. If you stumble over the words, so will the reader. It's the little details that add up to powerful prose.

Every Trick in the Book

You can use the narrator's voice to reflect much more than the moods of your characters. The narrator's voice can mimic the environment and the overall tone of your book. Let's use a life-threatening snowstorm to show a few examples.

Active Adjectives

A few well-placed adjectives can add up to an overall sense of cold:

> She trudged through a *crusty* snow bank so dense she nearly collapsed in exhaustion only halfway through it. *Cold* flakes beat against her *numb* cheeks.

Vibrant Verbs

Seek out verbs that are distinctive or dramatic. Instead of saying "snowflakes fell," pick a more potent verb:

> The flurry of snow *flailed* at her raw skin. She *shuddered* and *curled* her numb fingers into fists.

Right Rhythm

Use sentence length to catch the right rhythm of the situation:

> Cold. So cold. No reprieve. Hell, they would die here. Black fingers. She had black fingers! She couldn't feel them anymore. They were dead. She would be, too, if help didn't come soon.

Magical Metaphors

The right metaphor or simile at the right time can encapsulate the exact feelings you're trying to convey:

> The snow went on forever, as far as the eye could see. Farther, even. It lay before her like a pristine white shroud, newly woven and anxious to wrap her in its cold, permanent embrace.

When you write your first draft, don't over-analyze these elements. Get your story down, then go back and examine each sentence. If you carefully choose the right verbs, rhythms, and metaphors, you will be well on your way to writing exciting fiction.

Say What You Mean

"Say what you mean, and mean what you say" is a good motto for any writer—novelists included! Just because you're writing fiction doesn't mean your work can be vague and meandering. When I started out, I had a naturally rich and lush style. Someone in my critique group once said about a particular sentence: "That was beautiful! But what did it mean?" I realized then that it's not enough to write beautifully. The words have to make sense. Since then my writing has become much more concise.

A romance novel seems to beg for a beautiful writing style. But regardless of style, your writing must communicate clearly. Look at what you've written carefully. Are you being precise? Try to envision the images you've created. Do they match? Do they make sense? Do they follow logically? Do they create a clear picture? Remember, you are your first editor! Be ruthless with yourself and you just might spare yourself the pain of rejection.

Stop the Presses!

While you should carefully edit your work, be careful not to edit the life out of your manuscript. Cut out the fat, but don't cut to the bone. Your style is determined by your word choices. So choose the words that please you, and if an editor has a problem with them, she'll let you know.

A Real Character!

At some point you might want one of your characters to narrate a story. Gothics are narrated by the heroine. Ideally, the narration should reflect the heroine's outlook and natural way of speaking.

You can use a minor character as a narrator, too, but sometimes that's limiting, especially in a romance. After all, how much detail can a minor character really give about a love scene between the hero and heroine? Actually, in my medieval romance, *The Maiden's Heart,* I glossed over that issue entirely—and my narrator was a monk! I got away with it because the monk had written the love story in an illuminated manuscript, so the only time his presence was felt was in written asides that were few and far between.

Voice Checklist

Writers usually have to feel their way into their own voice. Once you hear it often enough, you'll start to recognize it. In the meantime, here is a checklist to think about as you cultivate your own unique writing style.

- ❏ The style of my writing is my own.
- ❏ I am not imitating someone else's style.
- ❏ I've started to identify words I would use to describe the mood, tone, or style of my work.
- ❏ I feel as if I've found my niche.
- ❏ The kind of romance I'm writing is appropriate for my style.
- ❏ I have resisted the urge to let my narrator blab about future events.
- ❏ All my characters have different voices.
- ❏ I have chosen words designed to communicate to the reader, rather than words designed to impress her.
- ❏ My dialogue sounds natural.
- ❏ I have given a flavor of a dialect without making it too hard to read.
- ❏ I've allowed my narration to reflect the mood of the characters or the environment when appropriate.
- ❏ I have used active adjectives, vibrant verbs, the right rhythms, and magical metaphors.

The Least You Need to Know

➤ Most successful authors have a unique voice.

➤ To find your own voice you must keep writing and polish your prose.

➤ Every character should have his or her own way of talking.

➤ Don't overdo dialects or you'll frustrate the reader.

➤ Tighten your sentences until each one says exactly what you intended.

Chapter 10

Conflict: The Magic Ingredient

In This Chapter

➤ Why you can't write a romance without conflict

➤ Two kinds of conflicts are better than one

➤ Building to the big crisis

➤ Not every conflict has to be a Greek tragedy

➤ The best way to make your book absolutely compelling

➤ No magic solutions allowed!

Isn't it ironic? The one genre that most celebrates the concept of love is the one genre that depends most on conflict. Without conflict, you don't have a romance. Conflict is the gas that will fuel your story. Luckily for you, you just pulled into the gas station. So fill 'er up!

"I Couldn't Put It Down"

Those five words are music to an author's ears. It's the ultimate compliment. If someone can't put your book down, it means you've succeeded in creating a compelling work of fiction. It also means that the reader will probably be waiting for your next book!

At first glance, you might think that a compelling love story is one in which love knows no bounds. The hero waxes poetic and proposes on bended knee, and the heroine spends all of her free time writing love poems to the hero—not so. A compelling romance is one in which there's enough conflict to raise that all-important question: How will these two lovers ever manage to overcome their differences and make it to the altar?

Creating Suspense

To keep the reader turning the pages, you first have to create characters that she cares about. I talked about that in Chapter 7, "Characterization: Heroes to Die for and Heroines to Cry For." Then, you have to make the reader wonder if they'll ever get together. That nagging doubt is raised when you skillfully introduce a series of obstacles or problems. These problems have to fall smack dab in between your protagonists and their most cherished goals.

Your characters' problems might be small (will their car make it to the next highway exit ramp with a flat tire?) or huge (will they keep the comet from colliding into the earth?). Ideally, your scenes will have a mixture of both, but you must have problems in order to build suspense!

Write On!

The "Show, Don't Tell" rule applies to villains. If you want to create a really nasty villain to supply the main obstacles, you have to show him (or her) in action. It's not enough to tell the reader how bad he is. Show examples of his villainy. That will make him a worthy opponent of your strong hero and heroine, and a legitimate concern to the reader.

Pothole on the Yellow Brick Road

I seem to be hung up on automobile metaphors. In this case, the metaphor is apt. An obstacle or conflict serves the same purpose as a giant pothole. Your characters are cruising along, driving toward their personal goals, when all of a sudden they come to a screeching halt. They can't move forward without falling into a pit. They've reached a conflict. They can try to go around it, backtrack and try to take a detour, or they can call in contractors to fill the hole on the spot, but they must deal with it one way or another!

Turn Up the Heat

No more Ms. Nice Writer! It's time to get tough. Not only do you have to give your protagonists problems, you have make those problems get worse. (Ouch!) Are you ready to be a meanie? If so, consider some of these techniques:

1. If a villain is causing problems, make him a strong villain so he can make things progressively worse.

2. Give the hero and heroine conflicting goals. This way, while they are falling in love, their progress toward their individual goals makes matters worse for the other and their relationship. Ultimately, they must chose between their goals and the one they love.

3. Let your hero/heroine inadvertently make things worse by their own actions. Maybe your hero reluctantly decides to take abuse from the villain because fighting back will make things worse for the heroine. Maybe the heroine hurts the hero's cause by being so honest she unwittingly gives away an important secret to the villain.

4. Let outside forces unexpectedly turn the tide against your protagonists. If the hero is trying to save a child from a burning building, the wind changes direction, and the flames shift toward the child's bedroom. If the heroine has been trying to prove her worth by making a killing on the stock market, the stock market crashes, and she loses everything.

The Shortest Story Ever Told

Without a progressive series of worsening conflicts, your story will be very short. In fact, it will be so short it won't exist. Stories without conflict are slice-of-life vignettes that have no forward motion, no suspense, and no plot. If you're thinking about writing a nice little love story that evokes wonderful feelings, that's great, but it's not enough. Mood will only carry a book so far.

Speaking of Romance ...

A by-product of a good conflict can be an increase in the sexual tension between your hero and heroine, according to author Ruth Owen. She says: "Conflict is the friction that makes the sparks fly between your hero and heroine. Face it, if Romeo's and Juliet's parents had said, 'Okay, get married,' the sexual tension between them would have been non-existent—and so would the story. I'm not necessarily talking sex. Some of the most powerful love stories ever written have been about people who don't make love. Think about Jane Eyre and Mr. Rochester. They barely kissed, but you could feel the sensual charge between them ... romance stories are about the sizzle, not the steak. And the sizzle comes from conflict."*

Contemporary Crises

One of the most pleasant aspects of writing contemporary romances is that you can probably relate to, or at least have a concept of, just about any problem you create for your characters. Even if the conflict is something you're not likely to face, you can imagine what the hero or heroine would feel like when dealing with it.

Think about how you'd feel if ...

➤ You were running nonstop for two weeks from a Mafia hit man who also happens to be your stepfather.

➤ You've just had your third patient die while you were performing routine surgical procedures, and you don't know why.

➤ You had to land a Concorde jet after the pilot and co-pilot became incapacitated from poisoned food.

You'd feel fear, anxiety, anger, frustration, guilt, apprehension, and/or terror. These are all emotions you've probably felt at one point or another. So remember them and use them. If your story conflicts don't evoke strong emotions in your characters (and you) they're probably not worth the paper they're written on! Can them and start over.

Historical Hitches

We tend to think of historical events as more dramatic, and in many ways they were. People faced a greater threat of mortality, disease, war, violence, and a host of other problems we are not forced to face on a daily basis. Fortunately for you, it's all fodder for conflict.

So your hero and heroine think all their problems are solved, eh? We'll see about that. Try throwing a plague their way. That will really complicate things! If you're worried about creating realistic historical conflicts, try the following suggestions:

➤ Do research to give yourself a better sense of what historical problems were really like. Don't forget first-hand accounts, like diaries, which are often more emotional and descriptive than textbooks, though not always factually accurate.

➤ Trust your imagination. Human emotions have changed little over the centuries. Your heroine would react to a brutal Viking invader with the same emotions you would. Just put yourself in her shoes.

➤ Don't worry about the reader's judgments. Do the best job you can researching what problems were really like way back when. There is always room for interpretation regarding historical events. Historians themselves frequently disagree on what happened in the past.

The Number-One Concern

Don't forget that you're a writing romance. So the number-one concern, plagues and mayhem not withstanding, is the romance. Sure, your lovers are being chased by a fire-breathing dragon or a demented serial killer, but how is their relationship developing in the meantime? The romance itself must face conflicts. Without problems in the relationship, all you will have is an adventure story. Frankly, nothing bores me more than to read a romance in which the hero and heroine declare their love early on and then proceed to chase a villain over mountain and stream for the rest of the book. That's not a romance! That's a romantic adventure.

It Takes Two Conflicts to Tango

Write On!

In historical novels, there are lots of opportunities to weave social conflicts into the lives of your characters. War and political intrigue offer characters a chance to take sides and make difficult choices, which inevitably leads to conflict. To the extent that you include these broader conflicts into your novel, you naturally broaden the scope of your story.

Speaking of adventure, there is nothing wrong with chase scenes and lots of action. In fact, you want some kind of movement in your book. It would be boring to place all your scenes in a single Victorian parlor, for example, and have the characters do nothing but talk about their problems.

The conflict should force your characters to make decisions and take decisive action steps. However, there is more to a well-written romance than action. You need two distinct kinds of obstacles to make the dance worth the price of admission.

Externally Speaking

Your romance should have some sort of external conflict. In order to overcome outward problems, the hero and heroine must grow and change. Those changes give them the added insight and maturity that enable them to make a commitment. External conflicts are the easiest to create and identify. Here are few things to keep in mind about outward obstacles:

1. **They are often visible.** We can see these things happening. They are outside of the characters. Examples: A raging wildfire threatens the heroine's homestead. If it burns, she'll have to go back to Boston. Or a villain chases the hero through the streets of New York.

Write On!

Be sure to foreshadow conflict throughout the book. Let's say the climax of your book involves a scene where your heroine must cross a high wire. Make sure that early in the book you let the reader know that she was forced to be a trapeze artist by her circus ring-master father, a career which she hated and ended when she fell and broke her back.

2. **They are often situational.** These are situations that cause turmoil for the characters. Example: The heroine might not get tenure because a new faculty department head hates her guts. Or an ATF agent falls in love with the fugitive he's been chasing across the country for five years.

3. **They should be tailor-made for your characters.** Example: If your hero is an artist with a studio in the Blue Ridge Mountains, he'd probably be upset if a land developer came in and bought up the nearest town. But that's a generic problem. To make it specific to the hero, have the developer also buy out the hero's lease and throw him out of his art studio. Better yet, how about making the developer the hero's older brother who vowed long ago to make him pay for being their parents' favorite? The brother buys up his lease, throws him out, then burns his paintings. Now that's a tailor-made problem! And it's more dramatic because it pushes all of the hero's buttons.

You want to choose external conflicts that truly affect your characters in more than a passing way. In fact, external conflicts should be directly tied to the essence of your characters, perhaps stemming from the characters' own internal conflicts.

Speaking of Romance ...

Romance author and teacher Jeanne Triner has some great observations about the role of conflict in romances. "The real art in writing romance comes from the pacing of the revelation of the obstacles and their resolutions," says Triner. It also comes from "the ability to convince the readers that they, like the writer, know the heroine better than she knows herself and must stand beside her until the end to help her fight her internal demons. This is why the existence of an internal conflict is so important. The external problems, the problems of the story, go on and are conquered by the characters without the reader's help. However, a good writer convinces the reader that the internal conflict is too big for the heroine to handle alone. She needs the wisdom and support of her friends."

Internal Affairs

The internal conflicts provide the meat of the story. These are the real issues that keep the characters apart long after the external problems have been resolved.

Let's say your hero and heroine, Ken and Karen, are firefighters working to control a forest fire. At first they hate each other because they work for rival cities (external conflict #1), but soon they learn to respect each other and love grows. Then, the fire worsens and threatens both their lives (external conflict #2), but they overcome that problem, too, when extra water is pumped in. So what's going to keep Ken and Karen apart after these are resolved? The internal conflict.

In romances, the internal conflicts usually revolve around feelings and/or beliefs. Here are a few possibilities:

> ➤ The heroine has always lived under an unlucky star, and she blames herself for her first husband's death. She thinks loving the hero will be bad for him and perhaps even kill him. Irrationally, she associates love with the death of a loved one.

> ➤ The hero dutifully goes to Vietnam and survives a massacre. He returns home and swears he'll do everything in his power to help POWs and MIAs. He becomes a congressman and does his job with so much dedication he has no time for love. When he finally falls in love and takes time off, he feels as if he's abandoning his friends who died in the massacre. He equates accepting love with turning his back on duty, which has been the driving force in his life.

Misplaced guilt, fear of rejection, pride, lack of self-esteem manifested in excessive ambition, inner fragility—these are all internal problems. Often, the characters are unaware of their internal conflicts so they are usually the last problems to be resolved in your story.

Think of your story as an artichoke. You peel away the outer leaves (the external conflicts) until you reach the heart (the internal conflict). That's the soft core of the character that is carefully hidden away and protected.

The Crossroad Collision

Continuing our car metaphor, your internal and external conflicts often drive on parallel roads. At some point, these roads should intersect. I'll give you an example: In my first medieval romance,

Stop the Presses!

You can have more than one external conflict in a story, but they should all be tied to the plot. One accident or natural disaster after another won't do. The problems must arise from who the characters are and what they do, and they should build to the big finish.

Lady and the Wolf, my heroine made a vow beside her brother's deathbed to become a nun and pray eternally for her brother's soul, but Lady Katherine was instead forced to marry. She felt guilty when she ended up falling in love with her husband and abandoning her hopes of eternal prayer. This guilt (the inner conflict) was present throughout the story.

The internal conflict really came to a head when it collided with the external conflict. Katherine had to retrieve a medallion in order to prove her husband's rightful inheritance and save his life. The medallion was buried with a corpse, so in order to save her husband's life (external conflict), Katherine had to dig up the medallion, risk eternal damnation for grave-robbing, and reconcile the guilt (internal conflict) that she felt about abandoning her prayers for her dead brother.

The corpse was a gruesome (emotional) reminder of her brother's fate. It forced her to deal with her unresolved guilt. Once that was resolved, she was finally free to love the hero without hesitation. In this story, the external conflict made the internal conflict much worse than it already was, which provoked change. In this case, the Black Moment was both internal and external.

Write On!

If you're writing a romantic comedy, do you still have to have a Black Moment? Yes—or at least a Dark Gray Moment. Simply tone down the conflict. With a heroine who's reluctant to marry, instead of blaming it on a former boyfriend who raped her, give her a former boyfriend (she didn't really love) who left her at the altar.

The Black Moment

The Black Moment, which you may remember from Chapter 6, "Plotting: Fresh Take on an Age-Old Story," is pretty much what it sounds like: a moment in which everything looks bleak and hopeless. It usually happens about four fifths of the way into your book. It's often the point at which the internal and external conflicts collide and really muck things up. Here are a few things to remember about Black Moments:

➤ At this point, the relationship must appear to be doomed.

➤ The relationship appears to be doomed because the characters are unable or unwilling to resolve the core inner conflicts keeping them apart.

➤ Both the characters and the reader can't see how the problem will be resolved.

It's important to make the Black Moment emotional. If your characters declare their love early on, for example, and spend the rest of the book running away from the villain, your Black Moment will merely be external. If your characters are hanging over a cliff by their fingers, the reader will be anxious for them to climb back to safety. But she would be even more eager for them to reach safety if she is still waiting for the hero to admit he loves the heroine. Readers go for emotion every time!

About-Face!

In order to reach your happy ending, the Black Moment obviously has to come to an end. Something usually happens to bring about change. It could be that ...

➤ The characters learn something they didn't know before.

➤ Events beyond their control make an about-face.

These changes open a door of opportunity. The characters, having grown wiser over the course of the book, decide to choose love, no matter what the cost. When they make that decision, they take advantage of the opportunity to resolve their problems.

Now I Understand!

At the turning point of the romance, your characters have to gain some insight that enables them to choose love. Romance author Jeanne Triner calls that the "Come to Realize" conclusion. The characters come to realize that love is more important than their problems.

Remember the Vietnam-vet congressman? He must come to realize that he deserves love. He must come to realize that he not only has a duty to his country and the men who died in the massacre, but he has a duty to himself as well. He has to let himself love to be a complete and whole person. Something in the external conflict triggers this realization. Perhaps his lover becomes endangered through his neglect of her. He realizes what he might have lost, and that she, as well as his veteran friends, deserves his devotion.

Move Over, Freud

Once you start thinking about internal conflicts, it's easy to over-psychoanalyze your characters. You don't have to give your characters deep-seated fears and abusive childhoods in order to make them reluctant to accept love. Sometimes it's just a matter of juggling a couple of serious issues—a tough situation, a bad previous relationship, a misguided personal goal, or a slightly cynical outlook. Mix two of these problems together and you have a major pothole on the road to love.

Stop the Presses!

Frequently, beginning writers overload their stories with psychological conflicts because they don't know how to explore the subtleties of lesser problems. To avoid that pitfall, you need to really live in your characters' shoes. Imagine what it's really like to have their problems, then imagine how they really feel about each other. You'll have plenty of reasons to keep them apart until the end of the book.

Cultural Clashes

A good alternative to the psycho-babble approach to character conflict is the clash of cultures or values. Your main characters will have a tough time allowing themselves to love if they think doing so violates a fundamental belief or value.

Clash of cultures is a traditional theme in Native American romances. The white woman and the Native American man must find some way to live together even though their cultures are vastly different. It works well in contemporary settings, too. What if your heroine has been living in a tent city for a year helping the homeless, and she unexpectedly falls in love with the millionaire corporate executive she's seeking donations from? Does she move into his mansion, or does he move into her tent?

Goal Versus Goal

Every character needs a personal goal. To heighten conflict, give your hero and heroine conflicting goals.

A good example is the historical romance that focuses on the conflict between the Welsh and the Normans. The invading Norman hero comes to Wales to take over the heroine's castle. He marries her to ensure his dubious claim to her birthright. She wants to get rid of him. He plans to stay. Goal vs. goal.

Stop the Presses!

Do not mistake petty arguments for real conflicts. There have been plenty of rejected manuscripts that include scene after scene of unreasonable arguments between the hero and the heroine. Unjustified temper tantrums will turn your heroine into a whiner and your hero into a bully.

A Clear and Present Danger

Your characters' goals should be very clear. If they are, it will be very clear to the reader when those goals are thwarted. Likewise, the conflicts should be clear. A number of smaller problems can come up and be resolved during the course of the book (i.e., flat tires, nagging mothers, a lost job, a fear of mice). But you should have no more than one or two major conflicts. They should be utterly clear to the reader, and they should pose a serious threat—if not physical, then emotional.

You don't want your characters to meander from one so-so problem to the next until the book comes to an unspectacular finish.

Don't Leave 'Em Hanging

If you build up to a big crisis or Black Moment, play it for all it's worth. Then, resolve the dilemma completely. If your readers invest their time and feelings in your book, they want to feel like everything is hunky-dory by the end. Don't leave any loose threads.

How can you accomplish this? Easy! Read your book when you are finished writing and note all the subplots. Then, check them off one by one as they're resolved. If you're planning a spin-off romance involving secondary characters, you obviously need to leave some elements of their subplot unresolved.

Beginners Beware!

Creating believable conflicts is a romance writer's greatest challenge. It can be tricky even for experienced authors. So if you're feeling a little anxious, relax. It might take a little practice.

Meanwhile, I want to warn you about two problems that tend to plague beginners. A simple warning just might keep you on track.

No Rabbits, Please!

To solve your characters' problems, resist the urge to pull a rabbit out of the hat to magically solve everything. Sure, circumstances can change, but the changes should be logical and they should be foreshadowed.

Example: Let's say you're writing a big romantic suspense novel. The villain is the hero's 26-year-old ex-girlfriend. She's a former Olympic gold medallist who turns into a *Fatal Attraction* type of stalker, and she's trying to kill the heroine. You can't resolve the big crisis moment by having the villainess die of a heart attack—not unless you foreshadow the heart attack by mentioning that she also abuses cocaine or steroids or has some other problem that might cause an athlete to unexpectedly keel over.

Example: Let's say your hero and heroine work in a shelter for troubled youths. The plot revolves around their efforts to keep the shelter from being shut down. The crisis point of the external conflict comes when they conclude they simply don't have enough money. Just as they are about to nail the "Closed" sign to the door, the heroine gets a telegram saying that an uncle she never even knew about just died leaving her a million dollars. Now that's one big rabbit!

> **Love Letters**
>
> **Deus ex machina** is a term used to describe an inappropriately miraculous resolution of conflict. It came from ancient Greek tragedies in which an actor playing a god would descend on stage in some sort of machine, as if from the heavens, to decide the drama's final outcome.

To avoid this pitfall, make sure that your hero and heroine solve the problems. No *deus ex machina*. Forget the rabbits! Remember, you're a writer, not a magician!

Unsustainable Conflicts

Beginning writers sometimes get half-way through a book before they realize their conflict isn't strong enough to carry them through to the end. That's usually when they put the book in a drawer and never dig it out again. To avoid this problem, you need to make sure you start the book with a strong major conflict. How do you do that?

1. **Plot your story out.** If you can't seem to finish the synopsis, it may be a sign that your conflicts are weak. Think the story through again until logic tells you that it will hold together. Then start writing.

2. **Get to know your characters ahead of time.** If you know their goals, weaknesses, and strengths, you'll have an easier time making sure the conflict is tailor-made to their personalities.

When I first began to write, I started and stopped numerous books because I didn't have strong conflicts. So, when I began *Lady and the Wolf*, I was determined to create enough plot and conflict to see me through to the end. I methodically planned that story out. As a result, it was the first one I ever finished. I fine-tuned the conflicts over the course of many rewrites, but it wasn't until the last rewrite, when I added an internal conflict, that the story finally took off. So you see, fine-tuning conflicts can be an on-going process. Stick with it!

You will be better at creating conflict than I was because you already know more than I did when I first started! You've also mentally laid the groundwork for the next chapter on emotion. So, get out the hankies and turn the page.

Conflict Checklist

Hopefully, you no longer feel conflicted about conflict. It's the key to a great romance. See how your story measures up to this checklist:

❑ I have one or two clear and obvious conflicts.

❑ The conflicts are tailor-made for my characters.

❑ I have internal conflicts in addition to external problems.

❑ The problems build progressively to a Black Moment.

❑ It is believable when my characters "come to realize" they can't live without each other.

❑ My characters have goals.

❑ I have resolved all the problems and subplots by the end.

❑ The resolution of the conflicts is a natural outcome of the plot.

❑ The development of the romance is paramount, regardless of other conflicts.

The Least You Need to Know

➤ Without conflict you have no story.

➤ Create conflicts that are both internal and external.

➤ Build your story to a Black Moment when all seems doomed.

➤ The obstacles to happiness you develop should be clear and specific.

➤ Do not resolve conflicts by magically pulling a rabbit out of a hat.

➤ Pick conflicts that are strong enough to sustain you throughout the book.

Chapter 11

Emotion: Tugging at the Heartstrings

In This Chapter

➤ Learning how to pump up emotions

➤ Involving your readers by raising the stakes

➤ Understanding the power of details

➤ Sending your readers unspoken messages

➤ Using rich language to pack a powerful punch

Have you ever cried at a Hallmark commercial? Be honest! If you have, you should definitely read this chapter. If you haven't, you should read this chapter twice. Emotion is the hallmark (pun intended) of every great romance. Make 'em feel like laughing. Make 'em feel like crying. But whatever you do, make 'em feel!

Finally! Men Who Talk About Their Feelings

In real life, getting a man to talk about his feelings is sometimes like pulling teeth—but not so in a romance novel! The hero may have to be dragged kicking and screaming to the altar, but by the end of the book, he'll admit it: He loves the heroine and can't live without her. And because you, the writer, are in control of his life (he-he-he, she snickers, gleefully rubbing her hands together), you can focus your story on the thoughts and feelings that lead up to his confession.

When the hero finally tells the heroine he loves her, you can almost hear the reader shout "Yes!" His admission reaffirms the reader's belief that, when pushed into a corner, even a man will admit that love is the ultimate reward. It's not enough for the hero to make love to the heroine; he must ultimately admit he loves her emotionally, as well as physically. That is the catharsis point of the book. That is the moment the reader has been waiting for.

Researchers recently conducted a study and discovered that men actually talk less than women do. In the course of any given day, a typical man utters fewer than half the number of words spoken by his female counterpart. Given this statistic, is it any wonder that men and women struggle with communication?

So, how does a writer from Venus portray men from Mars? Here are a few tips to keep in mind about your hero's emotions:

➤ He feels just as much as your heroine. In fact, his feelings may seem even more intense if he bottles them up, as men frequently do.

➤ If you write scenes from the hero's point of view, you can show his thoughts and feelings. If you don't get into his head, you'll have to show his feelings by his reactions to events.

➤ If your hero is a man of few words—the strong silent type—he can show his love through his actions. Just as in real life, actions often speak louder than words.

Heroines Just Like You

Your heroine may have qualities, values, strengths, and weaknesses that are different than yours, but her emotional reactions to events will probably be similar to your own. Emotions are universal. The only thing that varies from person to person is what triggers those emotions.

Here are a few tips to keep in mind about your heroine:

➤ She has more freedom to express her emotions than the hero does, just like women in real life. A reader will be more apt to accept a heroine who cries when she's angry than she will be a hero who reacts that way to frustration, for example.

➤ Your heroine shouldn't be a cardboard stand-in for you. It's tempting to identify with the heroine so much that she becomes almost a neutral observer of events as they unfold, but she is not you. She must have goals, conflicts, frustrations, joys, and triumphs all her own, which must be visible to the reader.

➤ Your heroine, like many women in real life, may temper her dialogue with qualifying statements. Men are often more direct. If a woman wants someone to leave the room, she might say something like, "I hope you won't be offended, but it may be best for everyone involved if you consider leaving the room, if at all possible." A man is more apt to say "Get the hell out of here."

Action and Reaction: Putting Feelings Before Plot

Romances are not generally read because of their plots. Readers are usually looking for emotion, though a good plot is still essential. As a writer, you're not going to put your characters through their paces simply to show the reader a course of events. If that's your intention, you may as well write an adventure story or a techno-thriller. Your purpose is to involve the reader in the characters' emotional development—which becomes evident as the plot unfolds! See how simple it is? (Yeah, right!)

Stop in the Name of Love

If your well-crafted plot starts to feel like a runaway train, put on the breaks. Allow your characters to …

➤ React to what's happening.

➤ Vent their feelings.

➤ Decide what to do next.

Stop the Presses!

Big emotion has to be justified or it will seem melodramatic. If you want your characters to react strongly, you have to create conflicts that warrant strong reaction. You also have to make sure your characterization is strong as well. If you put cardboard characters in a dramatic situation, the reader will simply yawn. A good romance is a triangle of strong plot, emotion, and characterization.

Once you've made sure you haven't short-changed your characters' emotional development you can continue your story. That doesn't mean the action has to come to a dead stop while your characters engage in group therapy. It just means you can't short-change emotional growth in favor of action scenes.

Take a Breather

How do you slow down a runaway plot? Unless it's a high-octane action thriller, you should allow some downtime. Give your characters, and your readers, a chance to catch their breath. That might mean focusing briefly on the subplot, or throwing in a scene that does nothing but allow the characters to have fun—quality time, to use the parlance of the times. Here are a few possibilities:

➤ Add a sensual scene in which the characters bathe each other.

➤ Get the characters alone and focus on their feelings.

➤ Draw out the first kiss, the first touch, the first glimpse of each other.

➤ Include a scene about a painful goodbye, a fun picnic, a poignant act of charity, or a giddy and breathless game of hide-and-seek in the woods.

In other words, create scenes where the action puts the spotlight on the emotion *du jour*. The point is to give your characters plenty of time and space to feel. And don't forget, not all emotions are painful or sad!

Write On!

After every action or plot development, ask yourself, "What is each character feeling now?" Your hero and heroine will react, at least internally, to every event. If they don't, then you're not allowing your characters to develop. Once you realize how each event affects your hero and heroine, let the reader in on the secret!

Show, Don't Tell

You have already heard the "Show, Don't Tell" rule. It's especially important when dealing with emotions. It's more effective to show emotional reactions, rather than to tell the reader what the characters are feeling. Here are some ways to show reactions:

1. **Dialogue.** How do your characters react with words? We can tell a lot about their feelings by what they say and by what they don't say. Sometimes lips clamped tight in stubborn silence reveal more than a litany of curses. An angry character might shout, a sad character might cry, and a reasonable character might analyze his feelings in a calm voice. Whatever the reaction, dialogue is a good and easy way to show it.

2. **Body language.** Another way to communicate what the characters are feeling is to show physical reactions—a trembling lower lip, a quick blush, clinched fists. These are all indicators of emotion.

3. **Choices.** What choices do your characters make as a result of an action? These choices can tell the reader a lot about the character and his/her emotions. If the hero walks into a room and sees that his lover has been molested, what choices does he make? Does he forgive and forget? Does he report the crime to the

police and wait for authorities to bring justice? Or does he quietly get a baseball bat, find the molester, and beat him to a bloody pulp? When we see these actions, we realize, without being told, what kind of hero he is. We also know how he feels without the writer having explained his emotions.

These are all different ways to show emotion. The last example, a character retrieving a baseball bat, is more powerful than telling the reader "He was really mad." Don't get me wrong. There is a time and a place to tell the reader what's happening with your characters, but when it comes to conveying emotions, showing is more effective than telling.

Reading Between the Lines

When a scene drips with emotion, the author has often used a variety of techniques—not to mention talent—to give you that overall impression. It's time for you to learn some of those techniques!

You want your reader to laugh and cry and feel like she's an integral part of the story. Here are two ways to clue the reader in to your character's emotions without hitting her over the head.

Scene Subtext

In acting classes, actors quickly learn something very important about the people they're trying to portray: What a character says and what a character thinks/feels are often two different things. Actors call the thinking/feeling part of that equation "subtext."

In the most interesting scenes, there is subtext beneath the surface of the conversation. That's especially true when there's sexual tension. If your hero and heroine are in a garden, they might be talking about roses, but they're thinking about who is going to make the first move. How can you convey the subtext and the underlying emotions of a conversation?

➤ **Let the characters' actions tell the real story.** For example: Your hero is talking about a long hot spell, but instead of looking at the sun, he's looking at your heroine's long and sexy legs. The location of his gaze is a dead giveaway to his thoughts.

Write On!

Actors have a lot in common with writers. Both try to create convincing and compelling characters. If you're feeling blasé about a scene, try to act it out. Get out of your chair and physically go through the motions, playing all the parts. You'll have a better idea of how to describe the action and how your characters would react.

➤ **Use innuendos and metaphors.** For example: If your heroine wonders out loud how the flower feels when a bee draws its nectar, her real meaning should be loud and clear! Metaphors can mask feelings that your characters aren't yet prepared to talk about.

➤ **Let the viewpoint character think to him-/herself.** For example: You can tell the reader the character's thoughts through an inner monologue or through the narrator. Here is a vignette using both. The inner monologue is italicized and followed by the narrator's interpretation of the character's thoughts:

> "I really don't like you very much, Lord Halifax," Julia said, resisting the urge to stroke his brow. *Damn him,* she thought, *he didn't deserve such affection.* He had trifled with her feelings. So she spun on her heels, leaving him to his solitude.

Granted, thoughts are just another way of telling, instead of showing, but they create a greater sense of intimacy than if the narrator tells the reader the same information.

Speaking of Romance ...

Author Jolie Kramer, who has great insight into the writing process, cites Stephen King as a master of details. Kramer says: "I think the reason we're willing to believe that horrible clowns live in the sewer or a writer's dark half has come to life is that King has made his protagonists so incredibly specific ... He doesn't write about birds. He writes about sparrows. He doesn't write about lunch, he writes about Cup-'o'-Soup. Specific. Detailed. And a direct conduit between the universe of the story and the universe of the reader."*

Detail-Oriented

It's one thing to have characters who are feeling strong emotions. It's another thing altogether to get the reader to feel those emotions as well. This is what you want to strive for. If the reader doesn't feel the emotions, she'll be a detached observer and will likely dismiss your writing as melodramatic.

To get the reader to go along for the ride, you need to do two things:

1. **Make sure your characters react to events in a way that's true to themselves.** Otherwise, your reader will sense something is wrong and will stop feeling and start analyzing the problem.

For example: You want your heroine to sob hysterically as a carriage rides off with all her worldly possessions. You need her to cry because it's a big turning point in the book, but when you write the scene, the heroine laughs instead because she always finds the humor in every situation. If laughing is unacceptable, then rework your story or your character. Don't force your heroine to cry to fit the needs of your plot, or it will ring false to the reader.

2. **Focus on details.** That's the best way to draw your readers into a scene. If you allow them to feel, smell, touch, and hear what the characters do, readers will put themselves into the characters' shoes and feel the same emotions.

   For example: Look at a brief description of a walk in the woods. One is a general description, and one is detailed.

   General. Colby walked down the path and enjoyed the sun on his cheeks. He felt invigorated and picked up his pace until he reached the clearing.

   Detailed. Colby walked down the gravel path, his heels sinking with each grinding step. Soon his heart pumped faster, and he turned his smiling face up to the warm, buttery sun. The scents of summer were in the air—newly cut grass and the promise of rain. He hurried on until he reached the carpet of daffodils that bobbed their yellow heads in the clearing.

Now you decide. Which one was better? Which one painted a clearer picture? Which one involved you more? That's the same one that will involve the reader.

Speaking of Romance ...

Award-winning author Kim Cates always creates heart-tugging romances. She says: "The key to emotion in a book is to create characters people can identify with and love because of their flaws and vulnerabilities, as well as their strengths. Then, put them in reach of what they want the most and threaten to take it all away. You key into emotions everyone has, realizing that whether it was 1814 or 1999 people want all the same things—to belong, to be secure, to be loved, to be safe, to be respected for who they are. And make sure that what they want *is* worth all the angst you give them. If a grown woman is still whining about not being invited to *the* party in junior high, people will get impatient."

High Drama

I'll never forget my reaction to a wonderful Harlequin Superromance I read many years ago. The characters were so real that when a friend of the heroine's died unexpectedly in childbirth, I literally screamed "No!" and burst into tears. I couldn't believe the author had gone that far, and I was upset with her for killing off a character I cared about. After I had a good cry, though, I was happy to have felt so much. Let's face it, in today's high-efficiency, high-tech world, sometimes you have to read a book just to remember how good old-fashioned emotions feel.

The plot twist in the Superromance had a strong impact for three reasons:

1. The author made me care about the characters.

2. The plot twist came as a surprise.

3. It was dramatic.

You can make similarly dramatic choices if they fit the kind of romance line you're targeting. In fact, when you're plotting your book, ask yourself if making more dramatic choices would work for your story. If the answer is yes, then make them. Remember, this isn't slice-of-life fiction.

Love Letters

Romance novels are not **high-concept** books. But you'll probably hear the term because it's a favorite publishing buzzword. High-concept novels have a concept or plot that *is* bigger than life and has never been done before—and it usually takes precedence over characterization. *Jurassic Park* by Michael Crichton, a novel in which dinosaurs are cloned from DNA and bred for a theme park, is a high-concept book.

Bigger Than Life

Albert Zuckerman is a literary agent who has written a wonderful book called *Writing the Blockbuster Novel.* Zuckerman writes that in each blockbuster novel there is usually one larger-than-life character: someone with boundless ambition who goes to the extreme to achieve his or her goals.

If you put those kinds of characters in a traditional romance, they would come off as kooky or abnormal, in other words not hero or heroine material. Does that mean your characters have to be mundane? Not at all! The greater the emotional swings your characters undergo, the more exciting your novel will be. The key is to take normal, yet distinctive, characters and put them in larger-than-life situations. In *high-concept* novels, a big situation or a unique plot twist is often more important than the characters.

Raising the Stakes

In good romances, the characters usually reach a point where they have to make difficult choices. They have to come up with extreme solutions to seemingly impossible problems. They have to take huge risks or face the possibility of failures larger than anything you or I will probably ever face. These are the hallmarks (that word again!) of exciting fiction.

To heighten the emotion and drama of your story, put your characters into tight corners, then let them find a way out. Let's raise the stakes on some boring setups:

Boring: Your hero is a duke who isn't sure if a beautiful, rich countess is the woman he wants to marry.

Exciting: Your hero is a duke who isn't sure he wants to marry a beautiful, rich countess. But after he's kidnapped by a cousin, beaten up, wrongfully discredited as illegitimate, and left for dead, he has to woo the countess and convince her to help him restore his rightful inheritance.

Boring: Your hero is a zookeeper who is not sure he really wants to get involved with the veterinarian recently hired by the zoo. He is laid back, and she seems to be the button-down, establishment type.

Exciting: Your hero is a zookeeper who falls in love with the zoo's new vet, only to discover she's heading up a research project involving controversial testing of the chimps in his care.

The heightened conflict in these setups will lead to greater emotion. That's your goal!

Difficult Choices

Dramatic situations produce greater conflicts. They also force your characters to make difficult choices. When your hero and/or heroine finally decide to choose a committed relationship, circumstances should make it a difficult choice. Your hero and heroine should have to sacrifice something for love—if only their independence or their misguided notions of who they are or what they stand for. If the sacrifice is even greater, then all the better.

Perhaps your hero is a cop who falls for a murder suspect. In choosing to stand by her, he risks being fired from the only job he's ever wanted just to prove her innocence. That's sacrifice. Because he has to sacrifice for love, the decision to embrace love will be that much more emotional, for him as well as the reader. Difficult choices heighten emotion.

Powerful Prose

An exciting writing style can make the most of emotion, even in an otherwise mundane story. I don't recommend that you rely exclusively on style, but it can sometimes make the difference between being published and remaining unpublished. Powerful prose does justice to powerful emotions. Let's look at a couple techniques.

Speaking of Romance ...

Jolie Kramer says the best way to create emotion is to give your characters difficult choices. She says: "Don't take the easy way out. Take your characters to the wall. Don't make them choose A or B. It's easy to choose right from wrong. Those choices tell us who the hero is and who the villain is. They don't illustrate character, though, and they don't evoke emotion. Now if you make your hero chose A at the sacrifice of B in order to get C—that's character! That's suspense. That's emotional. And that's where you'll suck the reader in."*

A Closer Look at Dynamic Verbs

We've already talked about active adjectives, vibrant verbs, and magical metaphors in terms of style, but how can they heighten emotion? Dynamic verbs act as conduits for feelings. They can add an almost electrical charge to your scenes.

Example: Instead of saying "He walked," say "He strode" or "He bolted" or "He meandered." These words are more specific. They paint a clearer picture of the character's emotions. They sound more active.

Example: Instead of saying "He angrily knocked on the door," say "He beat on the door." Beat is a stronger verb than knocked, and it takes away the need to use the adverb "angrily." Beating implies that he was angry. Omitting the word "angrily" tightens your prose and makes it more powerful.

No-Holds-Barred Metaphors

Critics of the genre sometimes claim that romance writers indulge in *"purple prose."* In particular, they condemn the use of adverbs. Adverbs are "-ly" words like tenderly, forcefully, reluctantly. ("She sighed tenderly.")

Critics also aren't too keen on romantic metaphors. I say tough beans to the critics. Rich language evokes emotions. The metaphor, in particular, can be a romance writer's best friend.

Metaphors, words or phrases that mean one thing but are used in place of something else in order to make a comparison, work because they add depth and dimension. They make linear thoughts multidimensional. If you say your heroine's hands are butterflies flitting around your hero's head, you show the reader not only the heroine's light, nervous touch, but you also evoke an image of a dainty and beautiful creature as well.

That adds to the reader's understanding of the character. And greater understanding allows the reader to feel more involved. The image of the butterfly will add to the emotions evoked by the heroine.

Empathetic Environment

The environment can reflect not only the mood you want to establish, but the characters' emotions as well. Talk about versatile!

For example, if your heroine is depressed, let her gaze out the window at a leaden sky (instead of a blue one) and listen to the oppressive sound of never-ending rain (instead of the cheery chirps of robins). The rain and the gray sky mirror and amplify her depression. Or you might deliberately choose to paint an environment that contrasts the character's moods—a fact that the character might find irritating!

Good Diversions

In Chapter 8, "Pacing: Timing Is Everything," I warned you not to take too much time to describe the scenery. It slows your pacing. However, it's okay if the description shows the reader something about the character's emotional state or if it establishes an important tone. Here's an example from my nineteenth-century romance, *My Fair Lord*:

> "She stared fixedly out of a rain-splattered pane of glass, focusing on the sundial in the garden. The sun cast the mounted timepiece in a brilliant ray of light, the kind that gloriously splays through dark clouds as in one of those dramatic paintings of the ascension of Christ. The sundial's brass gnomon sparked with light as it cast its long shadow on the hour of the day. So often, it seemed, shadows accompanied light."

The last line about light and shadows reflects the heroine's realization that her happiness is being overshadowed by darkness. The description added information about the heroine's state of mind.

Love Letters

Purple prose is a derogatory term used to describe overly descriptive or lush fiction. It evolved from the nineteenth-century phrase "purple patch," which described a brilliant or ornate literary passage in an otherwise dull work of fiction. It literally meant a patch of cloth that possessed the brilliance and gaudiness of the color purple. "Purple passage" is another variation of the term.

Write On!

Your reader will feel more in touch with the environment if she sees it through the eyes of the characters. If your hero reflects on his feelings about the ocean as he walks along the beach, it will have more impact than if the narrator offers details. When the hero reacts to the ocean, the reader not only sees it, but she also learns something about the character.

Emotion Checklist

You are now dealing with some sophisticated aspects of writing. In the next chapter, I'll talk about adding sensuality to your romance. Before I turn up the heat, though, here's a checklist on emotion.

❏ I allow time in each chapter for my lovers to explore their feelings.

❏ I show emotions through dialogue, body language, and the choices my characters make.

❏ I've hinted at subtext—thoughts and feelings below the surface.

❏ I've allowed my characters to react with emotions true to their personalities.

❏ I've used specific details to create a picture so vivid that my reader reacts to it emotionally.

❏ I've put my characters in the most dramatic situations possible.

❏ I've raised the stakes to force my characters to make tough choices.

❏ I've used dynamic verbs.

❏ The environment reflects, contrasts, or otherwise illuminates my character's emotions.

❏ I feel emotions when I read the most dramatic scenes in my book.

The Least You Need to Know

➤ You can't let the plot get in the way of your characters' emotions.

➤ It's better to show an emotional reaction than to tell the readers exactly what the characters are feeling.

➤ What characters say and think are not always one and the same.

➤ Use specific details to engage the reader's emotions.

➤ Giving your characters tough choices will heighten emotion.

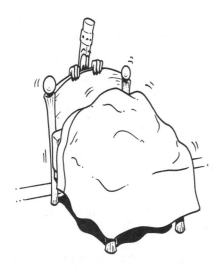
Under the Covers: Sex and the Single (or Married) Romance Writer

> ### In This Chapter
>
> ➤ Are you willing to write a love scene?
>
> ➤ Finessing the details
>
> ➤ Don't worry what Mom will think!
>
> ➤ The real purpose of a sex scene
>
> ➤ The real meaning of meaningless sex

Not all romances contain lovemaking, but many do. It's the natural outcome of courtship and commitment. To an outsider, writing a sex scene looks like a no-brainer, but a great love scene is far more difficult—and rewarding—than any outsider could ever imagine! But you're no longer a stranger to this great genre—you've learned the secret handshake. So, it's time to learn how the masters of the genre put the sizzle in their sex scenes.

Love Means Never Having to Say You're Sorry for a Sex Scene

If you ever decide to publicize your romance novel through the media, you may run into reporters who want to talk about nothing but sex. Journalists who don't blink an eye at gruesome murders sometimes lose their objectivity and turn into disapproving

Puritans when it comes to sexuality in women's fiction. Just remember—the reason most media outlets even chose to do articles on romance novels is so they can exploit the sex angle to raise their ratings or readership!

People who don't read romances assume that all we write about is sex. Of course, that's not true. If it were, we'd be writing erotica—sex for sex's sake. That's not our agenda. As romance writers, we create real characters in exciting stories who make love as a natural outcome of a loving relationship. What a wonderful and natural process!

The Curse of the Bodice Ripper

No matter how masterfully you write your story, no matter how sophisticated your style, or how deep your characters, or how profound your theme, at some point, some clod will ask you, "Is this a bodice ripper?" The term "bodice ripper" was given to romances written in the 1970s. That's when authors such as Rosemary Rogers and Kathleen Woodiwiss wrote wildly popular historical novels in which the heroine's clothing was invariably ripped to shreds in sexual escapades that were sometimes violent.

Speaking of Romance ...

Twenty years ago, rape fantasies appeared in novels that were soon dubbed "bodice rippers." RWA Hall-of-Famer Eileen Dreyer, who writes romances as Kathleen Korbel, says rape has no place in today's romances, which exalt the power of love: "Within the context of historicals, rape and abuse are sociologically accurate. So are head lice, scabies, the plague, filth in the streets, bodies that hadn't been washed in a lifetime, and bad teeth. We write not for an audience in the 1200s, but an audience in the 1900s."*

That's ancient history, but the ghost of those early romances still lingers in the minds of the public. Just remember you're not writing for the critics of yesterday. You're writing for avid readers of today's sophisticated romances.

Forget Aunt Tilda

You're not writing for Aunt Tilda, either. So don't bother to blush when you write your love scenes. And don't tone them down for fear of what your mom will think. She knows all about sex or you wouldn't be here! Write the best love scene you can. If you're true to your characters, it will be perfect. Remember, you're not your heroine, and you're not writing a biography. This is fiction. So go for it!

Was It Good for You?

You are the only one who really matters when you're writing a love scene, or any other kind of scene for that matter! You'll know when it's working and you'll know when it's not. Here are a few keys to writing natural and powerful love scenes:

1. **Try to write the scene in one sitting.** To do that, you can't analyze and judge every sentence. Just throw words down on the paper. Love scenes tend to have a rhythm and build to a climax (one can only hope!). So write like crazy and edit later.

2. **Get some perspective.** Put the scene away for a few days and then re-read it. Polish it as needed. Smooth out awkward phrases and rework lines that are inappropriately graphic, or if your descriptions are too vague, make them more graphic. When your book is finished, go back to the love scenes and rework them again. The more you know your characters, the more accurately you can portray their lovemaking.

3. **Strive for unique descriptions.** Don't take the easy way out by recycling phrases you've read a million times before. Lips are often described as rosebuds, for example, and heroes are often described as smelling musky and masculine. They're apt descriptions and hard to beat, but you can try!

4. **Reflect your characters' personalities.** If you simply focus on how bodies are touching and reacting, your scene will be generic. Make it unique by letting movements, touches, and sounds be particular to your characters. A virginal Amish heroine is probably not going to romp around like a French courtesan the first time she makes love. Her personality and emotions will affect her movements.

> **Write On!**
>
> Creating a conflict that keeps your hero and heroine apart will add to the sexual tension. The conflict might be external, such as the guy from the wrong side of the tracks falling in love with the senator's daughter. Or it might be internal, such as a reluctance to relinquish control.

Speaking of Romance ...

Silhouette Desire is one of the contemporary lines that allows sexual scenes, as editor Joan Marlow Golan explains. "Sensuality is a key component of the series, and there must be at least two fully consummated love scenes in every Desire submission. But remember, there's much more to a Desire than steamy love scenes—more than anything else, the sensuality comes from the emotional intensity that surrounds the hero and heroine coming together and overcoming the conflicts in their lives by helping each other. Internal conflicts especially can create an emotional connection, causing sparks to fly."*

5. **If your sex scene comes to a dead halt, work on characterization.** If you write a love scene organically—natural to the characters—you have to know them pretty well. If you throw your hero and heroine in bed and they refuse to make love, or if it seems mechanical and manufactured, you probably have to develop their relationship a little more. Rework the scenes leading up to sexual intercourse and make sure they make sense, flow naturally, and evolve the relationship. And if it's too early in the book for them to make love, substitute intercourse with lesser manifestations of intimacy.

6. **Don't forget the almost-love-scene.** If you want to increase the intimacy, but it just seems wrong or too early for your characters to have sexual intercourse, try the close call. Your characters can make love without doing the wild thing. Make the most of a stolen kiss, or have them strip naked and almost make love. Of course, there has to be a good reason to go to the brink and pull back at the last moment. You can't simply do it to tease the reader; it must make sense in terms of the development of the relationship.

The Writer's Comfort Zone

Your decision whether to include sex, and if so, how much, rests entirely with you. Some readers love hot romances. Others hate them. So write what you feel comfortable with and you'll find an audience who shares your tastes.

Testing the Waters

If you're not sure how you feel about lovemaking scenes, write one and see what happens! I was reluctant to include sex in my first novel, but after doing so I found out some interesting things about love scenes:

➤ They can be the most emotional and engaging scenes in your book.

➤ They enable the reader to see the characters' most vulnerable and endearing sides.

➤ A love scene may bring out the best of your skills because you can't phone it in when you're writing about passion. It's not like describing furniture. You have to be emotionally involved as a writer to convey the intimacy necessary for a great love scene.

➤ The best part of a sex scene is the emotional growth your characters undergo as a result of exposing themselves in such an intimate way.

Some Like It Hot ...

Some writers specialize in super-hot romances. They clearly enjoy writing about sex and their devoted fans enjoy reading about it. In the historical market, Susan Johnson and Bertrice Small have made names for themselves writing uninhibited scenes. The Silhouette Desire and Harlequin Temptation lines allow for explicit sex in the contemporary category market. Try reading a few sizzling romances. If you enjoy reading them, you may enjoy writing them as well.

... Not!

If writing about sex is out of the question for you, then explore the sweeter romance markets. Most single-title historicals have at least one lovemaking scene. If you're writing a squeaky clean historical, you might consider pitching it to a Christian Publisher.

Write On!

Young romance writers have a distinct advantage over their senior colleagues. Their first kiss is a more recent memory. But even if you're 60, you can recall your first experience with love. Close your eyes and take yourself back in time. Remember your first exhilarating brush with sexuality. A little memory, a little imagination, and a lot of writing skill are the perfect ingredients for great love scenes.

You have a number of options if you want to write a chaste contemporary romance. In addition to the Christian and teen romance lines, there is Silhouette Romance and Harlequin Romance as well as Avalon Books. Just remember, even in some of the sweet romance lines the sexual tension is high, even if the reader doesn't follow that tension to its ultimate conclusion!

Finessing the Details

So, what if you don't want to write about specific body parts, but you also don't want to close the door after the first kiss? What's a writer to do? Generalize. Finesse the details.

Sure, you can use metaphors like "his manhood," but if you don't feel comfortable with that approach, write around it. Here is a sex scene written in one sentence that describes sexual intercourse without specifics:

> "He carried her to the bed and kissed her everywhere, smoothing his hands over every intimate part of her, and by the time they joined, she was more than ready."

Obviously, this sentence is hopelessly boring and begs for more details involving the senses and emotions. But to make it specific enough to involve the reader, you don't have to give a blow-by-blow account of who put what where. You can make your scene specific by focusing on the senses. You can describe the feel of skin that's slick with sweat, or the masculine scent that remains on the pillow afterward, a cooling breeze on hot skin, or a guttural cry of release. These kinds of details can evoke very sexual images. That frees you from having to resort to the type of anatomical descriptions you might find in a textbook.

Stop the Presses!

A word of warning about sex scenes: They shouldn't be used as filler to pad a manuscript that's short on plot. That's about as smart as putting wallpaper over a crack in a wall. Fix the problem first and then add the wallpaper. You can have as many sex scenes as you want as long as they add to, instead of pad, the story.

Is There Such a Thing as Too Much Sex?

In a word, yes. Your book will have too much sex if you use it in lieu of character development or to flesh out (so to speak) a flimsy plot. Many avid romance readers confess that they skip sex scenes entirely. They just flip over the pages! They're not really interested in the lovemaking. They're interested in the love relationship.

How do you keep readers from flipping over your sex scenes? Here are two keys:

➤ Make the love scene integral to your story. In other words, if you cut the sex out of your story, you should be missing something. The story should have a gaping hole. If not, that means your love scene was superfluous. You need to go back and rewrite it so that something important happens.

➤ Let your love scene be an emotional turning point that leads to new insights, understandings, greater intimacy, or new decisions.

➤ Use the love scene to further explore issues that contribute to the characters' inner conflicts. If the reader gets a glimpse of the deepest fears and hopes of the characters, she'll feel much closer to the hero and heroine. In that way, sexual intimacy brings everyone closer!

The Meaning of Meaningless Sex

A meaningless sex scene is one that doesn't show the reader anything new about the characters. When your hero and heroine make love for the first time, it should change them as people. At the very least it will change how they see and relate to each other. It might also change how they see the world.

If your characters engage in one sexual romp after the other and never grow or change as a result, you're probably writing meaningless sex. Those are the kinds of scenes that bore many readers to tears, no matter how inventive the positions or how titillating the details.

Move It Along!

Every scene in your book should propel the story forward. That goes for the lovemaking scenes as well. If a sex scene doesn't reveal something new about the story or the characters, it probably should be cut. I say probably because sometimes a love scene can serve another purpose. It can set a mood or simply give pleasure to the reader after a long trek toward "happily ever after." Sex scenes and scenes involving joyful emotions can offer the reader a much-needed "breather" from the story's conflicts.

The Snowflake Theory

Every sex scene should be like a snowflake—unique. No two characters make love the same way. That's why writing a lovemaking scene is hard work. You have to really put yourself inside the characters' skin. You have to see how their emotions and hang-ups and hopes and desires manifest in the act of making love.

Write On!

Don't forget to include dialogue in your sex scenes. Readers sometimes get antsy when they see scads of black ink. Break up the monotony of narration with a few words now and then. Your characters don't necessarily have to have a running conversation, but sounds are a part of sex. You just may be pleasantly surprised at what your characters have to say in the moment of passion.

Sensuality Versus Sexuality

The difference between sensuality and sexuality is the difference between a movie like *Body Heat* and a military training film on the perils of sexually transmitted diseases. A sex scene will be mechanical if it doesn't include the senses.

Stop the Presses!

Beginners sometimes mistake accidental intimacy for sexual tension, e.g., she trips into his arms or he's forced up against her in a crowded elevator. Of course, accidents do happen, but really good sexual tension comes from actions motivated by a character. A smoldering look from across the room as the hero and heroine recognize their attraction can be far more powerful than stumbling into each other's arms.

The Sensibility of Senses

It makes sense to use all the five senses whenever possible, but especially in a love scene. Here are a few good reasons:

1. A person in love has a heightened awareness of everything about their lover—how she/he looks, smells, feels, sounds, and tastes.

2. Those in love see the world around them with heightened sensibilities—they notice beautiful sunsets and take the time to smell the roses. The world seems to mirror their newfound love.

3. The five senses define us as people. What a character sees, hears, or touches defines his world and sensibilities. A shallow corporate raider, for example, might revel in the scent of a crisp, new dollar bill but he might not even notice the rich, sweet smell of daffodils at the flower stand outside his corporate headquarters. What he smells tells us something about who he is.

How do you employ the senses in a love scene? Focus on them—methodically. Think about what the hero and heroine are seeing, feeling, touching, and smelling. Then, mention these details. A well-placed sense detail can make a love scene come alive. For example, whenever a writer mentions the smell of soap on skin, I can always smell it and instantly feel more involved in the scene.

In the Mood

A lovemaking scene without the proper mood-setting is like making love without foreplay; it's not nearly as gratifying as it could be! You should build up to a love scene with plenty of hints to the reader—growing sexual tension, the characters' recognition of their desire, resistance, then acquiescence.

As a narrator, you can help set the stage by focusing on sensual details in the environment. They're everywhere! For example, you can focus on the crush of velvet against skin, the sultry play of candlelight on a bed, or the heady perfume of blood-red roses. These kinds of details can definitely help get the reader in the mood.

Sexual Tension

Can you define sexual tension? What is it exactly? You might have a hard time defining it, but you probably have an easy time recognizing it. If you read a scene and find yourself getting aroused, breathlessly wondering when and if the couple will end the suspense, that's sexual tension!

The best way to build sexual tension is to meticulously focus on your hero and heroine. What are they thinking, doing, feeling, wanting? Specifically, what are they thinking about, doing for, feeling about, and wanting from each other?

Here are a few tips for building sexual tension:

➤ After every scene in your book, check in with your hero and heroine. Have you focused on their latest feelings for each other? How have they grown or changed?

➤ No matter how much action your scenes contain, don't forget to include sense-details. If your characters seem to be disembodied, talking heads, track where they are in every scene (where are they sitting or standing?). Put them in a place the reader can visualize and then add sense details.

➤ When you're plotting, be sure to include scenes that allow plenty of time alone for your hero and heroine to flirt and savor the moments when they touch.

➤ If your hero and heroine are acting more like brother and sister instead of red-hot lovers, adjust your characterization to change the dynamics of the relationship or let your characters do something dramatic or unexpected to change the level of sexual tension. Bold actions can spark flames to set your characters on fire.

➤ If your sexual tension seems to fizzle like a wet firecracker, zoom in your camera lens until the reader sees nothing but tight shots. Focus on the sensual lines of his lips, the almost translucent skin of her breasts, the provocative curve at the small of her back. The devil is in the details. The devil in a blue dress, that is!

Write On!

There are two reference books that come in handy for historical romance writers in particular. One is *Sexual Slang: A Compendium of Offbeat Words and Colorful Phrases from Shakespeare to Today,* by Alan Richter. The other is *The History of Underclothes,* by C. Willett Cunnington. Both are affordable trade paperbacks that contain information hard to find elsewhere.

Do Your Homework!

Be sure to use the proper terms when you write your love scene. Underwear by any other name is still underwear in a contemporary romance. But in a historical setting, you'll use other terminology. In the Middle Ages, men wore braies, for example. The phrase "making love" is a relatively new invention. You can certainly use it in narration, but in dialogue you might want to use historical words like "tup" and "swive" to describe sexual intercourse. *Webster's Ninth New Collegiate Dictionary* or the *Oxford English Dictionary* can tell you exactly when these words came into use.

Sensuality Checklist

This is the last of the seven chapters focusing on writing techniques. Up next, we prepare your precious package for special delivery to the world at large. In the meantime, double-check your skills at sensuality with this checklist:

- ❏ I am writing at a level of sensuality I feel comfortable with.
- ❏ I am writing to please myself.
- ❏ I am not preoccupied with how I think others will react to my love scenes.
- ❏ I've found new and unique ways to describe physical details.
- ❏ If I'm writing a contemporary romance, I've decided how I'm going to approach the issue of sexually transmitted diseases.
- ❏ My sex scenes reflect the personalities and emotions of my characters.
- ❏ My sex scenes keep the plot moving forward.
- ❏ I built up to my sex scenes with the proper mood and sexual tension.
- ❏ I've used sexual terms that are appropriate to my story's time and setting.

The Least You Need to Know

➤ You should include sex in your romance only if you feel comfortable doing so.

➤ If you include sex it should move the story forward.

➤ Every love scene should be unique to the characters.

➤ To build sexual tension you should focus on the five senses.

➤ Be sure to use sexual terms that are historically accurate.

Part 3

After the Romance: Bringing Up Baby

Once you've finished your romance novel, you'll rightfully feel like a parent, proud of your creation and a little protective over its future. But before you send your baby off to be accepted or (eek!) rejected, you have to dress it in its Sunday best. That requires polishing your prose, getting feedback on your manuscript, and learning the proper way to make a submission. At the same time, you'll begin your search for an agent and editor. In this part, you'll learn how to do all of these things. After laboring so hard over the birth of your manuscript, this part will seem like a breeze.

Chapter 13

Research Recap

In This Chapter

➤ Research doesn't have to be painful

➤ Ways to get the information you need

➤ Tips for contemporary romance writers

➤ Using the Internet to make research easy

➤ Narrowing the scope of historical research

You want just the facts, ma'am, nothing but the facts. And you want to make sure that the facts you gather are accurate. That's why research is so important. When you finish your manuscript, you should double-check your facts and details. Of course, if you're writing a historical you can't really even begin your story without research. So, let's start at the beginning—your subject.

Understanding Your Subject

Whether your romance is set during the American Revolution or during the computer revolution in Silicon Valley, you'll need to research before you even begin to plot. Why is that so important?

➤ Even if you know how the love relationship will develop, your characters will be affected by events around them.

➤ Any setting worthy of your book will have its own culture, style, and exciting events.

➤ If you don't understand the culture in which you're placing your characters, you may as well put them on the moon or have them falling in love in no-man's land.

The Good News About Research

Research isn't a necessary evil. It's an important and exciting part of your job as a writer. The more you research, the richer your story will be. Being able to create a historically accurate environment will help you create real characters. That's because characters are defined by the world in which they live.

Researching the events of your chosen period will also give you great ideas on how to plot your book. With my novel *A Dance in Heather,* I wanted to pick a dramatic moment in time, so I chose England in 1414. There were several significant things happening that year. There was the incredible Battle of Agincourt in which King Henry V defeated the French against all odds. There was the recent introduction of guns and gunpowder that spurred the decline of chivalry. There was also King Henry's persecution of the Lollard heretics. I wove all of these issues into my story. As a result, that book never lacked for dramatic twists and turns.

Write On!

If your story is starting to bore you to tears, go back to the library and do more research. Chances are you'll discover a tidbit of information that can help make your plot come to life. It might be an incident that affects your plot or additional information about customs and culture.

Speaking of Romance ...

Roberta Gellis made a name for herself with well-researched historical romances and is now writing historical mysteries. She says the first place for a beginning researcher to go is the children's library. "The books for 8- to 12-year-olds have more than enough accurate historical information for most historical romances. A second very good source is a well-written biography of an important or interesting person who lived in the period." Roberta also suggests you play around on the computer system at your library. Go to Key Word menu options and start with a key word from your period, like "medieval" or "regency." Then add a second word, say "medieval marriage" or "regency women." You'll end up with a variety of book titles to explore.

But I Hate Research!

If you hate research, don't panic. Not every romance requires it. Many contemporary romances are almost exclusively character-driven. The stories could be set anywhere and it wouldn't affect the course of the relationship. If that's the approach you'd like to take, simply pick a setting you're familiar with.

The Three Faces of Historicals

The history of the historical novel has been a long and interesting one—from the early days of women's fiction with Mary Renault, Dorothy Dunnett, and Victoria Holt to more recent stars like Kathleen Woodiwiss, Jude Deveraux, and Teresa Medeiros.

The emphasis in popular historical fiction has definitely shifted from history to relationships. Here are three approaches to historical fiction.

The Straight Historical Novel

Authors such as Mary Renault and Mary Stewart wrote historical novels in which romance played a minor role, if any. Today, most popular historical novels include a strong romance plot, and in many cases it's the main course. Historicals that don't fit into this category are usually rare literary historicals such as Charles Frazier's best-seller *Cold Mountain*.

The Heavily Researched Historical Romance

Authors like Roberta Gellis wrote romances with a great emphasis on history. Roberta's acclaimed medieval series *The Roselynde Chronicles* is a good example, as is Edith Layton's marvelous story about the princes in the Tower, *The Crimson Crown*, and any of Elizabeth Grayson's novels. However, this kind of history-rich romance is currently being overshadowed by what we might dub "Historical Lite" fiction.

Light and Fluffy

There's a new breed of historical romances that tickles the fancy and doesn't tax the brain. They're historical novels that have a humorous tone and involve a minimum of historical details, though the details included are well researched.

There is a similar trend in contemporary romances as well. Susan Elizabeth Phillips is a good example. Early in her career, Susan wrote expertly researched and fascinating multilayered novels like *Hot Shot* and *Glitter Baby*. Now she's writing shorter, simpler, funnier, and better-selling romances that emphasize characterization rather than setting and research.

How Much Research Should You Do?

You should include in your novel the amount of research that you enjoy reading yourself. However, bear in mind the latest trends in the marketplace. Readers seem to have shorter attention spans these days. None of us seems to have as much reading time as we used to. While some readers love to sink their teeth into a huge meaty historical, many more seem to be satisfied with *costume dramas*. At least that's what publishers believe. The challenge is always to write the best, most well-researched novel you can within the constraints of the latest publishing trends.

Love Letters

Costume dramas are books that contain very little historical research. In fact, the only way the reader even knows it's a historical is by the costumes worn by the characters.

The Path of Least Resistance

Whether you're writing a contemporary or a historical, chances are at some point you'll have to research something! You'll want to start with broad brush strokes and pencil in the details as you go. I believe very much in the fingertip approach to research. Start with anything you can easily get your hands on. For example ...

➤ If you're writing a contemporary romance about a bronco-riding hero, get your hands on that recent *Life* magazine article you saw on the subject at the doctor's office, rent the movie *Urban Cowboy,* and buy tickets to the rodeo that's coming to town next month.

➤ If you're writing about a medieval heroine who is forced to leave a convent to marry against her wishes, watch the next *Brother Cadfael* mystery (which is set in a monastery) on PBS, visit the local Renaissance fair, rent the movie *Lady Hawke* to get yourself in a medieval mood, or buy the new illustrated version of *The Canterbury Tales* that you saw in your local independent bookstore.

Does it sound like I'm advocating the lazy approach to research? I'm not. Really! What I'm encouraging you to do is understand your topic from a modern context. Multimedia treatments of history can give you a wonderful flavor of a period and can act as a springboard to more in-depth research. A movie such as *Braveheart* can't substitute for time in a library, for example, but it can inspire you to write about Scotland. It can also indicate a current interest in Scottish history, which is always good if you're writing popular fiction. You want your book to be popular, right?

Delving Beneath the Surface

Once you have a general feel for the subject, you need to go beyond the obvious. Think of yourself as a reporter. What do reporters do when they need to understand a subject? They ask questions—lots of them!

The Lois Lane Approach

Interviews work particularly well for contemporary authors. If you're writing a romance set at Cape Canaveral, you could probably wrangle an interview with a real, live astronaut about what it feels like to walk in space. But there's no way a historical author will ever be able to talk to a Knight Templar about his experiences fighting the Saracens!

Speaking of Romance ...

Lots of authors never visit the places they write about. Instead, they rely on books, videos, and the Internet. Their imagination does the rest. Nothing beats a visit to the place where you're setting your book, but traveling can be costly and time-consuming. Nora Roberts says she wrote her big hardcover *Montana Sky* without ever leaving her office in Maryland. She used the Internet and the telephone to get firsthand descriptions of the land. Since Nora is so prolific, if she visited every book location to do research, she'd never have time to write!

Ma Bell Is Swell

Modern technology is truly a researcher's best friend. Do you need some quick information about how diesel engines are made? Get on the horn and call an engineer. Do you want to know what the bird-of-paradise your hero gives your heroine smells like? Call your local florist. Just ask. You'd be amazed at how willing most experts are to share their knowledge. Here's a direct and open-ended way to ask for the information you need:

> "I'm wondering if you can help me. I'm trying to find out about (fill in the blank). I'm writing a book. Can you tell me about it, or do you know anyone else who knows something about this subject?"

Most experts will answer at least a few questions, especially when they find out you're a writer. That always impresses people. If they can't help you, they'll refer you to someone else. Get names and phone numbers, and keep following the trail until you find what you need.

A Wealth of Information

We're fortunate that America values freedom of information. In our country, there is a vast amount of information available free to anyone who asks. Our institutions are highly user-friendly. Here are the kinds of experts you can easily contact by phone:

➤ Company information specialists or public relations officials

➤ Professional associations

➤ College professors and research institutes

➤ City directories and chambers of commerce

➤ Think tanks and watch-dog groups

➤ Reference librarians

You can find phone numbers for these in the Yellow Pages or at the library. Just ask your librarian for help.

Write On!

Do your homework before you call an expert for help so you know what questions to ask. Also, be sure to list your questions in order of importance. While many experts are willing to help, they may not have time for an extended phone call. If you ask the most important questions first, you'll have what you need in case the interview is cut short.

Fishing with the Net

The Internet can be a powerful research tool, especially for contemporary authors. All you have to do is get on the Internet, type in the name of a search engine, then type in key words from your research topic. Up pop various Web sites, and off you go, clicking your way through a maelstrom of information. This can be a time-consuming and frustrating process, but one that's also extremely enlightening. There's a vast, convoluted, and amazing amount of information on the (what else?) information superhighway.

In many ways, the Internet is less helpful for historical authors. There are Web sites on all the popular eras, from the Middle Ages to the Victorian age. However, history is such a broad topic that many of these Web sites are too general to be of use to writers. Many sites do have good *bibliographies,* though. Once you have the titles of good research books, you can hunt them down in the library.

Mice at the Starting Gate

Are you ready to click that mouse? Here are a few ways to use the Internet for research:

➤ Use search engines such as www.yahoo.com, www.dogpile.com, and www.altavista. digital.com to pull up Web sites pertaining to your area of interest.

➤ Subscribe to mailing lists and newsgroups that attract experts in your field of interest. Sites like www.dejanews.com list newsgroups and mailing lists. If you join Romance Writers of America and subscribe to its list-server, you can probably learn about other sites by hobnobbing with other authors. A listserver is a type of Internet software that can direct e-mails to groups of people who share the same interests.

➤ Check out online libraries. Unfortunately, there are very few books that you can read word-for-word online. But you might find what you're looking for on Internet libraries such as www.ipl.org and www.elibrary.com. There are several hundred online dictionaries, which you can find by logging on to www.onelook.com.

➤ Check out other writer's Web sites. Jo Beverley's site is a good example. She has a variety of research information that can be useful to other writers. Her Web site is www.sff.net/people/jobeverley.

The Accidental Researcher

Do you have to know what you're doing when you research a novel? I hope not! I certainly never did. I stumbled my way through 15 years of research about the Middle Ages. Here are some of the happy accidents that happened to me over the years:

Love Letters

A **bibliography** is a list of publications a writer has referred to in the text of his or her book. The bibliography is usually found in the back of the book and lists titles and authors. That means bibliographies are a good place for writers to cherry-pick additional research books. There are also bibliographies that are listings of all of the works written on a given subject.

Write On!

A good reference librarian can be a writer's best friend. They know how to use the system to get obscure and vital information, so be kind to your local librarians. Don't be afraid to ask them for help. Remember to show your gratitude when you get it. There have been more than a few librarians mentioned in the acknowledgment pages of romance novels.

➤ In a suburban Chicago library I bumped into a wonderful and obscure medieval costume book that I've never seen anywhere else.

➤ In a suburban St. Louis library I found an incredibly detailed book on falconry written by a thirteenth-century Holy Roman Emperor that inspired my novel *Falcon and the Sword.*

➤ I did a general search on "history and marriage" on Amazon.com and discovered a book about spiritual marriages in the Middle Ages. It became the basis for my medieval romance *The Maiden's Heart.* The hero and heroine marry but decide to remain celibate (at least for awhile!).

Call it serendipity, or call it going with the flow, the best ideas for novels seem to come from these happy and unexpected discoveries.

Stop the Presses!

Once your book goes into editing the copy editor will likely challenge your facts and the way you spell historic terms. If you haven't made notes on your research, you'll have trouble defending or verifying your work. At the very least, keep a notebook listing your research books, their Dewey Decimal numbers, and the libraries where you found them so you can retrieve them easily.

Good, Old-Fashioned Books

Libraries are good places for wonderful accidents to happen. You can find books you didn't even know you were looking for! Finding a good research book can spark a great idea for a novel or inspire an important plot twist just when you need it most. If your local public library doesn't have much to offer on your particular topic, try these resources:

➤ University libraries

➤ Rare and used bookstores

➤ New bookstores, especially the superstores

➤ www.amazon.com, www.barnesandnoble.com, and other online bookstores

➤ Snail-mail catalogues, like Edward R. Hamilton and Dover Publications

➤ Book fairs

➤ The online site for independent bookstores (www.booksense.com)

University and public libraries frequently have interlibrary loan programs. This means that your local library can borrow books from faraway libraries on your behalf. This is a free way to get detailed books from specialty collections. I once borrowed a book on medieval birth control from a medical library at a university 300 miles away and never had to drive more than a half a mile to my local library to retrieve it.

The Research Pyramid

Once you find the materials you need, you should organize your search. Start with a good overview of your subject and narrow your focus from there.

1. Start with a broad understanding of your chosen time or subject. (How did people think? What did they believe in? How did they measure success? What were the predominant professions? What were the major sociological, religious, and political influences?)

2. Narrow your research to specifics that affect your plot. (Who were the ruling authorities and what control did they have over your characters? Were there any major battles or wars affecting your characters? Did any diseases or famines affect daily living?)

3. Finish off with the multitude of tiny details that affect daily living. (What did people wear and eat? How did they travel? What was housing like?)

Painting a Historical Canvas

The process of going from generalizations to specifics would go something like this for a historical novelist:

Let's say you decide to write a historical set in England. Start with a broad overview of English history. Read a book that ranges from the Dark Ages to Margaret Thatcher. Pick a period that you think you'd enjoy. Let's say it's the Middle Ages (my bailiwick!).

Read research books specific to that 600-year period. Look for events or a setting within that range that appeals to you. Pick a specific year. Try to understand the way people thought at that particular time—what did they believe in and how did they prioritize their lives? Were they mostly concerned about survival or socially one-upping their neighbors? Keep this in mind as you plot your book. The social context can provide some good outer conflicts.

Write On!

Many universities will let you buy borrowing privileges. It can be a good tax-deductible investment. Most colleges have such vast collections that you can find entire books about extremely small details. Sometimes it's just easier to buy your research books if they're still in print. If that gets too costly, buy the ones you know you'll use over and over and check out the rest.

Once your plot is set, narrow your research even further. Find out about castle building styles and how people ate, slept, and traveled. Give your hero and heroine appropriate goals and purposes. For example, she couldn't be a socialite because partying every weekend wasn't a priority in the Middle Ages, except for the occasional and expensive feast. Make sure the plot and the characters fit the period. Then, write your story.

Do additional research as you write, especially when you reach a scene that can't be written without further information. After the book is done, double-check your facts and make sure your phrases and words fit the era. Then pat yourself on the back. You've done a good job researching your novel!

Details, Details!

The more details you can use the more authentic your story will seem. That goes for contemporaries as well as historicals. Unfortunately, many nonfiction books don't provide the kind of details that are helpful to a writer. Historians often assume you know more than you do. Here are a few tips for finding specific details:

➤ **Look at children's books.** They are often written in a simplistic but very informative way that's perfect for writers.

➤ **Do hands-on research.** If your story is about women in a quilting bee, try your hand at quilting. A book might tell you about technique, but doing it yourself will tell you much more—the proper way to tie a knot, how painstaking the work is, how it feels when you prick a finger, and how fun it is to spend time with other women.

➤ **When hard facts don't exist, make a good guesstimate.** You can make up details that don't exist in research books. No one knows exactly how prehistoric people lived, for example, but that didn't keep Joan Wolf from writing a series of romantic prehistory novels.

➤ **When historians disagree over the facts, look at all sides of the issue and decide what you think is the most logical.** If that makes you nervous, add an author's note to your book clarifying the discrepancies in the history books.

➤ **Use literary license when necessary, but within limits.** You can move a minor historical event a year or two to fit your plot, as long as you explain that in an author's note. Do not make gross changes in history, though. Don't, for example, let the South win the Civil War!

The Intentional Researcher

There is a wealth of information available in books, if you know where to find it. The best sources will vary depending on your topic, but there are a number of places to start.

Encyclopedias

Encyclopedias, like *Encyclopedia Britannica,* are very generic but might be worth a glance. More interesting still are a number of specialized encyclopedias, like the *Encyclopedia of Military History* and the *Larousse Encyclopedia of Ancient and Medieval History.* The trick is finding one that relates to your topic.

Dictionaries

General dictionaries are handy to have at your writing desk. *Webster's Ninth New Collegiate Dictionary* gives not only definitions, but also the dates when words came into use. That's helpful for historical writers. I think of *Webster's Ninth* as the poor man's version of the *Oxford English Dictionary*. There are also some interesting specialized dictionaries, such as the *Dictionary of Mythology, Folklore, and Symbols* and *Merriam-Webster's Biographical Dictionary*.

My favorite is the *Oxford English Dictionary*. It is a massive, 12-volume set that includes every conceivable word in the English language, including its place and time of origin. Each entry also shows the word in snippets from texts throughout the centuries. You can find it at any well-funded public library. At home I have a cheaper two-volume condensed version. (The type is so small that the set came with a magnifying glass!)

Stop the Presses!

If you do a lot of research, congratulate yourself on your thoroughness. Do not, however, feel obligated to use every detail you find. Don't overwhelm the reader with minute details and intriguing little facts that don't advance the story. Use just enough research to make your story feel authentic, then get on with the plot.

Series Books

There are some excellent research books linked by a common approach to history, or by a single author. Your librarian can advise you on series that might be helpful to your topic. Here are few I know about:

➤ *Eyewitness* books. These are large picture books that can be found in the children's section of bookstores. There are also smaller *Eyewitness Junior* books. Each one focuses on a specific topic, like music, mummies, castles, and cowboys.

➤ *The Story of Civilization.* Ten volumes written by Will and Ariel Durant, these dense books give a good overview of history from virtually the beginning of recorded time to the French Revolution.

➤ *The Oxford Illustrated History of Britain.* Ten large volumes from the Oxford University Press. They give an overview of British history from the days of Roman rule to the twentieth century.

➤ **Frances and Joseph Gies's books.** This couple has written a series of marvelous books on the medieval time period. Subjects range from *Women in the Middle Ages* to *Life in a Medieval Castle.* Every aspiring medieval writer should start with these books.

➤ *Time-Life Student Library*. The editors of *Time-Life* magazines have issued a series of books on various civilizations and cultures that have lots of pictures that may inspire more than instruct. They do, however, have good bibliographies. *Time-Life*'s *The Old West* series is marvelous.

➤ *The Writer's Guide to Everyday Life* series. Writer's Digest Books has a series of research books filled with details helpful to writers. The *Everyday Life* series includes books dedicated to the 1800s, Colonial America, regency and Victorian England, the Wild West, and the Middle Ages.

There are a number of other series I have never seen, but are highly recommended by medieval author Roberta Gellis: *The Cambridge Medieval History, The Cambridge Ancient History, The New American Nation, The New Cambridge Modern History, Everyone a Witness* series, and the *Everyday Life* series. Check 'em out!

Love Letters

Periodical literature refers to anything published at regular intervals—usually articles in magazines or journals.

Atlas Shrugged

Do more than shrug in confusion over the lay of the land—look it up in a historical atlas. Libraries usually have atlases with maps of the world as it used to be. If you're writing in the old days, you'll want to have at least a general idea of boundaries and borders. Take a look at the *Rand McNally Atlas of World History* as well as the *Penguin Atlas of Ancient History* and *Penguin Atlas of Medieval History*. A membership in the AAA Auto Club is a good investment, especially for contemporary writers. The club sends detailed maps and tour books to members for free.

The Rest of the Story

There is so much available to the curious mind that there are reference books about reference books. There are also guides to bibliographies and *periodical literature* and books that tell you how to research. Ask your librarian for help in tracking down costume books as well as maps and atlases.

Research Checklist

Boy, what a fun chapter! I think it's time I wandered back into the library and did some more dreaming about my next book. How about you? Before we do, though, let's review what you learned. Then, it's time to move ahead and see what the world thinks of your creativity.

- ❏ I have included the right amount of research for the kind of book I'm writing.
- ❏ I have utilized the resources in my own environment, including books, movies, and events.
- ❏ I have asked enough questions to get to the heart of my research topic.
- ❏ I have given myself the pleasure of exploring a good library.
- ❏ I have subscribed to mail-order catalogues that might have books I need.
- ❏ I have researched enough to get a good sense of the big picture of my topic.
- ❏ I have included enough details to draw the reader into the world I'm creating.
- ❏ I have been careful not to overload my story with facts.

The Least You Need to Know

➤ To be a good researcher you should follow your instincts and ask lots of questions.

➤ Get a good overview of your topic before you nail down your plot.

➤ The Internet can be helpful, especially to contemporary authors, but if you're not online you can still find what you need through libraries and other sources.

➤ You don't have to be a professional historian to find the historical details necessary to write your romance.

➤ Don't be afraid to ask for help from librarians!

Chapter 14

Polish Until It Shines

In This Chapter

➤ How to approach a rewrite from ground zero

➤ A methodical way to fix nagging problems

➤ Common and correctable mistakes

➤ Two secret weapons to fight manuscript malaise

➤ Handy tips from a real pro

Before we talk about rewrites, there is something important you need to know. If you've completed a draft of your novel, you deserve a standing ovation. You have put yourself a cut above the rest. A finished manuscript is a major achievement, so go ahead and pop open that bottle of champagne!

After the bubbles have fizzled, and after you've spent a night dreaming about your upcoming publicity tour, it's back to reality. Most books don't sell until they've been thoroughly polished. The rewriting stage takes faith and patience. This is usually what separates the pros from the wannabes. So, you wanna be a pro? Then keep reading. More important, keep doing!

It Ain't over 'Til It's Over

I always say that writing is a business of delayed gratification. The first delay comes when you finish your first draft. You've slaved for weeks, months, perhaps even years. You've done the very best you can ... only to discover there's still more work to do!

Unless the proverbial "fat lady" sings when you type "The End," you're going to have do a rewrite or at least a little polishing.

Even Educated Pros Do It

Most writers have to polish their prose—even the best-sellers. As a beginner, you may have to rewrite virtually everything. Take heart, though. The more books you write, the easier it gets. The better your first drafts become, the fewer rewrites you'll have to do.

Feeling Your Way Through a Rewrite

Some pros write from beginning to end without stopping, then polish after the first draft is completed. Others write a few chapters, or even a third of the book, and go back to make sure that much is working before forging ahead. You'll soon discover what process works best for you. The important thing is to keep going until the book is finished. Endlessly polishing chapter one will keep you at square one forever.

Once More into the Breach

You may be wondering, "Do I have to rewrite the whole @#!*%& thing?" It depends. Obviously, after reading your book through, you'll know what to keep and what to discard. But here's the good news: Unless you're rewriting what's already perfect, your book will be better for your efforts. I have never done a rewrite that didn't improve my novel—even the revisions I reluctantly did at the request of my editor!

The Big Picture

There's something thrilling and wonderful about reading your book for the first time from start to finish. You've created a story that has never existed before. You know, or at least you should know, what an incredible achievement it is. What a gift to the world! But how do you approach your story with an analytical eye for editing and polishing?

> **Write On!**
>
> Even after you've polished, spell-checked, and printed your final draft, it's a good idea to have a friend read it to catch typos and missing words. They have a sneaky way of slipping by the author's eyes. Even professional proof-readers hired by the publisher goof up and let errors go to press now and then. So hedge your bets with a second pair of eyes.

> **Write On!**
>
> If you work on a computer, it's a good idea to print out a hard copy of your work now and then. Editing on computers is so easy that it's tempting to delete lines, paragraphs, even whole scenes, prematurely. A printout will give you the chance to retrieve good writing if you have second thoughts after slicing and dicing on your computer.

1. Pretend you're a reader and see what impressions you get. Try to read your manuscript in one sitting, if possible, to get a feel for the rhythm. Resist the urge to edit at this point.

2. Don't freak out if it's not perfect. Make notes on what worked and what didn't work. You may not know immediately how to solve your problems. Mull them over for a few days, and invite your subconscious to come up with some solutions. If you feel too emotionally involved, put the book away for a month to gain perspective.

3. Get feedback from a trusted reader or writer friend. Mom doesn't count. She's too biased.

4. After going through steps one through three, start to edit your book. Working on a hard copy (a computer printout) is a good way to start. You can then enter the changes into your computer. You can catch errors on paper that slip by unnoticed on the computer screen. If you're writing by hand, of course the pen will be your surgical instrument of choice. Eventually your handwritten work will have to be typed, which provides even more opportunities for editing.

Focusing the Lens

When you read your book through from start to finish with a critical eye, what should you be looking for? You should be looking at the wide-angle view as well as the close-ups. These are the things I watch for when I read my first drafts:

1. **Trouble spots.** The sections that drag or seem awkward or disjointed.

2. **Scenes that hum.** The sections that have a spark of life, that work great, or at least hold my interest.

3. **Missing pieces.** The scenes that I realize I need in order to fill in the missing blanks or to further develop the plot and/or characters.

4. **Sketchy parts.** Important moments that are sketched out but still need color and depth.

5. **Best and worst lines.** The great sentences that transcend prose and the hokey lines I'd be embarrassed to show anyone.

Stop the Presses!

If you decide to add a scene, don't forget to polish the ones that come before and after it. One should lead smoothly into the other. When you dropkick a block of copy into a chapter, it creates a domino effect that will have ramifications throughout the rest of your book, so polish, polish, polish!

What do I do once I identify these areas?

➤ Awkward scenes are rewritten, tightened, refocused, or cut.

➤ Scenes that work are kept or even expanded. I analyze what worked and try to do more of it in other parts of the book.

➤ Missing pieces of the puzzle are written and added.

➤ Sketchy parts are fleshed out and expanded. Character motivations, climaxes, and important plot points are clarified.

➤ Best lines are treasured, and the worst ones are ruthlessly cut.

Method to This Madness

You may be getting the sense that this is a methodical process. If so, you're absolutely right! First-timers often think that great writing is magic. It has a magical effect, but the process of creating magical writing can be quite painstaking. So, no matter how bad you think your first draft is, you can make it better with careful analysis and thoughtful corrections. And if it ain't over 'til it's over, don't judge your book until the rewriting process is done!

The Three "Rs"

After looking at the big picture, you may decide you're pretty much on track, but the manuscript still seems rough. There are a few simple ways of identifying nagging problems—those pesky little glitches that can add up to general manuscript malaise.

Read out Loud

Reading your story out loud is an excellent way to pick up on problems that flew by unnoticed on silent read-throughs. Often, our eyes see what we meant to write, not what actually made it to paper! Here are some of the problems a verbal read-through will reveal:

➤ Redundancies

➤ Stilted dialogue

➤ Missing words

➤ Slow pacing

➤ Illogical ideas and contradictory information

➤ Unnecessary scenes

As a beginner, you may want to read the entire book aloud. As you become more proficient, that won't be necessary. But this is a good technique to use with problem passages no matter how advanced your writing skills.

Rhythm and Blahs

The best romance novels have a pleasing rhythm to their sentences, scenes, and chapters. The stories flow and build and hold your interest. You want to have the same reaction to your own novel. There should be a natural rhythm, and one sentence should lead effortlessly into the next. If they don't, you have some editing to do.

How do you know if your rhythm is right on? You get so wrapped up in the story that you forget you're reading. You stop thinking about your writing style and become engrossed in the action. So how do you know when your rhythm is clunky? You stumble over sentences and have to re-read them, you grow bored, and/or you put the book down because reading it takes too much effort.

Write On!

If you want to find an interesting word to replace one that's mundane, get yourself a good thesaurus. A thesaurus looks like a dictionary, but instead of offering definitions it provides synonyms—words with similar meanings—and antonyms. My personal favorite is *Roget's International Thesaurus.*

Repeat After Me

One of the most common mistakes beginners make is using the same words over and over. Fortunately, it's one of the easiest problems to fix. In general, you should strive never to use a distinctive word more than once in a paragraph, or even on the same page. See how many times the word "boat" is used in the following example:

> Henry took the boat to the boat dock and tied it next to a boat owned by Mr. Carlyle. Then, he stepped into his boat, and it bobbed against the boat in the next slip.

Now let's edit out most of the references to boat and find ways to write around it:

> Henry took the boat to the dock and tied it next to Mr. Carlyle's schooner. Then, he stepped into his hull, and it bobbed against the water craft in the next slip.

Love Letters

A **synonym** is a word that has a meaning close to another word. The meaning might be virtually the same or slightly different. Synonyms for anger include wrath, ire, and soreness. So, instead of using the same old words over and over, pick a synonym now and then!

The solution to this problem is simple. Get out your thesaurus and find some *synonyms*. If you find yourself repeating the same adjectives and adverbs, consider cutting them instead of finding replacements. Adjectives and adverbs are often superfluous.

181

Something's Wrong, but I Don't Know What

So let's say you've solved the little bugaboos plaguing your manuscript, but there's still something "not quite right." If that's the case, you have to dig deeper. I suggest you look at two areas that pose a challenge to even the most experienced writers.

Show, Don't Tell ... Again!

This maxim shows up at every turn, doesn't it? If you've written a great scene, but it just doesn't feel as great as it should be, you may be doing too much telling and not enough showing. Note the scenes in your book that are flat. Then read through each one by itself and ...

➤ Find spots where you can add sensory details to make the scene more vivid. Focus on everything the viewpoint character is seeing, touching, smelling, hearing, and tasting.

➤ Find places where the narrator is telling the reader about the character's thoughts and feelings. Try to show those thoughts and feelings through dialogue or physical action instead of narration.

Love Letters

The **viewpoint character** is the person you choose to focus on during any given scene. The reader will see everything in the environment through that character's point of view.

Point-of-View Tune-Up

The second major bugaboo to look for in a bland scene is point of view. If a scene seems unfocused or too general, chances are you need to tighten your point of view. In order to do that, you should thoroughly understand what that phrase means.

Point of view is the position from which something is seen or considered. If you stand in the middle of a room and turn in a circle and write down everything you see, you are writing a scene in your own point of view. You would be the *viewpoint character*. If suddenly you described the color of your eyes, you would have violated that point of view because it's physically impossible for you to see the color of your own eyes. Only someone outside your viewpoint could see that unless, of course, you're looking in a mirror. Having a viewpoint character gaze in a mirror can be an effective, if somewhat overused, way to let your reader see what your main character looks like.

Sneaking in a description from outside of the viewpoint character is not "illegal," but it does muddy the waters. If you do it often, it will dilute the force of your scene, leaving it bland and vague.

Here are a few commonly held beliefs and/or suggestions about point of view to bear in mind:

➤ Sticking with one person's point of view in a scene or a chapter helps build the reader's identification with that character. Also, for the writer, one viewpoint is easier to handle than multiple viewpoints.

➤ Jumping from one viewpoint to another can be jarring to the reader.

➤ Be consistent. If you're consistently in your hero's viewpoint, let's say, resist the urge to jump out of his point of view for one sentence just so you can describe him. You can either wait until you reach a scene written in someone else's point of view, or you can be creative. Have him look in a mirror, gaze at a self-portrait, reflect mentally on his appearance, or describe his looks through details of his physical actions (e.g., "He smoothed the curled ends of his mustache and put on a hat to shield his fair skin from the sun").

➤ If you head-hop (jump from one character's viewpoint to another from paragraph to paragraph), be consistent with that as well. Do it from the start so the reader knows the ground rules.

➤ If you stick with one viewpoint per scene, be especially vigilant in group scenes. Scenes with lots of characters can be confusing and sometimes leave the reader feeling vague about who she should be rooting for. If you're in your heroine's viewpoint, for example, check back in with her every so often to see how she's reacting to the group around her. It will help ground your readers.

I generally, but not always, try to stick with one point of view per scene, except in love scenes. Then I like to focus on the physical sensations of both characters. There's no question that single viewpoint scenes are cleaner and often more powerful. Still, I love novels with multiple viewpoints. There are no rules on this subject, so handle it however you feel most comfortable.

Resetting Your Setting

So what if you have a scene that's working fairly well, but it's not exactly blowing up your skirt? Try a different *setting*.

For example, let's say you've written a pleasant courtship scene. Your hero and heroine are sipping tea near the fire in a drawing room. The dialogue is going well, but the scene seems static. Why not try a different setting? Keep the same dialogue, but put your characters on horses and have them ride through a beautiful spring meadow. Or, put them in a carriage that's pitching to and fro as it makes its way across a muddy spring road. The added action will give them more to react to. Who knows? Maybe the carriage will nearly tip over, throwing the heroine into the arms of your hero!

Cut!

Alas, my friend, there comes a time in every writer's life when she must get out the scissors and cut a scene entirely. Every scene must pass the "move the story forward" test. If it doesn't add something important to your story, it has to go.

Admitting that a scene isn't working doesn't mean you have failed as a writer. Quite the opposite! Being able to discern what's working and what's not is the skill that will ultimately lead to publication. Our words aren't sacred. They are a means to an end. And the end should be a great read.

How Do You Spell "Duh"?

In this day and age of computer spell-check programs, there is no excuse for misspelled words. When I first started writing, I actually thought I was a good speller. Boy, was I ever wrong! After years of writing, I've improved a lot, but I still employ my computer spell-checker. Even with that handy device, you have to pour over your manuscript carefully to look for the following:

➤ **Misused words.** Do you ever substitute their or there for they're? While all are spelled correctly, they obviously have very different meanings. Some computer programs will catch these errors, but don't count on it.

➤ **Word usage.** Read through your manuscript once just to focus on your use of words and phrases. Be sure of their meaning. Don't say "I could care less" when you mean "I couldn't care less." Delete *anachronisms*. For example, "King Arthur checked his watch" is a major anachronism since watches didn't exist in the Dark Ages! And make sure phrases and *idioms* are consistent with your chosen locale and time. "Hunk of burning love" was a phrase I'd bet a royalty check you'd never hear Queen Victoria say.

➤ **Grammar and punctuation.** Make sure you place your commas, dashes, colons, and semicolons in the right places. Poor placement can really make a manuscript look unprofessional. Consult Strunk and White's *Elements of Style* for proper usage or take a refresher grammar course at your local college.

Tips from a Top-Notch Talent

My friend Martha Powers wrote a dozen regency romances before she began writing hardcover mystery-thrillers. Her style is incredibly smooth and tight and worth studying. Here are a few of Martha's pointers on revising, as well as a few from my own bag of tricks:

➤ Don't use more characters than you need. Cut those who seem superfluous. If a character doesn't seem to have much of a purpose, get the hook!

➤ Don't repeat the same ideas or statement in a different way. Once is enough. Trust that your reader will get your point the first time.

➤ Intersperse character action and reaction throughout dialogue to show what's happening. Otherwise, you'll end up with talking heads. Actions help ground the reader as to what's happening visually. For example: "Put down the gun, Henry!" Neville shouted. He reached for it, stepping evenly across the Aubusson carpet until he reached the enormous mahogany desk. The gun was mere inches from his grasp. "Easy, Henry. Just put down the gun."

➤ Keep a running list of names so they don't end up sounding alike or starting with the same initial. If your heroine's name is Rachel and your hero's name is Rafe, readers will get confused. It seems like a silly detail, but it's so true!

➤ If a scene doesn't work, try rewriting it from another person's viewpoint. It may take off in ways you never imagined.

➤ Mention other body parts besides heads, hands, and fingers. Romance writers tend to focus heavily on the eyes. What about the ears or the nose?

➤ Use "action-reaction" sequencing instead of "reaction-action." For example, instead of writing "She ran from the room after seeing the ghost," write "She saw the ghost and ran from the room." The action of seeing should come before the reaction of running.

Stop the Presses!

You don't have to have an English professor's knowledge of grammar to use it wisely. You can use good grammar instinctively without knowing all the rules by heart. The important thing is to have a clean manuscript. To editors, reading a book with poor grammar is like hearing fingernails on a chalkboard. It sets their teeth on edge.

➤ Be careful with pronouns (he, she, it). Don't overuse them. Be sure to establish clearly who "he" or "she" is with a proper name (John or Sarah). In scenes with two or more people of the same sex, remind us now and then. For example: "Dave walked in the room. He saw John. He was mad." Who was mad? It's unclear. You must, above all, be clear.

➤ Avoid filtering phrases. They distance the reader. Instead of saying "She saw that the crowd was out of control," say "The crowd was out of control." Instead of writing "She felt that she deserved better," write "She deserved better." She felt, she saw, she thought, she knew, and she sensed are all unnecessary add-ons.

➤ Choose active over passive voice. Instead of saying "James was loved by Geraldine," say "Geraldine loved James." Geraldine is being active, and James is being passive. Geraldine should be the subject of the sentence. If you see lots of "was" or "is" words scattered throughout your book, make sure you're not using passive voice to excess.

Revision Checklist

Isn't it reassuring to know that there are ways to improve your manuscript? In the next chapter, you'll learn how to find out if your revisions worked. In the meantime, here is a checklist to help keep you on course:

❏ I have read through my manuscript at least once without editing it to get an overview of what's working—and what's not.

❏ I have noted places that drag or seem sketchy.

❏ I have noted scenes that work and analyzed why.

❏ I have read portions, particularly problem areas, of my book aloud.

❏ I have circled repetitive words and awkward sentences.

❏ I have noted areas that could use more sensory details.

❏ I have flagged places that could use more showing and less telling.

❏ I have considered whether any scenes could use more exciting settings.

❏ My grammar and spelling are up to snuff.

The Least You Need to Know

➤ Even the pros rewrite, so roll up your sleeves and get back to work!

➤ Read through your finished manuscript at least once as a reader and try to enjoy it.

➤ Flesh out sketchy scenes and add scenes when necessary.

➤ Read sections of your book aloud to catch poor pacing, choppy rhythms, and repetitive words.

➤ If something seems a little off, tighten your point of view and remember the "show, don't tell" adage.

Chapter 15

Feedback: It Hurts So Good

In This Chapter

➤ How to find out if your story is any good

➤ The best ways to get feedback

➤ Do you need to pay someone to edit your book?

➤ How to survive a bad review

➤ The difference between good and bad critiques

Dear Author:

We appreciate the opportunity to look at your manuscript. However, after careful consideration we have decided not to make an offer. While your style shows promise, the characterization was lacking, the plot was deadly dull, and the premise preposterous. If you're smart, you won't quit your day job. Oh, and by the way, don't bother to submit anything to us in the future. Of course, editorial opinions vary widely and we wish you luck in submitting your work elsewhere.

A rejection letter—especially one like this—is the most painful kind of feedback you can get. And while this example has been exaggerated to make a point, there are writers in the trenches who claim they've received rejections every bit as brutal.

You can't make anyone love your manuscript, but you can reduce the chances of a shattering rejection. You do that by making sure your book is ready for serious consideration. That means getting feedback before you send it to a publisher.

As a writer you'll get feedback every step of the way. You'll likely start with a critique group or partner, progress to editorial feedback, then it's on to comments (and sometimes zingers) from reviewers, until you have the thrill of receiving the ultimate feedback—purchases in the bookstore. Cha-ching!

Oh, *That's* What You Meant to Say!

One of the best reasons to get feedback is to make sure your words really say what you think they say. You know your hero and heroine intimately. How can you not after writing about them page after page? Just because you know and love your characters doesn't mean you have accurately portrayed them on paper. What you think you see is not always what the reader sees. You need some objectivity! Here are the kinds of questions you can ask an objective reader to answer:

➤ Are my characters sympathetic?

➤ Are their actions properly motivated and logical?

➤ Is the pacing adequate?

➤ Did the story drag at any point?

➤ Was anything confusing or silly?

➤ How would you describe my main characters?

➤ Did you catch any errors or inconsistencies?

➤ Does this need more work or is it good to go?

It's especially important to get feedback on your characters because romance novels focus so heavily *characterization*. Characters are tricky because …

➤ Your characters are defined not just by the adjectives you use to describe them, but by their own actions. You need to make sure the actions you've given them add up to the impression you want the readers to have.

➤ A poorly chosen word used to describe a character can give the readers a wrong and long-lasting impression of your character.

Love Letters

Characterization is your representation of a human being. It's the sum of all the brush strokes a writer makes in order to paint a three-dimensional fictional person.

Case in point: I recently gave a first draft of a novel to a friend. She said she wondered why I had created an unattractive heroine. Imagine my surprise! I thought of the heroine as attractive, though she was certainly no raving beauty. I went back and carefully reviewed my descriptions to see what had given my friend the wrong impression. Then, I purposefully added words to counterbalance the plain image I had painted.

Mother Doesn't Know Best

Your mother may love your writing, or your mother may hate your writing. Either way, take her opinion with a grain of salt. Mom may know best about many things, but there are two things she can't objectively tell you:

➤ Whether or not your book is publishable.

➤ Whether or not you have talent.

Write On!

Your family may be too biased to give you good feedback, but husbands occasionally prove themselves to be the exception to the rule. You presumably married your mate because he shares your outlook on life, so he can be a good source of honest, constructive criticism. He can at least comment on the male perspective. And of course, tell him you modeled the hero after him!

It's tempting to show your work to family members because, frankly, they have to love you. However, they don't have to love your writing. If you can expect support from family, then great! We all need encouragement. But if you know you'll receive hurtful criticism, spare yourself the pain and keep your writing to yourself. In any event, you'll need more objective feedback than family can provide.

Good Sources of Feedback

No matter who you turn to for feedback, you have to realize that all opinions are subjective. Have you ever loved a book that your best friend hated, or vice versa? The same thing will happen with feedback. One person will love your book, the next might rip it apart. So remember, someone's opinion on your work is just that ... someone's opinion. It's not gospel. Take it or leave it as you please.

Speaking of Romance ...

Pat White has served as the President of the Chicago-North Chapter of Romance Writers of America, a group that has met for nearly 20 years for critiques. Twenty-five to thirty or more members gather twice a month to share their knowledge about writing and the marketplace. "When you're just starting out you especially need feedback to get you on the right track and going in the right direction," says Pat. "We're really good at telling people how they can improve their writing or what things we know editors don't like. Therefore, we save them the time of writing books that aren't marketable and sending them out over and over again. Rather than learning it the hard way, aspiring writers benefit from our shared experiences."

Writer's Groups

I think a good writer's group is one of the best places to get feedback on a chapter or a manuscript. If more than one person reads your work, you can get a consensus of opinions. If 9 out of 10 people love your story, you know you're on track. If 9 out of 10 hate it, odds are you've got problems. Here's some advice to consider before you join a writer's group:

1. Make sure criticism given is constructive, not destructive. Comments should focus on tangible ways to improve manuscripts. Those who critique shouldn't spout negative comments just to prove how brilliant they are.

2. Make sure at least one person in the group knows more than you do. It's hard to learn when you're the teacher, although you can learn a lot from critiquing others! At the very least, make sure a few others are writing at your level.

3. Make sure members of the group are serious about getting published, preferably in the romance genre. If you want to be a successful popular fiction writer and everyone else wants to publish poetry in university journals, they won't understand your agenda, and you'll be frustrated by theirs.

4. Make sure a healthy dose of praise is given with every critique, but don't settle for flattery. If your group isn't skilled enough to offer insightful commentary, you're probably wasting your time. Even unskilled groups, however, can give you general feedback as readers, and that alone may have some value.

5. Make sure you put the critique in perspective. Put the critiqued manuscript away for a few days before you try to incorporate any suggestions. That gives your subconscious a chance to sort the good comments from the bad. When you look at the critiques again, you'll instinctively know which comments, if any, to heed.

It can be very helpful to read first chapters and synopses in groups. A cluster of writers can brainstorm and help you get off to a good start. You probably don't want to read every chapter, though, or re-read the same chapter a second time. At some point, you have to learn to trust your own instincts. And learn to trust them you will! When you learn to critique others, you are also learning how to critique yourself.

> **Write On!**
>
> One of the best ways to find a critique group or a potential critique partner is through your local chapter of Romance Writers of America. There are 8,400 members in 143 chapters throughout the world and cyberspace. Call the Houston headquarters at 281-440-6885 to find the chapter nearest you. You can also ask your local librarian or bookstore about other writers' groups in your area. Or, start your own group!

Classes

College classes or continuing adult education courses can be helpful. Class assignments offer you a deadline to strive for, and teachers are paid to give you feedback. Be careful, though, to find a good teacher. A bad one can damage your confidence and drive, and most literary teachers neither understand nor appreciate the romance genre.

Critique Partners

When you find a critique partner, you'll feel as if you've found a soul mate. It may take some time to find the right person. You want someone …

➤ Who shares your artistic sensibilities.

➤ Who appreciates your talent.

➤ Whose talent you appreciate in turn.

➤ Who is supportive and not jealous.

➤ Who can make helpful suggestions.

➤ Who benefits from your comments as well.

A critique partner can't give you the variety of opinions a group can, but she can give you her undivided attention. If the benefit is mutual, you both have a vested interest in nurturing your creative relationship.

Speaking of Romance ...

Historical author Elizabeth Grayson and contemporary author Eileen Dreyer (a.k.a. Kathleen Korbel) are close friends who have been critique partners for years. "Part of working with someone for a period of time is that you develop a trust," says Elizabeth. "I've gotten to the point where if Eileen points out something that isn't working, I know without thinking twice that she's right. I take what she says and figure out how I can address the problems she's raised. Sometimes I take the suggestions she's made for changes, and sometimes I come up with another approach entirely. In any case, it's having someone you trust to be honest about your work that makes the critiquing process so valuable."

Editorial Services

You can also hire a freelance editor to critique or edit your work. Debbie Macomber pays one of her former editors to edit her books before she hands the final draft in to her publisher. If it's good enough for Debbie …

A word of warning, though. Be sure you understand the costs involved before you hire a critiquing service. Some editors charge a couple thousand dollars for a completed manuscript. Also, check references to make sure the person you chose is worth the money. Where can you find a freelance editor? Ask other writers for suggestions, or check want ads in publications like *Writer's Digest*. You can also call the Editorial Freelancers Association at 212-929-5400, or log on to its Web site at www.the-efa.org.

The Good, the Bad, and the Ugly

Asking for comments on your book is a delicate proposition. Getting reactions to your work makes sense. If you want to get published, that means you're writing for an audience. Your work has to appeal to a large number of people if it's going to sell as popular fiction. At the same time, asking the wrong person, or getting the wrong kinds of comments, can be ruinous to your creative health. There are basically three kinds of feedback: that which is helpful, that which is hurtful, and that which is downright devastating.

Constructive Criticism

Most people can give you a reaction to your book as a reader, but this kind of feedback is pretty generic. Readers tend to say things like "I loved your book!" or "I really liked it" or "I stayed up until 3:00 A.M. just to finish it!" That's nice to hear, but if you ask the general reader why it was so good, she'll likely scratch her head, shrug, or say "I dunno. It just was!"

You need more specific feedback than that. A good critic will tell you ...

➤ What is working and why.

➤ What isn't working and why.

This kind of commentary usually has to come from another writer, but not necessarily one who is published. Not all published writers are capable of giving insightful critiques. Critiquing is a learned skill. When you find a wise critic, published or unpublished, prostrate yourself before her and ask for her feedback. If she does you the favor, take her to lunch to show your appreciation.

It's All Subjective

A bad critique is usually one in which the commentator relies solely on her subjective opinions. She may say something like this:

> "I liked your hero, but he really seemed inconsistent to me. He's a CEO but would a CEO really get mad like he did in chapter five? All CEOs are self-controlled. You really have to change that. And I think you need to take this out of the corporate Chicago setting and put the characters in a circus. Instead of having a secret baby, your plot should revolve around animal rights abuse. If you don't make these changes, I guarantee your book will never sell!"

What's wrong with this critique? Her criticism is too broad. She offers no concrete solutions. She's also judging the hero based on her subjective opinions of how a CEO should behave. She is playing God, rendering a verdict on the book's salability. And worst of all she's trying to rewrite the story in the way she would write it. Steer clear of critiques like this!

Write On!

When listening to feedback, carefully sift the chaff from the wheat. The grains of wheat are the comments that point out genuine problems. The chaff are the comments that criticize your voice or vision. Ignore the chaff. Just because a friend doesn't like your voice doesn't mean an editor won't and ultimately, the editor is the only one whose opinion matters ... until the book goes on sale!

Downright Nasty Comments

It's hard to write a romance. It's easy to tear one apart in a critique. If you sense you've been the victim of a hatchet job, throw the comments in the trash immediately! Then, be much more careful about whom you share your work with. The worst of the hatchet jobs come from critics who actually know enough to be taken seriously. If the person making a brutal critique makes sense regarding your plotting or grammar, you're unfortunately inclined to believe she may also make sense when she tells you you're a talentless rube who has no business writing.

One of the most hurtful critiques I ever received was from a well-meaning friend who took apart my story line by line and told me all the reasons why each line didn't make sense. Suddenly, I saw my story through her critical eyes and I wanted to stop writing. When you feel punched in the gut by an unnecessarily harsh critique, remember something I mentioned earlier that bears repeating:

We all have some talent. We could all use more. But we should all keep writing.

Speaking of Romance ...

Kathe Robin has been a reviewer for *Romantic Times* since 1981. Every month the magazine rates new releases on a scale that ranges from one star (acceptable) to five stars (extraordinary). Kathe says her supposed power over author's careers is greatly exaggerated. "If somebody loves Indian romances, and your Indian romance gets a three or a two rating, they're still going to buy that book. I don't think I can make or break a career. I can get somebody to pick up your book and look at it. I cannot make them take it to the cash register and open up their wallet and spend their hard-earned money, but I can make them at least consider your book, because it's gotten exposure."

Give as Good as You Get

By the time you get published, chances are you'll owe a debt of gratitude to a variety of people who helped you along the way. One way to repay that debt is to help others in turn. You can give an aspiring writer the kind of support and feedback you enjoyed when you were just beginning. There is a great and generous tradition among romance writers of training our competition. I suppose it's no surprise that people who write about love feel compelled to help others.

When Giving Is as Good as Receiving

On a less altruistic note, critiquing others can be good for your own writing. When you see others making mistakes, you can more easily recognize your own. When you see others writing well, you can analyze why and apply the same principles to your writing. Editing someone else's manuscript teaches you how to edit your own. So, you may as well learn to do it right.

Rules to Critique By

Some people have a real knack for critiquing. Fortunately for those who don't, it's a skill that in large part can be learned. If you're going to critique for other writers, here are a few tips to keep in mind:

1. Understand the writer's intended market and vision. If she's trying to write broader women's fiction, your comments will be very different than if she's trying to write a category romance.

2. Understand your own likes and dislikes and don't let them get in the way. If you can't stand quirky, humorous writing styles and that's exactly what you've been asked to critique, you may want to take a pass because you won't be objective.

3. Don't try to rewrite the writer's story, but do identify what works and doesn't work—diplomatically! Don't say "The hero sucks!" Say "I had some problems with the hero." Then be specific about the problems and suggested changes.

4. Don't play judge and jury. You may think you know what will sell and what won't, but only a fool would declare such opinions as facts. Often, it's the books that seem unmarketable that end up selling because they're refreshing and unique! So stick to comments about technique and leave the editorial content to the writer.

Stop the Presses!

Don't fall into the mistake of thinking that criticizing a manuscript is the only way to give important feedback. Sometimes it's just as valuable for a writer to learn what she's doing right. Even published authors sometimes have no idea what's right with their writing. Praise beautiful lines, exciting moments, and good plot twists. The important thing is to be specific.

Write On!

Most publishing houses are big conglomerations that keep staff at a bare minimum. Sometimes editors are so overworked that they don't have time to give their authors feedback on anything but their final drafts. That means the friends who critique you now will still be needed after you become published. So be kind to them. You'll owe them big time!

197

Editorial Feedback

The kind of feedback every writer would like to get is from an editor. Ideally, of course, you'll get a phone call from an editor saying she wants to buy your book, but even a rejection can be positive ... really!

Congratulations! An Editor Hates Your Story

If an editor hates your story, you are to be congratulated. A rejection means you've actually gathered the courage to submit your work. Many writers never get to that point. So look at the bright side and pat yourself on the back.

Not all rejections are created equal, by the way. As a beginner, you'll typically receive one of three responses from an editor:

➤ A form rejection letter

➤ A personal rejection letter

➤ A personal letter suggesting changes in your story

If you get a personal rejection letter, it means the editor cared enough about your book to take the time to respond. If the letter explains why your book was rejected, you have some valuable feedback to consider. Since it's just one editor's opinion, it's feedback you can incorporate or discard.

Do I or Don't I?

What should you do if you receive a letter hinting that the editor might look at the book again if you make changes? It's up to you. You have to decide if the suggested changes fit in with your vision for the book. A letter like this is encouraging, though, and you'd do well to consider it closely. Just be forewarned that even if you do make the changes it won't guarantee a sale.

Early in Judith McNaught's career, she was told by an editor that *Whitney, My Love* was too long and should undergo major editing. Not only did Judith refuse to take this advice, in a fit of defiance she lengthened her manuscript! She ended up selling the longer book to Pocket and it became one of the most memorable and successful romance novels in recent memory.

Review This!

Since we're into positive thinking, let's assume that like Judith you, too, will succeed in finding a publisher. That's when your precious baby will be sent out into the world at large and face a very different kind of critique—book reviews!

Great reviews can put you on cloud nine and bad ones can put you in the depths of despair. In spite of the potential for pain, though, every author wants reviews. The more your book is reviewed, the more people will read about it and possibly buy it.

The Grand Scheme

If you're worried about getting a bad review, let's put a few things into perspective. Most newspapers don't review romances, so most readers won't see a review of your book before deciding whether to buy it. Even with a bad review your book can still sell well. However, many dedicated romance readers subscribe to *Romantic Times* magazine and review publications such as *Affaire de Coeur* and *Rendezvous*. Some booksellers even post these reviews in their stores. Barnes and Noble has allied itself with *Romantic Times* and posts the magazine's "Top Picks" list in its stores.

Cyber-Critical

There are a number of new online romance sites that feature reviews. A word of warning, though. Many of them aren't for the faint of heart. The anonymity of cyberspace seems to lend itself to a slash-and-burn approach to reviews. So, don't go there unless you have on your creative armor. It's unclear how many readers actually read online reviews, but if you want to cover all the bases, ask your editor to send review copies to the romance Web sites.

Going Mainstream

Romance novels are increasingly being reviewed in industry magazines that have overlooked the genre in the past. The *Library Journal* and *Publishers Weekly* have recently made a commitment to review more romances. This is a very positive development for writers. Many librarians use these publications when deciding what books to buy. My local librarian told me that if she doesn't see a romance reviewed in *Publishers Weekly,* or *P.W.,* as it is widely known, then she doesn't know it exists.

> **Write On!**
>
> Once you start getting reviews, your publisher will keep them on file. The glowing quotes you see on book covers often come from reviews of the authors' previous books. It's handy to keep your own file as well, in case your publisher overlooks a good review in an obscure publication.

Speaking of Romance …

Many readers discover their favorite authors in libraries. That's why Romance Writers of America is putting a big effort into romancing librarians nationwide. Author Cathie Linz, a former librarian herself, is the RWA librarian liaison. She encourages readers and writers to share their love of the romance genre with their local librarians. "The way a genre is perceived is the way libraries and librarians handle that genre," says Cathie. So praise your librarians if they catalogue and regularly purchase romances, and direct them to the section for librarians on www.rwanational.com.

Taking Reviews in Stride

Now that you know how important reviews can be, let me try to impress upon you how unimportant they can be as well. Some of the novels that have received the highest acclaim among romance writers have received lousy reviews. And a number of authors who get panned in review magazines go on to great success with readers. (All the *Star Wars* movies have been panned. Do you see George Lucas crying?) I've said it before, and I'll say it again—creativity is subjective, so don't jump off a cliff if your first book gets a bad review. Some writers don't even read their reviews! I guess they feel what they don't know can't hurt them.

The Ultimate Feedback

We've talked about feedback from many sources, but guess whose feedback counts the most? The readers'. The ultimate feedback comes from the readers who plunk down their hard-earned money for your books. If you have a following, you have a career. So write the best book you can and hope that the publishing fairy will be good to you long enough for you to develop a readership in the marketplace.

Feedback Checklist

In the next chapter, we'll talk about the pros and cons of hiring an agent. Before you submit your work to an author's representative, though, make sure you've gotten enough feedback to know your manuscript is the best it can be. Complete this checklist:

❑ I've received enough feedback to be confident that my story has the effect on readers that I intended.

❑ I've thought carefully about whom I'm going to give my manuscript to for feedback.

❑ I'm careful to differentiate between helpful and useless comments when I receive feedback.

❑ When I give feedback I am careful to avoid rewriting the other person's work.

❑ After reading a critique of my manuscript, I allowed myself a cooling-off period before deciding what to keep and what to discard.

❑ I have reminded myself lately that all writing is subjective.

❑ I've promised myself that no matter how painful a critique or a review might be I will keep writing.

The Least You Need to Know

➤ It's good to get feedback on your book before you submit it.

➤ Try to get feedback from someone who knows as much or more than you do about writing.

➤ A good review can help, but a bad review won't necessarily sink your career.

➤ Writing is extremely subjective, so let criticism roll off your back and keep writing.

Chapter 16

Hiring an Agent

> ## In This Chapter
>
> ➤ What an agent can and can't do for you
>
> ➤ Agents to avoid
>
> ➤ The truth about big-time agents
>
> ➤ Getting your foot in a door labeled "Do Not Enter"
>
> ➤ An important tip about agent contracts

"My agent" are two words just about every aspiring writer would love to say. Once you finally have an agent, you may feel like giggling whenever you utter those bon mots. Next thing you know, you'll be wearing sunglasses and saying things like "I'll have my people call your people and we'll do lunch." After struggling to write on your own for so long, having an agent can almost seem unreal ... and somewhat pretentious.

So, do you need an agent? Are they really all they're cracked up to be? And how the heck do you get one? These are the burning questions every writer wants to know, so let's find the answers!

Do I Need an Agent?

When most writers ask that question, what they're really saying is: Do I have to have an agent in order to get published? Or to be even more specific: Can I sell my book without having to pay an agent's commission? Here's the answer: You can submit your own work directly to an editor, and you can even negotiate your own contract. But it's not easy.

Just because you don't have to have an agent doesn't mean you won't want one. This is an issue you should think through carefully. Here are a few guidelines to follow:

You May Need an Agent If ...

➤ You plan on having a long, successful career.

➤ You aren't assertive when it comes to negotiating.

➤ You would write for free if they'd only let you see your book in print.

➤ You aren't good at financial details and record keeping.

➤ You have a really hot book that could be a big best-seller.

You May Not Need an Agent If ...

➤ You're a one-book wonder ... and the book isn't a blockbuster.

➤ You have great business acumen and you're a firm negotiator.

➤ You plan to stick to category romances and feel you know enough about the business to make sure you're getting as much as the market can bear.

Stop the Presses!

Don't bother to query an agent until you have at least one completed manuscript. The agent won't know if you can successfully finish a book until you do. Of course, there are exceptions to this rule. Some topics are so hot that an agent will salivate even over a partial manuscript. That's rare, though. So get to work and finish that book!

Going It Alone

A number of category romance authors work without agents. That's in large part because there isn't all that much room for negotiation with category contracts. The advances and royalties are pretty standardized. So why share 10 percent or 15 percent of your income with an agent if you can get as good a deal yourself? Harlequin-Silhouette, the biggest publisher of category romances, willingly works with *unagented* writers.

Some single-title authors also negotiate their own contracts, but not many. To negotiate a single-title romance yourself you have to study the market closely because money advances vary wildly. You also have to be courageous enough to demand what you're worth. Too often writers are so eager to be published they settle for little more than vacation money and a pat on the head. Only later, after the thrill of being published wears off, do they realize they sold themselves short.

The Publisher's Preference

While many publishers are willing to buy a manuscript directly from an author, they frequently prefer to work with an agent. In fact, an increasing number of publishers won't even look at manuscripts not received through an agent. Editors like working with author's representatives because …

➤ Agents know the ins and outs of the business and can negotiate a contract more efficiently than many authors can.

➤ Agents are less likely to let themselves be taken advantage of. Sure, the publisher's bean counters want to pay authors the least amount possible, but editors know that an author who gets cheated may raise Cain later on when she realizes she should have received a better deal.

➤ Agents are less emotionally tied to the manuscript and won't get their feelings hurt if the publisher offers less money than expected.

Four Reasons to Hire an Agent

There are a number of very good reasons to hire an agent. Here are a few:

1. A good agent will in all likelihood know the market better than you do. She'll know the preferences of various editors and which editors are looking for your kind of manuscript. That increases your chances of finding the right editor. It also reduces the amount of time wasted sending your book to the wrong person.

Love Letters

An **unagented** writer is one who doesn't have an agent. It's a standard industry term used to describe an author who submits a manuscript without an agent. Guidelines usually indicate whether or not a publisher will look at unagented manuscripts.

Stop the Presses!

Your editor will not only edit your manuscript, she'll also negotiate your contract on behalf of your publisher. If you resent her negotiations over money, your resentment could taint your feelings about the editorial process. If you choose to negotiate your own contract, you'll have to be vigilant about keeping your feelings out of the negotiation process.

Love Letters

Submitting a book **over the transom** means you mail it in uninvited. The **slush pile** is the huge stack of unread manuscripts in which an uninvited manuscript ends up, gathering dust. A **multiple submission** describes a manuscript that is being shopped around at a number of publishing houses simultaneously.

Write On!

There's a good reason that agents get a quicker response from editors than writers do. Editors trust agents' opinions. If an agent likes your book enough to take it on, the editor knows that it probably has merit. Agents filter through bad manuscripts to find diamonds in the rough that editors are often too busy to find themselves.

2. An agent can get a quicker response. If you send your manuscript *over the transom*, it could sit in a *slush pile* for months. A decent agent can often get a yes or no response to a submission in a matter of weeks, or even days. It's not uncommon for authors to wait six months to a year for a response.

3. An agent can multiple submit and play one publisher off of another. A number of publishers don't allow *multiple submissions* from authors. An agent, however, can auction a manuscript if it's a single-title that he thinks is really special. He can pass around your book to a handful of editors and give them a bidding deadline. That would be difficult, if not impossible, for a beginning writer to do.

4. Having an agent who believes in you can be vital reinforcement if you have a hard time selling your beloved manuscript. There have been a number of books published simply because a dogged agent wouldn't give up—even after dozens of rejections. It's enough to bring tears to my eyes!

5. Agents know how to read and interpret contracts. They can also track royalty payments and handle other paperwork that sometimes makes creative people break out in hives.

One Reason Not to Hire an Agent

I can only think of one reason not to have an agent—the commission. Agents charge between 10 percent and 15 percent of whatever you earn. Most agents charge 15 percent, and some also bill you for expenses. Ouch!

Where Did the Money Go?

Fifteen percent doesn't sound like much until you actually get your check—minus the 15 percent! After you get done paying your agent's commission and forking over income and self-employment taxes to Uncle Sam, you may end up keeping less than half of your advance. So, you want to make sure you have an agent who is worth your hard-earned money.

Sweetening the Pot

There are two ways that an agent can make his commission more palatable. He can reduce the percentage when and if you start rolling in the dough. After all, the more you make, the more your agent makes. Fifteen percent of nothing isn't nearly as good as 10 percent of a big advance.

Some agents will also agree to split payments. It's standard practice for the publisher to pay you by writing a check in your agent's name. The agent deposits the check in her account then writes you a check for the same amount minus her commission. Under the split payment system, the publisher writes two checks—one made out to you and one made out to your agent. That way you get your money faster. That's always good news if your electricity is about to be turned off in the middle of a snowstorm!

Speaking of Romance ...

Agent Evan Fogelman is the recipient of a Lifetime Achievement award from Romance Writers of America and has served as the RWA liaison to the Association of Authors' Representatives. He says writers shouldn't hire an agent unless they really need one. "If you have to ask the question 'Do I need an agent?' then you probably don't," says Evan. "When you feel a compelling need for the kind of career help, in terms of contract negotiations and business management and development that an agent can give, then you'll say 'I need an agent' and you can best go about the business of finding the right agent for you."

I'd Rather Do It Myself!

If you decide to negotiate your own contract, you need to be prepared. That means educating yourself about the business before you get that magic call from an editor saying she wants your book. You should …

➤ Network with other writers and ask them advice about negotiating contracts.

➤ Join professional organizations like Romance Writers of America, Novelists, Inc., and the Authors' Guild. The latter two are open only to published writers.

➤ Read about the business in trade books and magazines, like *Romance Writers' Report, Publishers Weekly,* and *Writer's Digest.* There is a great book on self-agenting written by Richard Curtis called *How To Be Your Own Literary Agent.*

➤ Determine what kind of advance you're worth and then have the guts to ask for it.

If you decide to pay a lawyer a one-time fee to look over your contract in lieu of hiring an agent, make sure she knows something about the publishing business. Writing contracts are unique.

Should you negotiate your own contract? Only you can decide.

Frankly, an argument can be made for self-negotiation. There aren't as many publishers today as there were even three years ago—the corporate takeover syndrome has hit publishing as it has every other industry, so it's easier now for an author to peddle her book. There are only a half dozen places to send it, instead of dozens.

Love Letters

A **commission** is the money an agent earns for selling a book on your behalf. He earns a percentage, usually 15 percent, of your income, but doesn't get paid until you get paid. The agent receives a commission on everything you earn, including income from foreign and movie rights.

Still, I think my agent is worth every penny I pay him. If for no other reason than he can brag about me to editors and make demands that I could never pull off with a straight face!

Great Expectations

If you decide to hire an agent, you'll expect a lot in return for the *commission* you pay her. Just remember, though, agents aren't miracle workers. Your expectations of your representative should be realistic.

What an Agent Can Do for You

A good agent can do a lot for you. He can talk up your book with editors and writers, he can send it out enthusiastically and persistently, he can ask for lots of money (although he may not get it), and he can try hard to make sure the details of the contract favor your interests, instead of the publisher's. Here is a brief overview of what you can expect from your agent:

➤ **Responsible accounting.** Your agent should make sure you receive advance and royalty payments on time and in the agreed upon amounts. He should have an escrow account for his own agency so that you get your money even if he keels over and dies. He should give you copies of all checks and financial statements from your publisher.

➤ **Responsible communication.** Your agent should accurately represent your wishes to the publisher and vice versa. You should receive copies of rejections when they're written, and you should hear detailed explanations when they're verbal. She should consult with you when deciding where to send your manuscript, and she should follow up on the submissions promptly.

➤ **Enthusiastic representation.** Your agent should be excited about your work and should push you enthusiastically. She shouldn't give you the short end of the stick in favor of other clients, and she shouldn't care more about preserving her relationship with editors than she cares about asking for what you deserve.

A really good agent will go to the wall for you. That's the best and, in many ways, the least you can hope for.

What an Agent Can't Do for You

We have all probably fantasized about the "I'm gonna make you a star, baby" kind of New York agent. We hope a big-time agent will discover us and get us a million-dollar deal. It's definitely possible (more on money in Chapter 20, "Advances and Royalties"), but it's unlikely if you're an unpublished romance author. Most romance writers who get million-dollar deals have been writing for years and have built up an audience that justifies a huge advance.

You want your agent to ask for beaucoup bucks, and in most cases she should, but you have to be realistic about the value of what you're writing. If you've written a 55,000-word Silhouette Romance, you're probably going to get an advance of around $5,000. No agent is going to get $1,000,000 for a category romance, even if she's the great and powerful Oz!

What else can't you expect from an agent? An agent can't ...

➤ Make you more talented than you already are.

➤ Sell poorly written books, at least not in today's tight market.

➤ Sell a proposal that isn't written yet.

➤ Make a publisher buy your book.

➤ Make a publisher want to work with you if you have a reputation as a holy terror.

➤ Tell you how to write.

An agent isn't a nursemaid or an editor, though a few do like to edit their client's manuscripts. You can't expect her to call you everyday with writing tips and encouraging words. You can expect her to sell a good book, and for as much money as possible.

Stop the Presses!

Being a literary agent doesn't require a degree, an education, or even knowledge of the publishing industry. Anyone can hang a shingle outside his door and call himself an agent. So, writer beware!

The Perils of Pauline's Bad Agent

Pauline had a promising career, but then she hired a guy named Bob who hung a shingle on his door that said "Agent for Hire." Pauline thought any agent, even a bad one, was better than no agent at all. Boy, was she wrong! In the space of five years, these are the perils Pauline encountered:

➤ Bob took an overly hostile approach to negotiations, and Pauline's editor decided she wasn't worth the hassle.

➤ Bob never forwarded rejection letters from other publishers, so Pauline had trouble figuring out why new editors were rejecting her work.

➤ Bob talked big but never followed through on anything, so Pauline felt great, but found her income going down instead of up.

➤ Pauline thought she should dump Bob, but she didn't want to hurt his feelings. By the time she did get rid of him, the market had tightened and she couldn't get published again.

➤ After she dumped him, Pauline found out Bob was cashing and spending her royalty checks. He skipped town and hasn't been heard from again.

What a nightmare! This is obviously an extreme example, but it should serve as a warning. Just because someone claims to be an agent doesn't mean he's honest or knowledgeable about the business. Check out references and credentials before you hire anyone. And if you think he might be a bump on a log, take a pass until an opportunity to work with a good agent arises.

You're the Boss

Most writers have a tendency to look at agents as saviors or demigods. If you feel this way, remember this simple fact: You're the boss. The agent is your employee. Granted, an employee you respect greatly. But if an agent handles your career badly, his career will continue long after yours has floundered. Here are a few words of advice on dealing assertively with an agent:

➤ Ask questions. Ask him what career plan he has in mind for you, how he will handle your money, and what he thinks he can do for you.

➤ Be clear with him about the future you see for yourself.

➤ Once you hire an agent, speak up if you need information or more attention, but don't expect a lot of hand-holding. An agent expects you to act like a professional—albeit a creative and sometimes insecure professional!

Write On!

You pay your agent, but since it is a percentage of your advance, he won't get a dime until you sell a book. So if you're unpublished, your agent is taking a big risk representing you. Will he get a return on his investment of phone calls, FedEx bills, office overhead, and time? Even though there are lots of agents, they aren't exactly fighting over unproven authors.

The Vision Thing

In 1981, Sandra Brown sold her first category romance to the now-defunct Dell Candlelight Ecstasy line. I'm not privy to Sandra's bank account, but it's probably safe to say she didn't get rich off her first book. In 1987, she made the calculated and somewhat risky move to mainstream. The decision paid off beautifully when Sandra hit the *New York Times* Bestseller list in 1990. Since then, she's had more than 35 titles on the *New York Times* list. She recently signed a three-book, $16 million contract with Warner. Not bad, eh? Clearly, Sandra and her agent had a far-reaching vision of her career.

Debbie Macomber is another author who continually plans for the future. She and her agent, who live in different cities, meet once a year for a summit. They spend a few days focusing solely on Debbie's career. Maybe that's why Debbie also gets million-dollar contracts. These authors had visions of best-sellers dancing in their head, and now they're dancing all the way to the bank.

If you are going to make a commitment to an agent, you want to make sure you both share a vision of where you're going. Think not only about this book, but your next one, or your fifth, or even your fiftieth. Dream big, then write like crazy!

Speaking of Romance ...

Agent Irene Goodman meets periodically with her authors for "summit meetings" to discuss their careers. "I also meet regularly with publishers about specific authors—not just the regular business lunches, but office meetings with key people and a written agenda. I ask them what their plan is for this author and what their goals for her are, I suggest marketing and promotion ideas, I bring up any issues or concerns that need to be addressed and solved, and I present my own visions for the author's successes and how to achieve them. While publishers are often full of energy and good ideas, they can sometimes grow complacent."*

Stop the Presses!

Consider before you pay an agent a reading fee. The AAR (Association of Authors' Representatives) won't allow its members to charge reading fees. Granted, some legitimate agents charge fees to cover the cost of their valuable reading time. However, I have never met a romance author who had to pay an agent to get her manuscript read. If you want an agent, hire one that won't charge you to read your book.

Where Do You Find One?

Now that you have a better idea of whether or not you want an agent, the next question is how do you get one? Where do you start your search? After hearing about the perils of Pauline, you'll want to make sure you only query agents with good reputations.

Networking

One of the best ways to get the real scoop on agents is to talk to other writers. If a prospective agent gives you the names of several clients, call them and chat. Granted, an agent isn't going to refer you to writers who hate him, but you can still glean important information. Find out how quickly he forwards royalty payments, for example, and what his strengths and weaknesses are.

An even better way to get the lowdown on agents is to conduct your own ad hoc survey. Ask every writer you know who the best and worst agents are. Bear in mind, though, that opinions are often little more than thinly veiled gossip. While one writer may hate an agent, the next will think she walks on water. The best agent for you is someone who fits your needs, not the needs of other writers.

AAR (Association of Authors' Representatives)

Ideally, your agent will belong to the Association of Authors' Representatives. I have to admit I didn't even know what the AAR was when I hired my agent. The organization has strict requirements for membership, including a code of ethics agents must sign and procedures for grievances. So, if you're concerned about the honesty and reliability of a potential agent, this organization is a good place to start. You can request a list of AAR members by sending a self-addressed stamped envelope to the organization at 10 Astor Place, Third Floor, New York, NY 10003. Check out the AAR's Web site at www.bookwire.com/aar.

Does that mean you shouldn't use agents who don't belong to AAR? Not necessarily. You might stumble on a good agent who doesn't have enough of a track record to qualify for the organization, but you should know why your agent doesn't belong to the AAR. The answer may tell you a lot about his level of experience and/or his professional intentions.

Let Your Fingers Do the Walking

You can find lists of agents who have at least a minimum track record of sales in *Literary Market Place*. That's the publishing world's equivalent to the Yellow Pages. You should be able to find a copy in your local library.

Write On!

In some industry reference books, agents list their better-known clients, so look for an agent representing authors who write books similar to your own. One who only represents literary novelists such as Joyce Carol Oates and Gore Vidal wouldn't be a good choice for an aspiring romance writer. Instead, hone in on agents with a strong list of women's fiction clients.

You can also buy a handy reference book called *Writer's Market* at any major bookstore. A new edition comes out each year. The *Writer's Market* lists every book and magazine publisher's guidelines. There is also a section listing agents. (Only agents who took the time to respond to the book's survey are included, so an agent you're interested in might be missing.) *Writer's Market* is a must read for any beginner who wants to contact an agent or publisher. It will tell you what kinds of material an agent will represent, the percentage of his commission, recent sales, and guidelines for submission. It also has a "Book Publishers Subject Index" categorizing the publishing houses by what kinds of books they put in print. Another useful book is *Writer's Guide to Book Editors, Publishers, and Literary Agents, 1999–2000: Who They Are! What They Want! And How to Win Them Over!* This book lists agents' clients, which can be useful information.

Hot-Shot Agents

Once you start chatting with other writers, you'll quickly learn which agents are the big names known for getting their clients mucho money. If that's the kind of agent you want to query, then go for it. You owe it to yourself to try for the best. Don't be surprised, though, if your query is rejected.

Typically top agents will be interested in you only if …

1. You have a proven track record of successful novels.
2. You have a big blockbuster novel already completed.

Top agents like to make money. They can do that by turning already successful authors into superstars and by selling big novels that have the potential of finding a huge audience. Generally, they're not interested in unpublished authors who are strictly writing genre fiction. The payoff in commission for a category romance isn't big enough. To work with a big-time agent you have to have big-time plans for your career and the material to get you where you want to go.

Stop the Presses!

If you search simultaneously for an agent and editor, don't rush through your entire list of potential editors. If you end up with a stack of rejection letters taller than the Empire State Building, there's not much an agent can do for you. With so many publishing mergers, there aren't as many editors as there used to be. That leaves fewer alternatives for the agent to pursue.

Which Comes First: Agent or Editor?

That question is a little like the chicken or the egg conundrum. Do you have to have an agent in order to submit to an editor? No, but a growing number of editors won't look at unagented submissions. Unfortunately, many agents won't look at you unless you're already published! What's a writer to do?

Simultaneous Search

Consider conducting a dual search. Query editors and agents at the same time. Usually agents respond more quickly. If an agent takes you on, he can negotiate for you if the editor comes through with a contract. If the editor contacts you before the agent, no problem! That's a great reason to call the agent and nudge him along. Agents are always more interested if they know an editor is thinking about buying your book.

If you get an offer before you get an agent, it's perfectly okay to tell an editor, "I'd like to have an agent negotiate the contract. I'm in the process of hiring one now. I'll have my agent call you as soon as that process is complete." Or you can even ask the editor for several recommendations on agents to query.

If your main reason for getting an agent was to get your foot in the door at a publisher, you may decide to forego hiring a representative. Just remember, if you negotiate your own contract, you don't necessarily have to accept the first offer! Publishers usually expect a counteroffer, especially when negotiating a single title. That's why it's important to know the terrain before you get behind the wheel yourself.

Catch-22

What if your dream agent won't consider unpublished authors and your dream editor won't consider unagented submissions? That's a problem! You could settle for your second choices and start the query process or you can start networking and see if you can get a published writer to recommend you to the agent and/or editor you had in mind.

Personal recommendations count for a lot in this business, as in many others. Meeting agents and editors in person at writing conferences is another way to get around the Catch-22 that frustrates so many beginners. (See more on networking in Chapter 24, "Romancing the Industry," and find out how to query agents and editors in Chapter 17, "Finding an Editor.")

Stop the Presses!

Before you sign a contract with a book publisher, make sure your agent didn't sneak in a clause tying your agent to any future deals. While the book contract should mention your agent as your chosen representative, it should not state that he or she will negotiate your next contract. If you find such a clause, have it removed before you sign on the dotted line.

The Last Word on Agents

A quick word about agent contracts: When you hire an agent, she will send you a contract clarifying the terms of your relationship. It should be fairly simple. Read it carefully. A decent contract will enable you and the agent to amicably end your relationship with a few weeks notice. Don't sign a contract that binds you more permanently than that. Of course, even after you part ways your agent will continue to get a commission on any books she has already sold. Remember that you're not an indentured servant. You want a quick out if you realize the relationship isn't working.

The best author-agent relationship transcends the commitment on paper. When you find an agent you click with, you won't need a contract to cement your relationship. You'll be united by a common and noble goal—getting your book into print!

Agent Checklist

Review this checklist to make sure you're prepared to snag an agent. In the next chapter we'll talk about catching an editor's interest.

❑ After careful consideration, I've decided I really need an agent.

❑ If my contract negotiations will be simple enough for me to handle, I'll forego an agent and keep the commission myself.

❑ I've checked out references or at least talked to other writers about the agent I'm thinking of signing with.

❑ I have a vision for my own career, and it is clear enough to articulate to an agent.

❑ I'm clear on what I want an agent to do for me, and I can communicate that clearly.

❑ I have realistic expectations of what an agent will do for me.

❑ I'm professional enough to know my agent isn't there to hold my hand and call me everyday to cheer me on.

❑ I have completed at least one manuscript before trying to query agents.

The Least You Need to Know

➤ You don't have to have an agent in order to get published, but it helps.

➤ An increasing number of publishers won't accept submissions from writers without agents.

➤ Network with other writers to get your foot in an agent's door.

➤ Getting an agent doesn't necessarily mean you'll get published.

➤ An agent can be an important part of your support system.

➤ Agents don't make money until you make money.

Chapter 17

Finding an Editor

In This Chapter

➤ What editors want in an author

➤ The editor as gatekeeper of your career

➤ The kinds of edits you can expect

➤ How to find an editor that's right for you

Let me tell you the story about how I met my first editor at the Berkley Publishing Group. I met Hillary Cige at a cocktail party as part of a conference put on by the Missouri Chapter of Romance Writers of America. I didn't know who she was or I wouldn't have had the courage to say hello. In blissful ignorance, I introduced myself and the conversation continued something like this:

Hillary: "Hi! I'm Hillary Cige. What do you write?"

Julie: *(Gulp. Hillary Cige is the editor from Berkley! Oh, no! What do I say?)* "Oh, uh, I, uh, well, I write dark medievals." *(Thinking, "You couldn't possibly like those. No editor has so far.")*

Hillary: "I love dark medievals! Send it to me."

Julie: *(Gulp. Double gulp. Eyes widening.)* "Okay!"

It was as simple as that. With those eight words Hillary, bless her heart, launched my career. And you know what? It just might be that easy for you, too! In this chapter, you'll learn not only how to get an editor, but how to keep the relationship going for a long time to come.

Write On!

Early on, you should be careful not to go over your editor's head. Don't complain about her to other staff members. Don't call the publicity or sales department without her knowledge. Don't call her boss to countermand her decisions. Once you become an established author, you'll have a reason and a right to deal directly with other departments. Until then, let your editor be the conduit of information.

A Powerful Mentor

Editors are a little like fairy godmothers. With the wave of a magic wand, they can turn our manuscripts into books. With a simple nod of approval, they have the power to validate writers' lifelong dreams of being published. Is it any wonder that we tend to worship the ground they walk on? Editors are very special people, but they're still people. That means you have to brush up on your people skills to work with one.

A successful author-editor relationship requires a delicate blend of personalities, creativity, and power. The editor has the power. You have the creativity. Together you blend your personalities to produce a fruitful relationship. When you become very successful, the balance of power will shift, but we'll talk more about that later.

The Go-Between

An editor is the gatekeeper who will control virtually every decision affecting your book. She (or he) is the ultimate go-between. Your editor is the one who will …

➤ Make an offer on your manuscript, after getting approval from the publisher.

➤ Negotiate the contract with you or your agent.

➤ Make sure the contracts department sends you the contract and advance money.

➤ Suggest revisions, if necessary.

➤ Edit your finished manuscript.

➤ Act as an advocate for your book during the long process of getting it into bookstores.

➤ Consult with the art department to develop a (hopefully!) great cover.

➤ Pitch your book to the sales department so that the reps are excited about selling it to buyers and distributors.

➤ Ensure that the publicity department sends galleys or advance reading copies to reviewers.

➤ Collect reviews and track sales.

➤ Try to talk the publisher into buying your next book (if the sales and reviews were good!).

And you thought your editor would just pencil in commas and colons! As a matter of fact, that's the one thing your editor won't do. Your editor will do line edits, that is to say, edit each line for content. But a *copy editor* is the one who checks for grammar and spelling.

Guardian Angel

Aside from being your advocate on the business end, your editor will hopefully nurture your creativity as well. A good editor is like a guardian angel fluttering unseen over your shoulder. She'll give you the space to write your own story, but she'll be there to help if you get into trouble.

Do Your Homework!

To find a mentor and guardian angel in the publishing industry, you must be prepared for one. You should …

1. Have a marketable manuscript.

2. Research the field of editors before you seek one.

3. Know how to make a professional submission.

Eenie, Meenie, Minie Editor

We talked in earlier chapters about making your manuscript the best it can be. In the next chapter, you'll learn how to make a submission. Let's focus now on finding the right editor.

Love Letters

A **copy editor** is someone hired to go over your manuscript with a fine-tooth comb. The copy editor is often a freelancer. She will focus on grammar, punctuation, spelling, and word usage. She'll occasionally comment on plot points, but this is rare.

Write On!

If you are rejected by the one editor in all the world you were certain would love your work, don't despair. Keep submitting your book until it clicks with the right editor. You might be surprised at who that turns out to be. And remember, all it takes is one editor who's willing to give you a chance. They don't all have to like your book!

Crediting Editing

An easy and important way to pick an editor is to look at the acknowledgment pages of your favorite novels. Frequently writers will either dedicate a book to their editor or at least mention him on the acknowledgments page. Once you identify a favorite author, find out who edited her work. That might be a good editor for you to approach.

Bear in mind, however, that best-selling authors often work with editors at the highest echelon—a senior editor, executive editor, or even the publisher. Chances are you'll get your start with someone far lower on the totem pole—an editor or assistant editor.

Category Editors

Finding the right editor to approach with a category novel is a little simpler. Send away for the publisher guidelines. Each line will list a senior editor. Address your query to the senior editor of the line you're striving for. Once you start networking with other writers, you might find the name of someone who works under the senior editor whom you can approach. Newer editors and those lower in the chain of command are sometimes eager to find their own stable of talent and therefore, presumably, are more receptive to queries from unpublished authors.

Write On!

If a published author offers to recommend your book to her editor, jump at the chance. The author can't make her editor like your work, but she can almost guarantee the editor will take a closer look than she might have otherwise. It's not what you know ...

Ye Olde Network

Networking comes into play at every turn in your quest to become published. If you want to find out who is buying what, talk to other writers. This is one of the main reasons that the Romance Writers of America has become the biggest genre writing organization in the world. We romance writers really know how to network!

Here are the kinds of questions you can find out from other writers, published and unpublished:

➤ Are any editors looking for your kind of book?

➤ Which editors are actively looking for new talent?

➤ What new lines are being created that might be right for you?

➤ Who are the nicest, best, most brilliant, powerful, (you fill in the blank) editors in the romance genre?

➤ Who will accept submissions and/or who is willing to meet unpublished writers at conferences?

Spell the Name Right!

Even if you can't network with other writers, you can get the names of editors from publications like *Writer's Market* and in market updates in *Romance Writers' Report,* a monthly RWA magazine. In *Writer's Market,* the book publishers list their addresses and editorial staff. It's a good idea to call the publisher's switchboard to make sure the editor you want to query is still working there. Editors come and go as quickly as football coaches. And be sure to double-check the spelling on the name. There is nothing worse than misspelling an editor's name!

Don't Waste Her Time

Once you've figured out which editor to approach, make it count! Don't waste her time, or yours, by being anything less than 100 percent prepared. That means having a manuscript you truly think is worthy of publication and knowing your book fits in with the editorial guidelines of the house you're querying. Here are two mistakes many other unpublished authors have made that you should definitely avoid.

1. **Don't send in your book hoping for a rescue mission.** If your book has problems, an editor isn't going to fix them for you. Editors don't have time to toil through numerous revisions. They want manuscripts that are ready to go or easily fixable. If you sense your book has problems, seek help elsewhere before you approach an editor. (See Chapter 15, "Feedback: It Hurts So Good," which deals with critiques.)

2. **Don't send your book to a publisher who doesn't publish your kind of fiction.** Duh! Sounds obvious, doesn't it? But an amazing number of editors say they are bombarded with the most inappropriate manuscripts imaginable. Don't, for example, send fiction to a nonfiction publisher, or a romance to a science-fiction editor, or a ghost story romance to a romance line that doesn't accept supernatural elements. Why ask for rejection in this way? It's a waste of time.

Speaking of Romance ...

Maintaining a good relationship with your editor just makes sense. Nobody enjoys working with a holy terror, including editors. Here's how Leslie Wainger, the executive senior editor of Silhouette Books, puts it: "If someone is horrible to work with and fights for no particular reason on every score, her books had better be incredibly good and better sell incredibly well. Because if they're not, and you're sitting there going, 'Her sales aren't that great, and I might like her books personally, but they could be better, and she's really awful to work with ...' Well, what's the incentive to keep buying that author?"*

She Wants You!

We all know how low the odds of getting published are. You've probably either received a rejection already or you've heard about them. Now here's the good news: The editor you approach wants to like your book. She wants it to be the newest sensation in the publishing industry. She wants it to be something new and different and exciting. She wants your book to be a best-seller. Why?

➤ Editors love good stories.

➤ Editors are always looking for new talent.

➤ Editors enjoy discovering tomorrow's superstars.

➤ Editors look good to their bosses and colleagues when they buy successful books.

Could you be the next Nora Roberts, Jude Deveraux, or Dara Joy? You'll never know until you submit that book! So you go, girl.

What an Editor Is Really Looking For

There are two things editors look at when they decide whether or not to accept a book for publication. First and foremost, they look at the book. Second, they look at you, the author. Are you someone they can work with? If they sense you're more trouble than you're worth, they'll take a pass on your book, unless it's so brilliant they can't resist it.

The Book

What are editors looking for in a book? Pretty much the same thing that readers are looking for. They want a story that will excite them and hold their attention; one that's so absorbing it will make them forget they're reading a book. Most of all, they want a book that you feel passionately about. No write-by-numbers or mechanical efforts. They're looking for magic.

The Author

Editors are looking for writers who can make their publishing house money, not to put too fine a point on it. It's a crass reality, but gone are the days when publishers took the time to cultivate talent or published books for literature's sake. If you're going to sell to a major publisher, your books need to be profitable. That means not only do you have to write a great book, but you may have to promote it as well.

Write On!

When you approach an editor, it's a good idea to let her know you have plans for the future. You can mention that you have other books ready to be published or great ideas for new ones. In the romance genre, it can take a number of books before an author even makes a blip on the radar screen. So editors want tenacious authors willing to work hard and not give up.

The most financially successful romance writers treat their careers like businesses. They spend an enormous amount of time promoting themselves and/or their novels. You don't have to worry about that at this point, but editors hope to find authors who will at least treat their writing as a profession instead of a hobby.

In today's money-driven market, editors are looking for writers who ...

➤ Treat writing as a business.

➤ Are willing to promote their books.

➤ Have talent and have taken the time to learn to write well.

➤ Meet deadlines and don't make commitments they can't keep.

➤ Respect the editor's time restraints and opinions.

➤ Can write at least one book a year.

➤ Plan on having a long career.

The authors who fit this profile are the ones who have a shot at climbing to the top of the best-seller lists. Of course it helps if you're a brilliant writer, but some of the most talented authors are so creative they can't discipline themselves to write consistently or reliably. They're sometimes one-book wonders.

How Do Editors Edit?

Every writer dreams of having an editor. Actually getting one, though, is a mixed blessing. Before you're published, you have the pleasure of writing for yourself. Once you begin to work with an editor, you have to please her as well.

After nurturing your manuscript from infancy through childhood and the troublesome teen years, you may feel a little defensive if an editor asks you to change something. After all, you've worked hard on your creation—it's all yours! Well, if you want to get published, it's a cooperative effort. After the editor carefully reads your book, she may suggest changes.

What You Can Expect

Your editor's comments will be wide ranging. She may ask for revisions on any of the major elements of your book: plotting, characterization, language, tone or mood, and pacing. Here are a few examples of the kinds of comments editors make:

➤ In chapter two, on page 12, your heroine seems a little selfish when she tries to shut the hero out of the room. Can you come up with a different reaction that doesn't seem so unsympathetic?

➤ Pacing in chapters four and five seems to slow a little. I think you need to combine these chapters. You might consider cutting the scene in the woods since it doesn't really advance the story.

➤ Your hero doesn't seem to relate to anyone. He's a loner and never talks. The only time he really seems to come alive is when he's alone and thinking about his life. He doesn't even really come to life with the heroine except in the lovemaking scenes. Can you come up with a way to have him interact more significantly with others? Maybe create a secondary character who is the only one he's ever related to, or something of that nature?

The comments you're likely to get will vary depending on your editor and the manuscript. Most editors will be diplomatic about how they suggest changes. Now and then you'll hear a horror story about an editor who is a frustrated writer pulverizing an author's novel. Generally, though, most editors will respect your ability to create. They simply want your creation to be the best it can be.

Speaking of Romance ...

"When I find weak spots in a manuscript," says Berkley senior editor Judith Stern Palais, "I write a revision letter to the author. For less involved changes, I can explain what's needed in broad terms. For major structural and plot changes, I need to give writers a road map in chronological order by page number, chapter number, etc. Both first-time writers and established ones respond well to this type of letter because anyone would find it hard to alter a manuscript if told 'the middle sags—can you strengthen it?' The author is so close to the book by this point that she might not be able to see what bothers an editor."*

When the Ball Is in Your Court

If you're like most writers, you'll be inclined to believe your editor when she says changes are necessary. The trick is to take her advice and make it your own. If you don't like her suggested ways to solve a problem, you can come up with solutions. The important thing is to keep an open dialogue.

Of course, you might have the misfortune of running into an editor who has no talent or understanding of the writing process. If that's the case, you have the right to refuse to make revisions. Bear in mind, however, that it might end your relationship with that publisher. If you find yourself in that situation, consult with your agent or your writer friends about the best course of action to take.

Power Shift

Once you become a multipublished author, you will grow more confident in your knowledge of the industry. You may one day know as much about writing, editing, and promotions as your editor. If you have that kind of knowledge and a good track record in sales, you will be in a position to throw your weight around. If so, do it gracefully. The

Write On!

You can be respectful and grateful to your editor, but don't forget to be assertive, too. The squeaky authors get the most grease, er, rather attention and money. You and your agent can demand editorial support together: The good cop/bad cop routine comes in handy. Playing the bad cop is sometimes the best way an agent can earn her commission.

prima-donna authors who make the lives of their editors miserable are invariably the ones who have a painful fall from grace when their sales lag. If you're a good person as well as a good writer, your editor will do everything in her power to keep your career alive when times are lean.

Editor Checklist

You're just about ready to contact a publisher. In the next chapter we'll talk about the best way to query or submit to agents and editors. Before you take that big step, though, run through this checklist.

- ❑ I have a manuscript that is as good as it can be.
- ❑ I've researched the market and have a general idea of which editors would be most likely to buy my manuscript.
- ❑ I've double-checked the spelling of the editor's name and her job title.
- ❑ I'm prepared to present myself as a writer serious about succeeding in the publishing industry.
- ❑ I'm prepared to work hand-in-hand with an editor on revisions as long as I believe they will improve my manuscript.
- ❑ Once I have an editor I'll treat her respectfully but will assert my own interests in the course of becoming published.

The Least You Need to Know

➤ Editors seem like the all powerful Oz, but they're people with feelings, hopes, and dreams, just like aspiring writers.

➤ The more professional you seem, the more interested an editor will be in buying your book.

➤ Most editors won't force revisions, but they will strongly suggest them ... and you'll wisely accept them unless they're absolutely unacceptable.

➤ It only takes one editor to believe in you for your career to begin, so hang in there until you find the right one!

Chapter 18

Submissions: Laying Your Heart on the Line

In This Chapter

➤ How to avoid an automatic rejection

➤ Taking advantage of writer's guidelines

➤ What to include in a query letter

➤ The pros and cons of multiple submissions

➤ Following up on your submission

Did you know that some people never get around to submitting their manuscripts to an agent or editor? They go to all the trouble of writing, but never quite get it in the mail. And some who actually do mail off a manuscript tuck it away in a drawer after the first rejection letter. It's easy to understand why people stumble at the finish line. It takes courage to face the possibility, or the reality, of rejection.

To reduce the chances of a "thanks, but no thanks" response, you need to learn how to make a proper submission. The hard part—writing a book—is over. Now begins the exciting process of trying to get it published.

Hear Ye! Hear Ye!

Sending your manuscript off to an agent or an editor takes not only courage, but also chutzpah. It's your way of saying, "Listen up, world, I have something worthwhile to say, and I want you to hear it!" And you're absolutely right. You do have something important to share with others. That's why it's so critical to make sure you give your book every chance of being accepted. Wouldn't it be tragic if your novel was rejected over something as mundane as the poor quality of your copy machine? It would be heartbreaking. Don't let this happen to you!

How to Avoid the Trash Heap

One of the easiest ways to get a form rejection letter is to make a dumb mistake with the presentation of your manuscript. Here are a few examples of things you shouldn't do:

➤ Print your book with colored ink or on colored paper so it stands out.

➤ Single-space your sentences to save paper.

➤ Send in a handwritten manuscript to give your submission a personal touch.

➤ Send in an unrequested manuscript against the editor's wishes because you're just certain she'll want it once she sees it.

➤ Send your romance to an editor who doesn't buy romance because you're convinced she'll start buying romances once she sees how good yours is.

These seem like ridiculous mistakes, but an amazing number of aspiring authors make them every day. Since you know better, you're way ahead of the game.

"How-To" Know-How

They say knowledge is power. So let's give you the power to make an effective submission. The best way to do that is to understand exactly how an editor wants to be approached. Fortunately, many publishers offer very specific guidelines. Follow them to the letter and you'll make a professional presentation. Let's look at all the elements involved in making a rejection-proof submission, from content to appearances to cover letters. Putting all the pieces together requires painstaking attention to detail, something that we creative types sometimes struggle with!

Guidelines: The First Step

If ever there was a time to follow the rules, it's during the submission process. Harlequin Enterprises receives 10,000 submissions a year and can publish only 780 of them. Silhouette Books are swamped with 4,000 submissions competing for 350 spots. Editors receive so many manuscripts that they have to weed out the good from the bad. The first books to be plucked from the garden are those that weren't properly submitted. Unfortunately, some good books end up in the weed pile that way, so read the rules carefully!

If the publisher you're targeting offers free writer's or manuscript guidelines, send away for them before you mail in your manuscript. They'll tell you the names and titles of acquisition editors, how to approach them, and how to prepare your manuscript. If the house doesn't provide guidelines, you can at least find out whether they accept multiple submissions and material without an agent by looking in *Writer's Market*. If the publisher isn't specific about how your manuscript should be submitted, follow standard industry guidelines, which are also spelled out in *Writer's Market*.

Tip Sheet, Anyone?

Some publishers also include tips with their guidelines called tip sheets. You can get tip sheets and/or guidelines from most publishers by sending a request along with a self-addressed stamped number 10 size envelope.

Here's the gist of a few, though not all, of the helpful tips from the 1999 guidelines from Avon Books:

➤ Have fun and let your unique voice shine through.

➤ Your book can be wildly innovative or a more traditional story with a new spin.

➤ Hook the reader with a strong opener and keep the story sizzling.

➤ Avon editors will consider supernatural or magical romances, but they're not interested in futuristic or science-fiction romances.

> **Write On!**
>
> *Writer's Market* is an invaluable tool and an education in itself. New editions come out every year. It lists editors of consumer and trade magazines, as well as book publishers, agents, and script buyers. Best of all, this comprehensive reference book gives detailed instructions on submissions and teaches you how to do an accurate word count.

Editors' preferences change from year to year, so make sure you get the latest guidelines. Who knows? Maybe Avon Books will launch a sci-fi romance line next year. Keep up with the current trends. It will help you choose the right publisher for your novel.

It's All in the Presentation

Guidelines will also give you very specific directions on how to physically submit the book. Read these instructions carefully. Creative writers often have a hard time with mechanics, but it's important that your package contain all the right elements.

Here are some general guidelines that will make your presentation acceptable to most publishers and agents:

➤ Print your manuscript on plain, white, letter-quality bond 8½-by-11-inch paper. Do not staple it or otherwise bind it in any way.

➤ Double-space your lines. No single spacing!

➤ Do not justify your right margin. In other words, the right margin should be a jagged line, rather than straight. And margins should be at least 1 inch wide on all sides. You can make your left margin 1½ inches wide to allow room for handwritten edits if you want.

➤ Type only on one side of the paper—on the front, but not on the back.

➤ Use a standard typeface (font) like Courier, Courier New, or Times New Roman. Definitely no fancy script styles! They're too hard to read. Use 12-point type size.

➤ Use a header at the top of every page except the title page. Header styles vary, but typically the upper-left side of the header should include the name of your book and your last name. On the far upper right side put the page number. Your synopsis should include the word "Synopsis" some place in its header to distinguish it from your chapters.

Speaking of Romance ...

Editors see it all, and that's why they appreciate seeing good-looking submissions. "Having a professional presentation is important," says Berkley editor Cindy Hwang. "Not only is it much easier to read if it's neatly typed, it gives me a more favorable impression of how seriously the author views his/her work. In my opinion, submitting a manuscript for publication should be compared to submitting a resumé for a job. The first thing you learn about resumés is to check for typos and errors—it's just common sense to do the same for a proposal or manuscript."

Essential Elements of a Professional Submission

Once you've made sure your manuscript is in good shape, you should focus on the other pieces of your submission. Your package should also include:

➤ **A cover letter.** Keep it to a single page, if possible. (And only one side of the page!)

➤ **A *synopsis*.** Bind it separately with a paper clip.

➤ **Title page.** This goes on top of page one. The book title and your name should be centered in the upper third of the page.

"My Romance"

by
Jane Doe

In the lower-left quadrant of the page put your agent's address and phone number, or your own if you don't have an agent. Also include your word count and the targeted romance line (if you're targeting a specific line).

➤ **Self-addressed stamped envelope.** This is commonly called a SASE. It should be big enough to hold your manuscript, so the editor can return it to you in case of (sniffle, sniffle) a rejection. Make sure the envelope has enough postage to handle the weight. Harlequin-Silhouette recommends you send international postage coupons or an international money order for submissions to lines handled by editors in Canada and England. If you don't want to pay for your manuscript's return trip, tell the editor she can throw it away in case of a rejection. Include a self-addressed, stamped postcard for her to send you to let you know your manuscript was rejected.

➤ **A notification postcard.** If you want to know if you're manuscript arrived, don't call the editor. Simply include a clean white postcard, which can be purchased at the post office. (No scenes of Niagara Falls or the Lincoln Monument!) Address it to yourself and on the blank side write something simple like "Manuscript received." The editor can drop this in the mail to let you know your book arrived.

Love Letters

A **synopsis** encapsulates the plot of a novel from start to finish, either chapter by chapter or in a looser narrative form. The length can range from 1 to 65 pages or more. Some publishers, like Harlequin-Silhouette, request short synopses. While your synopsis should be concise, the length should be dictated by the depth of your story.

Once you have all the elements together, you can bind them to your manuscript with one large rubber band. Don't go crazy and wrap it up in layers of twine or tape. You want your material to be secure, but you shouldn't make the editor work too hard to open it. She might give up! Besides, manuscripts that arrive in packages as impenetrable as a Brinks truck look amateurish.

Appearances Count

Everything in your submission package, including your manuscript, should look neat and professional. That means the printed words should be clear and dark and there should be no frayed corners. You don't want the editor to think your book has been beaten up making the rounds to every editor in New York!

By the way, don't send your only copy. It could get lost. It's expensive to copy a whole manuscript, but the peace of mind is worth the price. Keep the original and send a good, clean copy to the editor. Once your book is accepted for publication, the editor will probably ask for a copy on a computer disk, but of course that's only if your book was written on a computer.

The Importance of Being Queried

There's a good chance that the first thing you send a publisher will be a query letter or a *partial,* not a full manuscript. Most editors don't want to look at a complete book unless they've requested it. They decide whether they want to see it based on what you tell them about your book in a query letter. Some editors also want to see the first three chapters and a synopsis. The writer's guidelines will tell you what sort of query to send.

Love Letters

A **partial** is a portion of the manuscript, usually three chapters and a synopsis. If your chapters are short, your partial can consist of more than three chapters. Usually editors like to see at least 50 pages of a manuscript.

Passport to Publication

The query letter is so important that it scares many authors. It's the key to the kingdom, so you have to do it right! A good query letter will do the following:

1. Introduce you and your writing-related background.

2. Tell the editor or agent briefly about your story.

3. Entice the editor or agent into asking to see the manuscript.

How do you do that? Very skillfully! You may be a fabulous novelist, but if you can't write a good query letter you'll have a hard time getting your book in front of an editor's or agent's eyes.

A Tricky Letter to Write

Query letters are challenging because you want to include the right information and the right amount of it. You want to make yourself look appealing, and you want to make your story sound riveting. That means you have to be confident without bragging; concise, yet warm and friendly; businesslike, yet creative. You have to set just the right tone. And ideally you'll snag the agent or editor with an intriguing first line. Holy cow! That's a tall order. Here are a few hypothetical examples of good and bad query letters.

Write On!

A query letter should not be unnecessarily formal or verbose. It should include important information, but the information should be presented as concisely as possible. You're not getting paid by the word! Editors and agents are busy people—they want you to cut to the chase. They also expect that as a writer you'll be able to communicate quickly and with a writing style that's easy and pleasing to read.

> Dear Ms. Stiller:
>
> This is your lucky day. You have a chance to represent the next blockbuster romance that's sure to knock Nora Roberts off the charts. I've written an uproarious romance set in San Francisco about a 30-something gal who is desperate to tie the knot …

(The address line is too impersonal and the content is presumptuous and too braggy.)

> Dear Ms. Stiller:
>
> I've just completed a 55,000-word romance that exhibits all the characteristics elucidated in your writer's guidelines. It's set in San Francisco and involves a young woman's quest for marital bliss. It would be an honor for me to submit my book to your establishment. Please let me know at your earliest convenience if a submission would be satisfactory to you …

(The style is too formal and doesn't give the editor any glimpse of the author's natural writing style or the tone of the book.)

> Dear Ms. Stiller:
>
> What's a nice girl like Jenny Brown doing on the ledge of the Golden Gate Bridge when her fiancé is waiting for her at the altar? That's exactly what Jenny has to figure out over the course of a 55,000-word humorous romance set in fabulous San Francisco. You see, Jenny desperately wants to get married, but at 35 she still hasn't managed to find the right guy and she doesn't know why.

233

I wrote this romance after I attended graduate school at Stanford University. I've written ...

(This is much better. The style is warm, engaging, creative, and still informational.)

What to Include

You'll want to include as much information as you can pack into a one-page letter. The more the editor knows about you and your story, the more able she is to make a decision about whether or not to request your book. Here are a few things to include, not necessarily in this order:

➤ Your book title and storyline

➤ The line you're targeting (unless it's a single title)

➤ Engaging or salient elements

➤ Word count

➤ Whether or not the book is complete

➤ Writing contests or writing awards you might have won

➤ Whether or not this is a multiple submission (which Harlequin-Silhouette, to name one, won't accept)

➤ Information about you—as long as it relates to the book or to your writing career

Editors don't want to hear that you have 10 children and a menagerie at home unless these kids and live wild animals served as the inspiration for your novel. Editors want to hear about your writing experience.

Don't panic! Just because you're not published doesn't mean you don't have experience. Tell the editor about the writers groups you belong to, magazine articles you've published, or even articles you've written for your local chapter of RWA. They want to know you are serious about your writing. The same information should be included in query letters to agents. If you don't have even this much experience, then obviously don't raise the issue in your letter. The editor's biggest concern is the plot of your novel.

Write On!

While you're writing your book, start thinking of ways to expand your writing credentials. That way you'll look more professional by the time you're ready to submit your novel. Write newspaper or magazine articles, for example. If you can't get anything into the big-town paper or the big women's magazines, write something for your local gazette or an obscure trade magazine. Everything counts!

What Not to Include

Setting the right tone for a query letter is essential. Sometimes what you don't say is as important as what you do say. Here are a few comments to avoid in your query letter:

➤ My mom really loves this book.

➤ I hope you like it because I really need the money.

➤ You'll see that my book is better than the trash being written by Authors X, Y, and Z.

➤ This book has been rejected by every other editor in New York, so you're my last hope.

➤ My manuscript is 500,000 words long, and I refuse to cut any of them.

In other words, you don't want to say anything that will make you sound unprofessional, desperate, indiscreet, or stubborn. Find good things to say about your book without being cocky or boastful.

What Happens Now?

After you've written the best query letter you can (and after someone else has proofed it for errors!), send it off with a SASE and wait for a reply. If the guidelines say you can send a synopsis and/or chapters along with the query, take advantage of the offer.

Think of the query as an information tool. It helps the editor determine whether she might like your book. If she sees a story line that piques her interest, chances are she'll ask to see your book. If she doesn't ask for it, it just means you saved yourself the time and expense of sending your book to someone who really wasn't interested in the first place.

By the way, you can query more than one editor at a time. However, you sometimes get more attention if your letter indicates that you're offering the editor an exclusive look at your book.

The Category Query

Harlequin-Silhouette editors like to see a two- or three-page synopsis with the query letter. The synopsis gives you a better chance to pitch your story. Here are a few things to bear in mind about the short synopsis:

➤ Its inclusion means the description of your story in your query letter can be very brief.

➤ The synopsis should give the editor an understanding of your characters, internal and external conflicts, and the setting.

➤ Though brief, the synopsis should be as dramatic and engaging as possible.

Speaking of Romance ...

Melissa Jeglinski, an associate senior editor at Harlequin American, has good advice regarding queries. She says: "A dramatic opening—a catch phrase or a flashy sentence—will pique our interest. Say something interesting about yourself, or your story, right off the top. If you choose to open with a question, do *not* make it one that can be answered with a simple yes or no. For example, "Are you interested in a romance about an angry man and a frightened woman who fall in love?" The answer very well might be "no." But a question like "Why was Amy so afraid to believe that Donald really cared for her?" is intriguing and makes the reader want to find out the answer."

The Category Conundrum

The query for a category romance is especially important since there are only a few places to sell category romances. If you write a book aimed at the Harlequin Duets line, for example, and your query is rejected, you may not have any other place to send your book—Duets is the only category line aimed at outright humor. That means you have written an entire manuscript for naught, unless it can be rewritten to fit another line or market.

To get around this problem, some experienced authors query editors after they write three chapters and a synopsis. They don't complete the book unless an editor asks to see it. The downside, of course, is that you have to write like mad to complete the manuscript if an editor requests it.

If you're a beginner, it's best to finish your manuscript. You won't become an accomplished novelist until you polish a few novels. Just be sure to carefully research the market to make sure the line you've chosen is the one that dovetails with your writing strengths. If you write an intriguing story and write a decent query letter, chances are a category editor will want to look at your book.

To Multiple Submit or Not to Multiple Submit— That Is the Question

You can send your book to one agent, or to many; to one publisher or to many. The choice is yours, with some restrictions from publishers. Let's look at the pros and cons of multiple submissions.

The Time Factor

The main advantage of sending your book to more than one agent or editor is that you can shave off the response time. If it takes three to six months to even get a rejection letter from an editor, that quickly adds up to years if you do one submission at a time. If that's the case, why doesn't every author make multiple submissions at the same time? There are two main reasons:

1. Some publishers won't accept multiple submissions.

2. If you receive rejections from every conceivable editor at once, you've exhausted all your options in the event that you later decide to hire an agent or improve the manuscript.

Editor's Edicts

How does the publisher know whether or not you've submitted your manuscript elsewhere? It's incumbent on you to be honest. Of course, some authors fudge it. Practically (not morally) speaking, that's okay until two publishers want to buy your manuscript at the same time. If you haven't been honest about a multiple submission, the publishing houses involved just might get mad enough to withdraw their offers. Then you can beat your breast and cry "A pox on both your houses!"

Stop the Presses!

Some aspiring romance writers fall into the bad habit of never completing a book. They write three chapters and a synopsis in order to enter a contest or query an editor, but they never actually complete anything. Just remember, you will never sell a book unless it's complete. And you won't really know whether you can complete a book until you do it at least once.

If you want to speed up the process without making multiple submissions, send out multiple queries and then decide which house to send your book to based on the level of enthusiasm of the editors' responses.

Approaching Agents

It is perfectly acceptable to query as many agents at the same time as you wish. It's a little nerve-wracking, though, when two or more say they want to see your book. It's somehow more personal than when you have to juggle interest from two publishers. If you choose one publisher over another, you're rejecting a corporation. When you choose one agent over another, you're rejecting someone's individual services. I'm sure it's a problem you'd love to have, but how do you handle it without making enemies?

If three agents say yes to your query, pick the one you think you'd like the most. Send your manuscript to him immediately. Tell him he's your first choice, but you have interest from other agents and, therefore, you'd like a response in a week. Then, follow up with a phone call after he's had a week to look at your book. If he rejects it, send your manuscript to your second choice, and so on. You do not have to tell the other agents what you're doing. What they don't know won't hurt them. And, trust me, they won't be waiting with bated breath for your manuscript, unless you have a hot, hot book. And in that case, they would have called you right away to schmooze you into accepting their representation.

Another way to handle this situation would be to call all three agents. Tell them you have interest from other agents and you want to get to know them over the phone before you decide whom to send your book to. Sounds audacious, I know, but agents aren't IRS agents. They want to work with authors they can get along with. If they ask to see your book, a phone call isn't out of line.

Write On!

If an editor who has requested your manuscript doesn't get back to you within the time frame she promised, give her a grace period of a week or two, then follow up with a phone call or a letter. If she says she needs more time, ask her when you can expect to hear from her. That gives you a date to follow up again if necessary.

Follow Up? Who? Me?

I once let a requested manuscript languish on an editor's desk for a year without following up on its status. Eventually, I received a form rejection letter. To tell you the truth, I was in no hurry to hear from the editor because I sensed a rejection was coming. The book simply wasn't good enough to be published. I knew it in my heart, although I didn't know how to make it any better than it was. This story has a happy ending, though. After a few more revisions, the book eventually was accepted by another (and better) publisher. There's a moral to this story, as well: Don't be as dumb as I was! Follow up on your submissions!

Lost in Space

A good reason to follow up on submissions is because all too often they get lost. You may call or write about your book's status months after you sent it off only to discover it never reached the publisher or disappeared in the mailroom.

Writer's Rights

Another good reason to follow up is that you have the right to know how your manuscript is progressing—especially if the book was requested by an editor who won't accept multiple submissions. If you have an agent, it's her job to follow up. If not, here are several ways you can find out what's happening with your book if you haven't heard anything within the publisher's predicted time frame:

> ➤ Some publishers, like Avon, suggest that authors send a postcard. Simply state your name, your manuscript, your address and phone, whether it was a partial or completed manuscript, and when and to whom it was sent. This will presumably nudge the editorial staff into looking into the matter.

> ➤ Send a letter to the editor asking her about the status of your book. Include a SASE or postcard.

> ➤ Call the editor. Many of them are amazingly open to phone calls, but keep your call short and friendly. Try to nail down the status of your book and a date when you might expect a decision.

When All Is Said and Done

Submitting your book to an agent or an editor is an exhilarating, nail-biting adventure. It's hard to wait for a response. To make the waiting easier, you can sit around drinking Mai Tais ... or you can start a new book! I highly recommend the latter. Okay, have one Mai Tai to celebrate the completion of the first book, but then get back to work!

> **Stop the Presses!**
>
> Sadly, some manuscripts can sit on an editor's desk for a year or more. If that happens to you, it's time to become assertive. Send the editor a letter diplomatically saying you need a response to your submission. If you don't receive a satisfactory reply, you can request the return of your manuscript.

Authors who write one book and wait for it to make the rounds have two problems:

1. They have too many emotional eggs in one basket. If it's rejected, they're crushed. They also remain unpublished.

2. If their book is accepted for publication, they have nothing else to offer the publisher, who might be in the mood to buy more than one manuscript!

So, don't rest on your laurels. Write on, my friend!

Submissions Checklist

In the next chapter, we'll talk about the good life—what it's really like to be a published author. Meanwhile, here's a checklist to go over one last time before you mail off your manuscript.

❑ My manuscript is free of typos.

❑ The copy is clear and easy to read.

❏ I've included all the necessary elements, including a cover letter, SASE, and the (optional) notification postcard.

❏ If I'm sending a query letter, it is succinct and professional, yet enticing to the editor.

❏ If I'm making a multiple submission to editors, I was up front about that in my query or cover letter.

❏ I have followed up after a reasonable length of time (e.g., a few weeks after the deadline promised by the editor).

The Least You Need to Know

➤ Send a number 10 size self-addressed envelope to the publisher requesting writer's guidelines.

➤ Follow submission guidelines to the letter.

➤ Make sure your query letter makes your book sound enticing.

➤ You have a right to follow up on your book's status after a reasonable length of time.

➤ If your submission doesn't look professional, it might be rejected for that reason alone.

Part 4
The Writing Biz

Romance writing is big business. If you have any doubt, just look at the growing number of romance authors appearing on the New York Times *Bestseller list: Nora Roberts, Jayne Ann Krentz, Tami Hoag, Sandra Brown, Linda Howard, Iris Johansen, LaVyrle Spencer ... and the list goes on. These talented authors are making big bucks. As well they should. They write fabulous fiction.*

In this part, you'll learn what it's like to be a professional writer and what qualities you need to become one. You'll get the real scoop on advances and royalties. You'll learn how to network and promote your novel. And last, but not least, I'll urge you to go for it! Dare to join the ranks of the most successful authors in the business.

You're Published, Now What?

Do you have it all planned out? You know what I'm talking about. Who is the first person you're going to call when you finally sell your book? Are you going to pop a bottle of champagne? Throw a party? How are you going to announce it to your writer's group? Who will you dedicate your book to? Where will you hold your first book signing? Don't tell me you haven't thought of these things!

Fantasizing about being a published author is half the fun of being a writer. Does the reality live up to the fantasy? Absolutely! And not exactly. Read on and find out what being a published author is really like.

Hurry Up and Wait

Remember when I said this is a business of delayed gratification? One of the delays comes after you sell your book. In all likelihood, it will be at least a year before it hits the bookshelves. My first book didn't come out until two years after I sold it! You can imagine my frustration. I would walk into my local bookstore and say, "I'm an author. No, really. I am. You'll see. Just wait." I was sure the store manager was about to call in the men in white coats to take me away. Why does it take so long to see your book in print? There are a couple of reasons.

The Wheels of Publishing Progress

It takes six months to a year for a book to work its way through the publishing process. Here are the general steps each manuscript must go through:

1. First it is edited by your editor, who focuses on the content of the overall story.

2. Then, the copy editor gets her shot, editing for grammar, punctuation, and accuracy.

3. The manuscript comes back to you for revisions, small or large, and approval of the edits.

4. The book then goes to the managing editor, who makes final decisions over any point that may be disputed between you and the copy editor.

5. The book is typeset and comes back to you for proofreading in the form of *galleys*.

This process can take seven or eight months. Meanwhile, the art department is developing a cover, copy writers are writing cover copy, and so forth and so on. A lot happens before you see your book in the bookstore!

Write On!

If you strongly disagree with a change in copy, politely say so in the margins of your manuscript and then write a letter of explanation to your editor. If you have a good reason for keeping something the way it is—even if it's just because you really like it that way—your editor will probably accommodate your wishes. This is your book, after all.

Love Letters

The **galleys** of a book are proofs of the typeset pages that will eventually go to press. They're printed on loose $8^1/_2$-by-11-inch sheets of paper, but the copy looks exactly like it will in book form. Since typos are easy to overlook, the author and a number of other eyes in the publishing house will proof the galleys before the book is printed.

Take a Number

Another reason it may take a while before you see your book in stores is that your editor has to find an opening in the publishing schedule. Books are planned several years in advance. If there isn't a slot in the lineup for you, your book has to wait until an opening appears. That's why it drives editors crazy when authors miss deadlines. A late manuscript may force the author to lose her slot in the publishing schedule, and there may not be another opening for a year or more to come.

Lucky Break

Looking on the bright side, when one author loses her slot in the lineup, it opens the door of opportunity for another author waiting in line. If you sell a finished manuscript that's ready to go, your editor might plug it in the lineup right away to fill a hole. Then you can enjoy the (almost) instant gratification of seeing your book on the shelves within a matter of months.

Gentlemen, Start Your Next Book

As I mentioned in the last chapter, as soon as you send off a book to an editor you should start a new one. It will keep you from obsessing about your completed manuscript, and it will ensure that you have another book to sell once you strike gold.

If you haven't started a second book by the time your first one sells, get busy! Most publishers want their romance writers to produce at least one book a year, give or take a few months. It takes that kind of productivity for an author to be noticed by readers in today's tight market. If you start your second book as soon as you sell your first one, it will be ready to go by the time your first one hits the shelves. Then, you can sell the second one and start a third one.

Write On!

Some prolific authors have a stack of finished manuscripts in their drawer by the time they sell their first one. They can conceivably sell all of them in one multiple-book deal. That's convenient if the publisher wants to flood the market with two or more books a year to quickly establish the author's identity.

Second-Book Syndrome

There's another reason to start your second book as soon as you finish your first one—you just might avoid second-book syndrome. This harrowing disease usually strikes authors who sell their first book and then start Book #2 after selling it on a partial. They begin to write and … boom! The doubts set in. Is this what my editor is looking for? Will this be as good as my first book? What if my first book was a fluke and I can't write another book? The only way to get through this dreadful self-doubt is to force yourself to finish your second book. After that, Book #3 will seem like a breeze.

The Honeymoon Period

There is a wonderful honeymoon period that lasts long after you sell your precious book. You feel on top of the world, and you're sure that the feeling will last forever. Here are the good things that will happen during the course of the publishing of your first book:

➤ You will feel gratitude and affection for your editor.

➤ Your editor will feel good about giving a new talent a shot.

➤ Your friends will ooh and aah about everything—phone calls from your editor, your new cover, your first book signing, etc.

➤ You're convinced this is the beginning of a long and successful career. (And it just may be!)

➤ You thrill over great reviews and signs that your publisher has big plans for you (like a great cover or an ad in an industry magazine).

➤ You rejoice over the fact that you had faith in yourself and the world is at last acknowledging your dream.

Nothing in the world beats the great feeling you'll have during the honeymoon period. If you're waiting for me to drop the other shoe, I won't do it—at least not in this paragraph! I want you to enjoy the rewards of your hard labor. There is no greater high for a writer than finally getting published.

An Exclusive Club

If you walk down the street, probably half the people you meet would like to have a book published. Very few have the discipline to see that dream through to its ultimate conclusion. If you are one of the few, you can congratulate yourself. You are in rare company.

Don't let it go to your head, though. There are tons of talented people in the world who, for some reason, never crack that nut. And sometimes getting published is just a matter of being at the right place at the right time with the right book, so don't be boastful. Be grateful and enjoy.

Speaking of Romance ...

Pamela Morsi, one of my favorite writers, shares these loving words of wisdom: "What we do as writers has value. It is important. Try to know that wholly down inside yourself. What you have created, this story, this novel, is not just a series of scenes moving along a line of plot. It is something that didn't exist until you created it. Like an alchemist making gold from iron, you have taken something as ordinary and everyday as language and made it into something precious: literature. Not everyone can do that, it's a special gift. And no one can do it the way you can, bringing your unique vision and life experience to the printed page."*

The Price of Success

Being a published author has its downsides. The unpublished friends you struggled alongside for so long all of a sudden may start treating you differently. Some may be jealous. Others may continue to be supportive, but if they don't become published they may lose interest in writing and your friendship may fall by the wayside. Not only that, but when you start to know more about the writing business than your mentors, you may be uncomfortable and feel a little guilty about your success. This is the unfortunate price any creative artist pays for achieving her goals. You have no choice but to move forward. You can't fail just to please your friends. In any event, true friends want you to succeed.

Stop the Presses!

The higher you go in this profession, the easier it is to become jealous of other writer's successes. That's when you must force yourself to remember why you became a writer in the first place—to create great fiction. If you're doing that, you've already achieved the ultimate success.

The Hazing

Once you become published, you feel you have the recognition and status you thought you deserved all along. But wait a minute! All of a sudden you're hobnobbing at conventions and publishers' dinners with authors who have a lot more experience and success than you do! Suddenly you're at the bottom of the totem pole again and you don't like it!

Sorry. That's the way of the world. There will always be those who have more experience and connections than you do and there will always be those who have less. Just try to remember that it doesn't matter whether or not Betsy Bestseller deems you worthy of a "Hello" at a writing convention. All that matters is whether readers buy your books. Ultimately, all that matters is that you feel good about the books you write. We tend to forget that that's how it all begins and ends … with the writing process.

You're in the Army Now

Something else important changes once you become published. You're no longer writing for yourself. You've joined the ranks of those who are expected to start producing on schedule. So stand at attention and shout "Sir, yes, sir!"

Stop the Presses!

If you run into trouble with your writing schedule, you or your agent can renegotiate your deadline, but do so only as a last resort. Unless your delay is caused by an act of God, your editor will remember that you let her down. She may not hold it against you the first time, but if it becomes a habit, your stock will slip.

Writing for Someone Else

Most writers are on their own while they create their first book. Every editorial decision is theirs alone to make. Once they sell that book and start to write another one for their eager publisher, though, things change. They begin to wonder if their first book was a fluke, and if their second book—and third and fourth—will measure up. Suddenly, they feel as if they're writing for everyone but themselves—their editor, the readers, the reviewers, their accountant. And their writing room begins to feel very crowded. So crowded, in fact, it may leave no room for creativity. What's a writer to do? Here's the secret solution you can use if you find yourself in this predicament:

Pretend you're still writing to please yourself.

This takes some practice. You have to shove aside all doubts and fears. You have to trust your own creative process, just as you learned to do while writing your first book. I think Eileen Dreyer (a.k.a. Kathleen Korbel) put it best when she said, "You write your first book on guts and all the rest on fear." You have to learn to stare down fear without blinking and then write your next scene. And the next. And the next. That's how great books are written, one scene at a time.

Writing Regularly

The other challenge for the newly published author is writing on deadline. You will have written your first book at your own pace. When you sell it, it's a done deal. But if you're lucky, your publisher will ask for a second book and eventually a third. You then get to pick a deadline for the completion of your next masterpiece. How do you do that?

➤ Calculate how long you honestly think it will take to write your next book.

➤ Give yourself plenty of room for life intrusions, like illnesses, vacations, children's crises, and writer's block.

➤ Try to fit your needs into your publisher's desired time frame.

If your publisher wants another book in six months and you want a year and a half to write it, compromise with a year deadline, but only if you think you can pull it off. Try to write as quickly as you can, but be realistic. Failing to meet a deadline is a sure way to get on an editor's bad side.

It's also important to craft a schedule that will allow you to produce quality fiction. With the current high price of paperbacks and a wide array of talented romance authors from which to choose, readers expect a good read. It's better to make your fans wait for a great book than to crank out a story that will disappoint them.

> **Write On!**
>
> Some authors refuse to sell on proposal. They only sell books that are complete. That way they can avoid the pressure of writing on deadline. However, many professional writers need money coming in on a regular basis. They sign contracts for unwritten books so that they can support themselves while they write.

The Pleasures and Pitfalls of Multi-Book Contracts

If someone offered you a three-book contract, you'd think you'd died and gone to heaven, right? Well, believe it or not, multiple-book contracts aren't always the prize they may seem.

The Ball-and-Chain Effect

If you make a lot of money off of a multiple-book contract, that's great. Bully for you. But if the contract locks you into a low advance for all three books, you're stuck, even if your first book is a smash hit. If you only write one book a year, a three-book deal ties you down for three years. In that situation, you'll feel imprisoned by your contract.

A Happy Medium

Many single-title writers prefer a two-book contract. It offers a couple years of security, but doesn't tie up their future. Many category writers go from one one-book contract to the next. The more successful authors, though, often receive multiple-book contracts. Since the shorter novels can be written faster, multiple-book contracts don't pin down category authors for years at a time.

In general, if your career is going well, your publisher will offer a multiple-book deal. That's because …

> ➤ They lock the author into a commitment at a guaranteed price.

> ➤ They reduce the amount of time spent haggling over contracts.

Speaking of Romance …

Betina Krahn is the award-winning author of more than 19 historical romances. She says writing for a living isn't as glamorous as others think it is: "I've given this a good bit of thought, and I've concluded that a great deal of the glamour associated with writing comes from *non-writers'* elevated but ill-informed notions about what we do. And since we who write were non-writers at one time, many of us still harbor these same delusions of glamour. We just think all the glamorous stuff is happening to writers who are a whole lot luckier and a whole lot more successful than we are."*

New York Times, **Here I Come!**

Whoa … not so fast, little doggie. Just because your book has been accepted for publication doesn't mean you're going to have a bona fide *New York Times* Bestseller on your hands, and it certainly doesn't mean you're going to be rich. Industry insiders say that with few exceptions a 500,000 copy print run is a bare minimum for making the *Times* list because you're competing with books that have print runs of between 800,000 and two million. You have to sell a heck of a lot of books in one week to bounce the likes of Tami Hoag and Stephen King out of the spot you plan to take. The odds are against you, my friend. Don't forget that as a first-timer your print run might be as low as 60,000 copies.

Not the Only Game in Town

As a beginning author, you have little chance of hitting the *New York Times* list your first time at bat. Most romance writers who've made the list had at least a dozen books under their belt. The *Publishers Weekly* best-seller list is also hard to score, but there are other lists that might be within your reach.

USA Today has an extended best-seller list on which newer authors sometimes appear. The top 50 books are printed every Thursday in *USA Today's* Life section. But the top 51 to 150 best-sellers are posted on the Internet at www.usatoday.com. Just click on the books section.

Frankly, this is a long shot as well. It's tough to make this list, especially when new celebrity and movie-related books are out. That's because *USA Today* tracks fiction and nonfiction releases on the same list, and your book has to compete with every title under the sun. If enough people rush out and buy your novel when it first comes out, you just might make it. Category romances appear regularly on this list.

Wonderful Waldenbooks

Romance writers owe a debt of gratitude to Waldenbooks because the chain goes to the trouble of tracking romance best-sellers—just for our edification. This is your best bet of breaking out of the pack. Waldenbooks tracks the top 10 best-selling category romances and the top 10 single-title romances each week. You can find the list on www.rwanational.com. If you make even the number 10 spot you can call yourself a best-selling author.

Speaking of Romance ...

Anne Marie Tallberg is the romance buyer at Waldenbooks. She says reaching the Waldenbooks romance best-seller list is certainly an achievement: "To put the list in perspective," she says, "Walden typically purchases all new romance novels, which can be 200 titles per month. The list is extremely responsive to the arrival of new books; often a book will only be on the list for a week. New authors have the best chance of appearing on the series side since Waldenbooks carries series in most stores in fairly high quantities. Harlequin–Silhouette publishes many new authors and with deliveries twice a month series books have twice as many chances to make the list."

Game Plan

If you want to be a best-selling author of any kind, you have to plan for success. That's something you and your agent can do together. If you don't have an agent, make up your own game plan. Here are a few things to think about as you try to track your way to the best-seller lists:

➤ What are your strengths as a writer and how can you exploit them more fully?

➤ Are you writing the kind of book that will reach a broad audience? If not, can you adjust what you're doing to make it more marketable?

➤ Are you writing fast enough to satisfy hungry readers? If not, can you write a little faster? The more readers see your name, the more they'll remember it. Or, conversely, are you taking the time to craft a phenomenal hit like *The Thorn Birds?*

➤ Are there ways you can better promote yourself, to your readers and to your publisher?

➤ What can you do to help your publisher support you? You're not the Lone Ranger, nor are you helpless. Think of yourself as a team player. Do all you can to make it a winning team.

Write On!

Every author expects to set the world on fire with her first book. It rarely happens. Hang in there, and six books later readers will finally notice you really are serious about writing. That's usually when they start buying your books and you finally register as a significant blip on the radar screen. Before you know it you're more successful than even you realized.

Most authors don't accidentally fall onto best-seller lists. They write good books and work like hell to grow their careers. So start planning now for your trium-phant arrival on the *New York Times* Bestseller list, and that seemingly impossible dream one day may be within reach.

The Ultimate Pressure

So what happens once an author hits the *Times?* Does she sit back and rest on her laurels? Is it finally time for her to relax and enjoy her success? No way. I once heard a panel of *New York Times* Bestselling romance authors talk about what being on "The List" has meant to their careers. They all said there are three things they think about now that they're so successful:

1. Staying on the list.
2. Rising higher on the list.
3. Staying longer on the list.

Once you achieve a high level of success, there is enormous pressure to maintain it. On the upside, you're paid enormous amounts of money once you reach that level. Every *New York Times* author on the panel said the amount of money she received for books exponentially skyrocketed once she made the *New York Times* list. You could probably handle a little pressure in exchange for a fortune, couldn't you?

What It Means to Be a Professional

Now I'm going to drop the other shoe. Yes, there will be a lovely honeymoon period with the publication of your first book, but the sheer ecstasy you feel over being accepted for publication will end. That doesn't mean your love of writing ends, though. It just means that writing for a living can sometimes be a drag. (Though it's still the best job in the world!)

Hey Diddly Dee, the Writing Life's for Me

How do you know when the honeymoon is over?

➤ You may procrastinate over writing.

➤ You may feel as if your editor no longer cares like she used to, or she may even be interfering in your writing process.

➤ You realize that not everyone in the world will sing your praises or even bother to read your book.

➤ Your book wasn't the instant best-seller you hoped it would be.

➤ You start to look enviously at other writers who seem to have better book deals or larger followings.

➤ You begin to think of writing as a job and not a passion.

Speaking of Romance ...

Best-selling historical author Rexanne Becnel was earning grocery money working part-time as a secretary when she first started writing. She was finally able to quit after her second book. "My husband and I had agreed when I had enough contracts and when I knew I was going to earn at least as much money as that piddly job, then I could quit," says Rexanne. "And being able to quit enabled me to spend more time with my kids. So as a full-time writer I have the best of both worlds."

If any of the preceding statements apply to you, it means only one thing: You're becoming a professional. A professional writes even when she doesn't feel like it. Even when she begins to think anything, including digging ditches, would be easier than writing for a living.

Overcoming Burn-Out

If you find yourself in need of an attitude adjustment, go back to the well and nourish your creativity. Writers don't make widgets. You can't crank out books without feeding your soul and subconscious. Consider these suggestions:

➤ Take a week off just to read for pleasure. If your eyes are weary, listen to a book on tape. Get excited about reading and it will help you become excited again about writing.

➤ Do the things you used to do to nurture your imagination before you became so busy meeting deadlines. Go to museums, listen to lots of music, wander through the library just for the heck of it, get out of the house and do something fun.

➤ Try new ways to cultivate your creativity. Read books like Julia Cameron's *The Artist's Way* which offer specific techniques to spark the imagination, like "morning pages." Buy "how-to" books on writing, even if you think you know it all. You might learn something new.

Write On!

Even if you become successful enough to earn a living at romance writing, you may feel oddly unacknowledged. That's because even your dearest loved ones may not understand the creative process involved in writing a book. Therefore, it's important to read books about the writing process. We live in an alternate reality, and it's important to have an alternate reality check now and then!

I Wanna Hold Your Hand

When you first become published, you may need constant reassurance that, yes, you really are a writer, and no, you're not a phony and a fraud, which is something many new authors think. Hopefully your agent and your editor will be patient and reassuring, but it's not their job to hold your hand. If you're going to be a professional writer, you have to assume confidence in what you do. As they say, fake it until you make it. After you have a few books under your belt, you'll begin to accept the reality and joys of being a professional writer.

Editorial Support

It's lovely when you receive praise and encouragement from an editor, but it's even better when you receive tangible support. What kind of support should you be looking for and asking for? Here are a few things your editor can do for you to put your career in high gear:

➤ Get you into a lead position on the publishing list as soon as possible. Lead titles get the most attention and promotion.

➤ Get you the prettiest, brightest, and most expensive cover as possible. That usually means lots of foil and embossing.

➤ Fight for you in editorial meetings.

➤ Put in your name when the publicity department wants to know who to offer up for signings at distributor conventions.

➤ Pitch your book at the next in-house sales convention.

➤ Agree to the biggest advance possible for someone with your sales record.

➤ Get your book a large promotion budget.

> **Write On!**
>
> Why would your editor need to sell the sales force on your novel? Because publisher sales reps have dozens of books to sell each month, especially after all the mergers in the publishing industry. The powerhouse publishers now have dozens of imprints, and the reps have to pitch every book from every imprint. You want the sales rep to know that your book stands out from the crowd.

These are all ways your editor can have a significant influence on your career. It's the kind of support you can bank on, and it's much better than praise. "You're wonderful" and a quarter won't even buy you a cup of coffee these days.

Once you start recognizing the difference between flattery and support, you will really be on your way to a professional career in writing.

The Least You Need to Know

➤ It may be a year or two before your book hits the shelves.

➤ Enjoy your first sale, because the bliss won't last forever.

➤ Be realistic about how fast you can write when setting deadlines.

➤ Making the best-seller lists takes time and career planning.

➤ Take time for yourself no matter how busy your writing schedule becomes or your creativity will dry up.

Advances and Royalties

All right, let's cut to the chase. I know why you're reading this chapter. In fact, you probably skipped Chapters 1 through 19 just to get to this one. Am I right? It's only natural. You want to know how much money you're going to make writing romances.

You probably have visions of dollar signs dancing in your head. You've heard how rich romance writers are. Is it true? Well … (drum roll, please) keep reading, because in this chapter we'll talk turkey.

Stop the Presses!

If you're lucky enough to get a nice advance, don't spend it right away. At least not all of it! Set aside roughly half of it for taxes. Then tuck away as much as you can for a nest egg. If you plan to make a living at writing, it's wise to have a year's income in reserve, in case the wolf comes prowling in between contracts.

The Cold Hard Realities of Cold Hard Cash

There is good news and bad news about money. The good news is that a handful of romance writers are very rich. Like millionaire rich. Like multi-millionaire rich. Which authors are rolling in the dough? Well, consider, if you will, two examples. Julie Garwood has at least 15 million books in print. And before her retirement, LaVyrle Spencer's books routinely sold in the neighborhood of 400,000 hardcover copies and more than 1.5 million in paperbacks, according to *Publishers Weekly*. I'm not privy to their bank accounts, but it doesn't take a rocket scientist to realize that these talented ladies are rich!

Now the bad news. There's a whole passel of published romance writers who don't even make a living wage. They may earn $10,000 a year, or $20,000, or even $30,000. While that sounds pretty good, after taxes it's not enough to pay a mortgage and the kids' college tuition. Why do some authors barely scrape by? The reasons are many, but to boil it down to the bottom line, they obviously haven't found the huge audience that writers like Garwood and Spencer have.

Going for the Gold

There are basically two ways to make a living in this business:

1. Hit your stride and consistently write at least one successful book a year if it's a single-title and two or three a year if they're category novels.

2. Hit it big with a runaway *best-seller*.

You can probably think of authors who've succeeded using both strategies. Megahits in women's fiction include *The Thorn Birds,* by Colleen McCullough; *Through a Glass Darkly,* by Karleen Koen; *The Shell Seekers,* by Rosamunde Pilcher; *Garden of Lies,* by Eileen Goudge; and *Outlander,* by Diana Gabaldon.

Then there are other superstar authors who've built a following around their names, rather than a particular smash title. Authors who took this tack include Nora Roberts, Elizabeth Lowell, Catherine Coulter, Sandra Brown, and Johanna Lindsey. They've written consistently year in and year out for decades with a quality that fans can count on. Their loyal readers buy their books regardless of titles or subject matter.

And there's a whole host of successful category authors who've built enduring and remunerative careers writing several titles a year, such as Jennifer Greene and Dixie Browning.

Category Cash

This may come as a surprise, but some category lines sell much better than others. For example, author surveys conducted by RWA indicate that the average Silhouette Desire and the average Silhouette Special Edition will earn about twice as much as a Silhouette Romance. The average income from a Harlequin Superromance will be roughly twice that of a Harlequin American or Harlequin Intrigue. In England, the Mills and Boon branch of Harlequin, which publishes Harlequin Presents and Harlequin Romance lines, pays the most of all—surveyed writers reported a $43,000 average earning per book.

The survey showed that the average advance for Harlequin-Silhouette books ranges from $5,000 to $9,000. Some authors reported advances as low as

Love Letters

A **best-seller** is a book that has appeared on a best-seller list. A best-seller that appears on a chain store best-seller list or a distributor's list might only sell in the tens of thousands of copies, where a *New York Times* Best-seller will sell hundreds of thousands, if not millions, of copies. So just because someone is a "best-selling author" doesn't mean she's rich.

$3,000 and some as high as $14,000. The higher end of the scale is presumably reserved for the most experienced authors who've developed a following. When you add royalties, those figures jump quite a bit. The income authors reported, on any given book, ranged from $6,000 to $58,000. That's not including the Mills and Boon imprints, which ranged from $25,000 on the low end to $82,000 up top.

Authors for Kensington's Precious Gems line report receiving a flat fee of $3,000 with no domestic royalties, but foreign royalties can add another $1,000 to $1,500. These romances are sold only at Wal-Mart stores at an affordable $1.96.

Speaking of Romance ...

A new poll conducted by Romance Writers of America shows that 19 percent of the category romance readers read specific authors only. Eighty-one percent read whichever books are released that month as part of the series. That's reassuring for new authors. It means readers will buy their books even though they're an unknown commodity. That's one reason why writing category romances is more of a sure bet than writing a single-title novel.

Single-Title Salaries

Single-title novels have the potential to make enormous sums of money. They also have the potential to flop. The books have to sell on the strength of the author's name, or the cover, or the concept. They can't rely on the publisher's name, like category books do. In fact, being a single-title author is such a risky proposition that some authors never earn more than their advance.

The average advance for a single-title romance can range from $3,000 to as high as $350,000 or more. So what does the average author earn? It's impossible to say. The average beginning advance is probably $5,000. The most successful historical authors who aren't huge names probably earn between $35,000 and $100,000 a year. A beginner might earn $12,000 or so a book over the course of a few six-month royalty periods. It's probably not an exaggeration to say that yearly incomes for romance writers span from $1,500 to $5,000,000. How's that for range?

The Dangling Carrot

If the money is so iffy in this business, why are so many people eager to give it a try? Because, the desire for artistic expression aside, there is a big fat orange carrot dangling in front of every writer, and it's a magical talking carrot. The carrot says, "Just think! You could one day be like Sandra Brown and get a three-book $16 million deal. You could be like Janice Graham, a Kansas schoolteacher who sold her first novel to Putnam in a three-book $1 million deal."

So is this miraculously loquacious carrot telling the truth? Yes, it is. These Cinderella stories about authors who hit the jackpot are true, and they're the ultimate enticement. That's why so many authors slave for so long for so little.

Yes, you can get rich writing romances. But you know what? Those who do get rich often earn every penny they make through blood, sweat, and tears. If you get $5,000 for your first advance and divide it by the number of hours you spent learning to produce a publishable manuscript, you will have earned about 10¢ per hour. So, when and if you ever do get rich from writing, I can only say, "You de man!" Or, as is more likely the case, "You de woman!"

Money Matters

So let's look at the two most significant money issues that you'll ever face: the advance and the royalties. You know what those are. The advance is the money you receive before the book comes out. It's a sort of prepayment in anticipation of future income. Once the book comes out, you get royalties, that is to say a percentage of every copy sold. But you don't get royalties until you earn back your advance. There ain't no free lunches in New York!

You may be wondering why do so many agents try so hard to get lots of money up front in the advance. Won't you get the cash eventually through royalties one way or another? Well, yes and no. But it's more complicated than that.

The Gift That Keeps on Giving

Let's look at the basic formula for the advance and royalties.

Suppose you get an advance of $5,000 and a royalty rate of 6 percent. That means you'll get 6 percent of the cover price of every book sold. Suppose your publisher prints 100,000 copies that sell for $4.99 each. Let's say your book does well and 70,000 copies are sold. To find out what you earn, use this formula:

$$70,000 \times \$4.99 \times \$.06 = \$20,958$$

Congratulations! You earned $20,958 on your book. Mind you, the payments may be spread out over a few years, so don't spend it all at once! And don't forget you have to subtract the advance from that sum.

Do the Math

Royalties are the moneys that you receive over and above the advance. Publishers usually pay them out twice a year, and you never know if you're going to get any royalty money until the check comes, or doesn't come, in the mail. Let's say you earned $20,958 (book sales × your royalty percentage) and you received an advance of $5,000. Here is how the royalty formula would work:

$$\$20,958 - \$5,000 = \$15,958$$

You have $15,958 in royalties coming because you earned that much over and above your advance. You have to earn out your advance before you get any more money.

Stop the Presses!

The royalty statements that you receive with your royalty checks twice a year will tell you how many copies of your book have been sold and how much you've earned. What they won't necessarily tell you is how much of your money the publisher is holding back in reserve for losses suffered if stores return copies of your book.

Write On!

You can sell the movie rights to your book, assuming your agent negotiated those rights. If a movie based on your book actually goes into production, you can pick up roughly $100,000. Although that rarely happens, it's not uncommon to have a book optioned: A producer pays you roughly $5,000, whether or not the film is ever produced, for one-year option to produce a film based on your book.

But what if your sales were dismal and your 6 percent of sales turned out to equal only $3,500? You still get to keep your $5,000 advance, even though you didn't earn it in sales. However, you obviously won't get any royalties. Worse yet, your publisher will either offer you only $3,500 for your next book or won't even want another book from you.

Here's a concept to bear in mind: If an author is paid what she's worth in advance money, she may never earn any royalties over and above that amount. If her advance was undeservedly low, she'll get a nice fat royalty check or two after the book comes out.

How Much Money Should I Ask For?

In general, you want to ask for as much money up front as possible. There are several good reasons for this approach:

Stop the Presses

You may as well prepare yourself now for lots of frustration over inequities in advances. While talented romance writers bang away at their keyboards in the trenches for a pittance, celebrities who couldn't write their way out of a paper bag snag multi-million dollar book deals. Frequently these books bomb. That's when you resist the urge to say: "I told you so!"

➤ You may need the money now. Why let it sit in the publisher's bank when that money could be earning interest in your account?

➤ The more money the publishing house invests in your advance, the more eager it will be to get a return on that investment. That's an incentive for the publisher to put some promotion money behind you to make sure you earn your advance. With a small advance, your publisher will not have the incentive to promote or support the book, and may leave your book to sink or swim.

➤ You deserve it. Sad to say, but in the romance genre publishers sometimes spend more money on the cover than they do on the author's advance. It just makes sense that the author who makes the book possible in the first place should be well paid.

➤ You may never get royalties. If your book does poorly, the advance may be all she wrote, so get while the getting is good.

The Slow and Steady Approach

Of course, if you get paid a lot of money and your book flops, your career might be over before it begins. In this tight market, publishers claim they can't afford to stick with authors who aren't immediately successful.

That's why some agents argue for a slow and steady increase in advances. If you earn a little more with each contract, you can build an audience as you go. If you hang in there long enough, you'll develop a readership. No publisher can sell books as well as satisfied readers can. On the other hand, these days publishers are increasingly hand-picking a few authors to get behind, and those invariably are the authors who are getting good advances and who succeed in the marketplace. So "Show me the money" might be a good mantra for every writer.

Speaking of Romance ...

"It's best to get as much money as you can," says Karen Solem, "but it's best to leave both parties happy at the end of the day." Solem has a unique perspective on advances. She created Silhouette Books, was once associate publisher of Harper Paperbacks, and is now a literary agent at Writers House, Inc. "You want your publisher to come back to you and want another book from you and want to pay you even more money. And there have been enough authors in the last two or five years who have been really struggling to find new homes because they've had problems earning out overly high advances. That's definitely a bad place to be because you're on a downward spiral."*

Royalty Rates

So you want more money, but your publisher won't give you a higher advance, eh? Then ask for a higher royalty rate! It will definitely put more money in your pocket.

Royalty rates for domestic mass-market paperback sales range from 4 percent to 12 percent of the cover price and can go as high as 15 percent or more. A good rate to start with is 6 percent. With single-title contracts you can also negotiate break points. In other words, you might receive 8 percent on the first 150,000 copies sold and 10 percent on anything over and above that amount.

Taxation Terror

Writers pay a shocking amount in taxes. Actually, any self-employed person does. It's just that writers are blinded with money signs when they first see the amount of their advance. They don't realize how much they'll be paying to Uncle Sam and their agent.

263

What's the Damage?

Let's say you're in a 28 percent marginal income tax bracket thanks to your spouse's good job. Assuming your advance won't kick you into an even higher tax bracket, add a 15.3 percent self-employment tax onto that. Throw in another 5 percent or so for state income tax. Now add the 15 percent you pay your agent. That totals up to 63.3 percent. That leaves you with only 36.7 percent of your income. If you earn a $5,000 advance, you get to keep only $1,835. Now picture in your mind the painting by Edvard Munch titled *The Scream*. That says it all.

Stanching the Flow

What's an author to do to keep the money from flowing out the door? First and foremost, keep track of your expenses. You'd probably be surprised by how much you're spending on postage, office supplies, conferences, and travel. They're all tax deductible. Consult a good tax accountant, preferably one with knowledge of publishing, for further ways to lessen your burden. An accountant can also recommend appropriate tax-free Keogh and SEP IRA plans.

Stop the Presses!

Andrew A. Mitchell is a CPA in Upper Montclair, New Jersey, who specializes in auditing publishers and preparing writers' taxes. He says authors should never assume royalty statements are accurate. Carefully review all figures and meticulously record your writing expenses. Those two steps will help put more of your earnings in your pocket.

There are no magic bullets to kill the tax monster. Some authors who make big salaries incorporate, but many accountants say the benefits of incorporation don't outweigh the hassle of the resulting increase in paper work. There are a few authors who creatively interpret the IRS code, but you should jockey with the IRS code only if you know what you're doing and only at your own risk. The safest thing to do is to set aside roughly half of your income for taxes as soon as you get it, and then write like crazy to make more money next year.

Is the *%!#! Check in the Mail Yet!?

Writing for a living isn't like working at the local five-and-dime. You don't get a paycheck every two weeks. Most publishers pay out royalties twice a year, typically July 1 and January 1, or some variation thereof. A word of warning: That doesn't mean you get paid on those dates! It usually takes a few months for the contracts department to calculate what you earned and cut the check.

As for payments on your advance, you'll receive checks according to the time table negotiated by you or your agent. Usually you get something like half the advance on signing the contract, a fourth of the advance on the approval of your proposal, and another fourth on completion of the manuscript. If you're selling a book that's already finished you'll get one big check for the whole amount a few months after you sign the contract. Yes, I did say months, not weeks. Most publishers are in no hurry to pay. They apparently have never heard of the phrase "starving artist."

Reasons to Keep Your Day Job

The best advice you'll hear after you get published is "Don't quit your day job." Even though you've sold a book, it may take a few more sales before you earn enough to comfortably pay your bills. A number of published authors write novels on the side, putting in a few hours of writing before or after work. They keep up this difficult routine until they're sure that they can support themselves as novelists.

If you're smart, you won't quit until you are making enough as a writer to see you through day in and day out. As a full-time novelist you'll have to pay for your own insurance and retirement plan, plus self-employment taxes. Considering you only get paid a few times a year, you really should have a nest egg as well.

When Do I Get a Raise?

Hopefully you will get at least a little more money with each advance. If you received $5,000 for your first single-title romance, hopefully you will earn $7,000 or even $10,000 on the next one. The only reason you shouldn't get a raise is if your publisher can prove your sales aren't progressively increasing. It's difficult to argue with hard figures. That's why it's important to understand as much about the business as you can. You need to be able to see the difference between cold hard facts and smoke and mirrors.

Some agents like to double their client's advances with every contract. That was easier to do in the 1980s and early 1990s when it seemed the sky was the limit in the romance genre. Now, for a variety of complex reasons, the growth in writers' incomes has slowed drastically. Study the market to determine the monetary value of your work, then ask for as much as you can reasonably hope to receive. Actually, you should probably ask for more than you're worth so that after you come to a compromise you will end up with what you deserve.

Write On!

Most writers dream of writing full-time, but just because you have all day to write doesn't mean you'll be writing eight hours a day. The more time you have to write the more you may dawdle. The extra time will, however, add more quality to your life. All work and no play ...

Speaking of Romance ...

If your book doesn't earn its advance, your career isn't necessarily over. Aaron Priest, a highly respected New York agent, says, "Books that publishers make big profits on often don't earn out. If you sell a book for $20,000 and it doesn't earn out, it's almost certainly not going to be profitable. If you sell a book for $500,000 and it doesn't earn out it could very easily be profitable."* That is to say if the publisher's profit margin is big enough it can take a hit on the advance and still make a profit, at least on books with the potential for big success.

Making the Most

How can you make the most of your money-making potential? There is no formula for success in the publishing industry. Each author has to find his or her own way. Of course it all begins with writing a great book, but there are a few general tips that can't hurt and hopefully will help:

Write On!

The writers who see the biggest increases in their advances are usually the ones who have the ability to jump ship. Interest from other publishers always makes an author's current publisher sit up and take notice. Some authors even write for two publishers. So if you want to earn more, write more.

1. **Understand the business side of writing.** The more you know to ask for the more you'll get.

2. **Know the value of your writing.** Don't sell yourself short but don't insist on 10 times more than you're worth.

3. **Always strive for exciting book ideas.** Editors and publisher sales reps work harder to sell ideas that are new and fresh.

4. **Create a niche for yourself.** Develop a unique approach or type of fiction that readers can count on.

5. **Develop a hook that will bring readers back.** Consider doing a series of books that revolve around the same characters, town, or family.

6. **Don't let your writing become tired.** Find a way to get excited about it if you start to take it for granted.

7. **Make your publisher's life easier.** Be helpful and friendly and learn what every-one on staff does to support your book.

8. **Promote yourself and your book.** Writing a book isn't enough; you must let the world know it's there.

9. **Take risks.** The occasional and calculated risk can zoom you past your current limitations when you need it the most.

10. **Invest in yourself.** Treat yourself to whatever office equipment, conferences, books, classes, or promotion expenses you really need to push your career to the next level.

In the next chapter, we'll talk a little more about laying the groundwork for a long and successful career. These keys are just the beginning.

The Least You Need to Know

➤ The more you understand publishing the better equipped you'll be to ask for what you deserve.

➤ You can expect to pay roughly half your income to your agent and the IRS.

➤ You don't start earning royalites until you've earned out your advance.

➤ Romance writer's incomes range from $1,500 to $5,000,000 per year.

➤ Surveys show that the average category romance advance ranges from $6,000 to $9,000.

➤ Single-title advances usually start around $3,000 and go as high as $350,000 or more.

Chapter 21

Acting Like a Professional

In This Chapter

➤ What you need to do to become a pro

➤ Rules that professional writers never break

➤ How to hobnob with industry insiders

➤ Learning the business side of writing

➤ Turning dreams into realities

Don't cry over spilled milk. If you don't have something nice to say, don't say anything at all. Do unto others as you'd have them do unto you. Be kind to your web-footed friends, for they might be somebody's editor.

In case you're wondering, I'm not regressing to my childhood. I'm simply quoting these familiar bromides because they offer important keys to professional behavior. When you come right down to it, being a professional is just a formal way of being nice, albeit with an ulterior motive. In this chapter, you will learn how to be a professional in the writing profession and how to plan for a long and successful career.

On Becoming a Pro

Have you ever heard the phrase "Fake it 'til you make it"? That's good advice for new and aspiring writers. Every bit of professionalism you exhibit will prepare you for success in the future and will likely be remembered by those around you. Becoming published doesn't instantly make you a professional. It's really the other way around. Being professional is what enables you to become published. And being professional helps turn the newly published author into a pro.

Stop the Presses!

One way to become a professional is to dress like one. Don't wear cut-offs to book signings and writers' conferences. And don't dress like a Valkyrie to draw attention to the fact that you've written a Viking romance. That doesn't mean you have to wear a severely tailored navy blue business suit. Simply choose a look that suits you and is appropriately professional.

Signs of a Professional Writer

One way to become a professional writer (in addition to getting published) is to act like one. How do the professionals behave? Here are a few characteristics I've observed in the top professional romance writers:

➤ They make writing a top priority, writing regularly, even daily.

➤ They associate with other writers, making good friends and few enemies in the process.

➤ They keep gossip and professional envy to a minimum.

➤ They reluctantly tolerate their insecurities and cultivate their confidence.

➤ They learn about the business side of writing and consider themselves the captain of their own ship.

➤ They learn from failure and never give up on the dreams they hold dear.

What Makes a Pro a Pro?

You would be amazed at just how savvy the top writers in the romance genre are. Women like Nora Roberts, Linda Howard, Iris Johansen, Julie Garwood, Catherine Coulter, Kat Martin, and Heather Graham are consummate professionals. They are super-talented as well as disciplined, and they know the ins and outs of the business like the back of their hands.

Speaking of Romance ...

Judith E. French and her daughter Colleen Faulkner both write historical romances. They have some good advice about how to be treated as a professional. "Many writers who work at home complain that family, neighbors, and friends don't take them seriously. They continually receive requests to pick up Mary's dry cleaning, wait for the Smith's washer repairman, or baby-sit a neighbor's sick child. Just say 'No.' If you expect others to regard you as a professional, you must do so. You must respect yourself if you want your family, agent, and editor to do the same."*

You don't become a romance superstar if you don't know nothin' 'bout birthin' no babies. Every book is a baby that requires hard labor. And most of the labor comes not from the writing end of it, but from making sure the baby gets the best chance it can in the publishing world. That requires following some basic rules of professionalism. The rules aren't written down, by the way. That would make it too easy. Only those smart enough to figure them out make it to the top. So let's figure them out right now!

Write Like a Pro

The pros in the romance genre have impeccable writing skills. Each book reflects their knowledge of writing. Some stories will be more entertaining or more popular than others, but every one will be polished and will appear seamless to the reader. How do you obtain this level of skill?

Learn from Others

Study other writers. Analyze the books that move you. Make a mental note to employ tactics that work. You may notice books that have surprising twists, powerful verbs, sophisticated emotional insights, tight pacing, real characters, reoccurring symbolism, driving narration, a delicious tone, or a raw sense of honesty. Figure out how the author pulled off these devices and try to incorporate some of them into your next book so your work can achieve a level of sophistication, too.

Nothing but the Best

Have zero tolerance for sloppiness. Learn to be a perfectionist in the areas of grammar, punctuation, word usage, and facts. Question the structure of every sentence, the clarity of every thought, the pertinence of every paragraph, the impact of every scene, and the emotional tally of every chapter. Make every component count.

Stick to Your Creative Guns

Honor your vision. Once you master the basic skills, the thing that will set you apart and make your work worthy of a readership is your singular vision of the world. Even as you hammer away at the mechanics, you must listen to the soft melody of your soul. Let each book hum with this unique song. This is part of what will distinguish your voice. It's what will clarify your themes. It's you on paper. Recognize your vision and then devote every book to that cause.

> **Stop the Presses!**
>
> As you learn to become professional, don't forget to nurture your creative side as well. Read books like *Bird by Bird,* by Anne Lamott; *Writing Down the Bones,* by Natalie Goldberg; *The Artist's Way,* by Julia Cameron; and *The Writing Life,* by Annie Dillard. These books speak to the creative side of writing. They reaffirm and nurture our basic instinct to create.

Fill Your Bookshelf

Create a body of work. The writers we consider true pros write consistently and produce numerous books. This approach gives you a chance to develop an audience and improve as a writer. Think of yourself not as an "artiste," but as a craftsman.

While you don't have to reinvent the wheel every time, each book should be better than the last in some subtle or not-so-subtle way. The more books you write, the less pressure you'll put on yourself judging the merit of each one and the more merit each one will have as a result.

Professional Affiliations

You can write in a cave, or in Hawaii as Johanna Lindsey does. You don't have to belong to any organizations in order to be published, but it helps. Belonging to groups like Romance Writers of America and Novelists, Inc. increases your opportunities to network and make friends who will support your professional goals.

Even Educated Pros Do It

Writers' organizations are incredibly helpful to aspiring authors, but they also offer support and recognition to those who are at the top of the industry. For example, RWA has an Honor Roll recognizing any member who has appeared on the best-seller list of the *New York Times* (top 15), *Publishers Weekly* (top 15), and *USA Today* (top 50). Jennifer Blake, Loretta Chase, Elaine Coffman, Brenda Joyce, Carla Neggers, Mary Jo Putney, Diana Palmer, Virginia Henley, Karen Robards, and Lisa Kleypas are just a few of the authors on the Honor Roll.

Staying Current

Being in professional writing organizations also helps you stay on top of issues affecting your career such as …

➤ Corporate takeovers and buyouts

➤ Standard publishing procedures regarding money and contracts

➤ The hiring and firing of editors

➤ The creation and dissolution of imprints

➤ Helpful hints about promotions

Can you imagine spending a year writing a book for an imprint that, unbeknownst to you, has been dropped from a publishing program? That's the kind of disaster that strikes when you aren't up to date on the publishing industry.

Code of Conduct

The pros are those who can be counted on to conduct themselves professionally. What does that mean from the publisher's point of view? It means the writers are reliable and consistent, ambitious and dedicated. It also means they don't make their editors' lives a living hell by failing to keep commitments.

Meet Deadlines

This rule is simple to understand, but sometimes hard to follow. Even though your editor may drag her feet about keeping her commitments, that's no excuse for you to slack off on yours. The writers who faithfully turn their books in on time are the ones who earn the respect and gratitude of their publishers. They're also the ones who are called on to fill in on special projects with tight deadlines. If the editor can't count on you to keep your place in the publishing lineup, she may not bother to even schedule you until she has your next book in hand, which causes a lag between your last book and your next.

Why do authors miss deadlines when they know they're so important? There are a variety of reasons:

➤ Writer's block or problems with the book

➤ Procrastination

➤ Failing to make writing a priority

➤ Life intrusions (illnesses, divorce, relocation, etc.)

One way for you to avoid missing your deadline is to give yourself plenty of padding in your schedule. When your editor asks you what deadline you can live with, be realistic and pick a date that will allow you to finish your book no matter what crisis comes up.

Stop the Presses!

Another important reason to turn a book in on time is that you can be fired if you don't. If you fail to meet the deadline, your editor can use that as an excuse to break the contract. In 1997 when HarperCollins decided to scale back its publishing list, it cancelled 70 contracts because the authors missed their deadlines.

Cheerfully Do Revisions

If your editor asks you to do revisions that will improve your story, do them with a smile. It can be torturous to go back to a manuscript you thought you'd never have to lay eyes on again and rework it one more time. Granted, you love the book, but it was so much work the first time!

In spite of these feelings of reluctance, don't complain. Remember—it ain't over 'til it's over, and revisions are a part of the process. Most authors admit that by the time their books are ready to go to press they're so sick of them they never want to read them again. That's the kind of work it takes to make a manuscript publishable.

Treat Your Editor Like a Client

As you learned in Chapter 17, "Finding an Editor," your editor will be your greatest ally and champion in your publishing house. Treat her as you would a valued client you don't want to lose. Consider these approaches:

➤ Express your gratitude when your editor does something to help you or your book.

➤ Don't nag her with unnecessary phone calls. Use e-mail and faxes when possible, since they don't demand her immediate attention.

➤ Don't harangue her about perceived slights. Keep a cool head if you think you're being given short shrift. Let your agent be the bad guy, or carefully check out your concerns yourself in a calm conversation with your editor.

➤ Keep your editor informed of your accomplishments, most of which she probably isn't aware. Send her copies of articles about you from your local paper, mention a speaking engagement, or a string of book signings you've arranged. Quietly toot your own horn so your editor never takes your efforts for granted.

➤ Send gifts now and then. Unlike writers, editors don't have the potential of getting rich from their work. The best they can hope for is a good salary and pleasant clients, so be sure you're one of the pleasant ones. A small gift for the holidays or a box of chocolates to say thanks is always welcome.

Know the Pecking Order

Once you have a book or two under your belt, you should start to get an idea of the chain of command in your publishing house. You should also know who does what. Get to know as many people in the company as you can. The more people you become friendly with, the more you'll have in your corner, and the more you can turn to for advice as your career expands. Here are a few of the people you should try to get to know during conventions and/or visits to New York:

➤ The editorial staff, including senior editors, editors, and assistant editors.

➤ The publisher, who usually only spends time with authors who are at the top or on their way up.

➤ Folks in the publicity department.

➤ The sales reps and directors of sales.

Write On!

Just how important is the sales staff? Very. They are the ones hitting the pavement, going from buyer to buyer and store to store. They know what's selling and what's not. That's why editors sometimes go to the sales staff before they buy a book to see if the sales reps think they'll be able to sell it. If the sales people say "No way!" the editor may pass on buying your book.

Sometimes the sales staff can give you good advice on what kind of promotions you might find effective. The publicity department can help you set up signings and other events. Don't expect a lot of attention from them, though, until you start to become well established.

Hobnobbing with the Powers-That-Be

You want to maintain good relationships with the people who have the power to move your career forward. Obviously, you need to meet them in person to do that successfully. If you start calling the sales and publicity people willy-nilly, your editor will hear about it and might think you're trying to go over her head. Once you meet staff members in person, then you have an excuse to call them, especially if they indicate they'd welcome a call from you.

So where do you meet "industry insiders"? At conference cocktail parties and during visits to your editor in New York. You can bump into editors and publicity people at national RWA conferences. The sales folks are often available at distributor conventions, which your publisher will send you to when you become more established. The American Booksellers Association's (ABA) annual BookExpo America is a good place to hobnob with behind-the-scenes professionals. You can buy a ticket yourself or ask your publisher to get you a pass. Some authors travel across the country just for the chance to attend the ABA convention.

Stop the Presses!

Some writers spend an enormous amount of time online "chatting" in cyberspace with other writers about the business. While this can be a valuable way to network, it sometimes leads to pointless arguments, hard feelings, and nasty gossip. Try to make sure your networking efforts remain positive. And remember—when you're online talking about writing, you're not writing.

Don't Burn Bridges

As you become more of an insider yourself, you'll develop an important network of relationships that can last your entire publishing career. It's important to treat these relationships with care. No scorched earth policies are allowed. The world of publishing is very small. Editors hop from one publishing house to another with frightening speed. If you leave one house because you hate your editor, you might be stuck with her again in a couple of years when she lands a job at your new publishing house. So be nice even when you don't want to be. Enter laughing and exit with grace and style.

The network of romance writers is very tight, too. Rumors fly faster than fur in a dog fight. Be very careful about the company you keep in gripe-fests. Carelessly spoken words of criticism all too often come back to haunt you.

Communicate Clearly

Your editor can't help you achieve your goals if she doesn't know what they are. Sure, she wants your books to succeed, but she probably has dozens of authors to think about. You are the one who cares most about your career. Share your ideas with her in an assertive, but nondemanding way. (Let your agent do the demanding!) You have every right to have opinions on all matters. Whether you choose to communicate them to your editor directly or through your agent is up to you. You can comment on …

➤ The kind of book cover you hope to have.

➤ The kind of back blurb you'd like.

➤ The kind of promotions you hope your publisher will do and the ways you plan to promote the book yourself.

➤ The ads you'd like your publisher to place.

➤ Ideas for special projects, like anthologies or theme books.

As a first-timer, you may not have the courage to talk frankly with your editor about these matters, but you should gather your courage as your career progresses. Editors are usually impressed with authors who involve themselves in an intelligent way. Just make sure your clear communications don't come out as demands. You definitely catch more flies with honey than vinegar when it comes to editors.

Speaking of Romance …

Many of the top-selling romance authors are top-notch businesswomen as well as creative writers. Sandra Brown has steered her own career to the pinnacle of success. "I wouldn't hand my career over to anyone else to manage anymore than I would have given my children for someone else to rear," says Sandra. "My agent has other clients. My publisher has other writers. But this is a one shot deal for me, so I keep well attuned to every aspect of it."*

Give and Take

When all is said and done, your relationship with your editor, and your agent, is a matter of give and take. You give and they take. Just joking! Your relationship with them is like any other. You get to know their strengths and weaknesses and they learn yours as well. If your editor lets you down on one matter, give her some slack. Chances are she'll come through on another issue. If you give her understanding, she's more apt to be patient with you. Patience and understanding help cement lasting relationships.

Open for Business

When you begin to write for a living, you may as well hang a shingle outside your door because you will essentially become a cottage industry. Keeping your own personal writing industry chugging along is more than a full-time job. That's why most of the successful romance writers have a personal publicist and/or some sort of secretarial help.

Until you start to make some serious dollars, though, chances are you'll be handling these details yourself. In the Information Age, instant communications and stiff competition allow few authors the luxury of doing nothing but writing. At some point, you have to juggle publicity concerns, book signings, media contacts, and speeches.

Speaking of Romance ...

One way to reduce the number of interruptions is to rent an office. Debbie Macomber is a big advocate of this approach. For her it's a worthwhile investment. "I put at least 10 to 20 percent of my advance back into promoting my books. I do this by hiring a publicist, maintaining a reader list and a bookseller list, and supporting an office outside of my home. My career is a business. This isn't a hobby or a sideline for me."*

Juggling Commerce and Creativity

Just when you sit down to start writing the climax scene in your book, the phone will ring. It's the president of the local women's social club asking you to speak at their next meeting. You handle the details, hang up, and type a few more words when the phone rings again. It's the library association president who wants to give you details about your signing at their next convention. Then the publicist at your publishing house calls to ask you if you can sign books at four Wal-Mart stores this spring. And your editor calls to say your galleys will arrive that afternoon on your doorstep. Can you have them back in New York in a week? And the printer calls to say he still needs the transparencies for your new cover if you're going to have your bookmarks in time for the release of your book. At this point, you want to throw the phone out the window!

How do writers deal with business interruptions and still manage to write? Not easily. Some authors take calls only in the afternoon and let their answering machines take the rest, but by the afternoon things start shutting down in New York and it's not easy to reach people.

Other writers take calls as they come and learn to refocus quickly on their writing. Still others encourage people to communicate with them through e-mail or the fax machine instead of the phone. The key is to protect your writing time and at the same time deal with business matters in a timely fashion. If you can't handle the business side of writing, you'd better keep your writing as a hobby.

Write On!

Once you become published, do yourself a favor and buy a fax machine. It's a fabulous way to communicate with your editor and publicity department. Sometimes information and copy have to be sent immediately. Another good investment is a computer with Internet capabilities. E-mailing notes and even chapters to your editor allows for instant communication.

Miracles of Modern Technology

Fortunately, we live in an age when communication is almost mindlessly easy. You can now e-mail chapters back and forth to editors. You can fax proposals for instant feedback. You can copy promotional items in the comfort of your own office. And you can screen your calls to make sure you only answer those with a 212 area code. (That's New York, in case you were wondering.) There is a host of wonderful technology that will make your life easier. Invest in this equipment. Not only will these time-saving devices give you more writing time, they're also tax deductible.

The Big Picture

I know it's hard to imagine now, but one day you may be a force to be reckoned with in the publishing industry. You may be a powerhouse best-selling author. What, you can't picture that? Then use the most precious tool of the trade—your imagination. See yourself as a successful author. See your name on the best-seller lists, picture yourself on a publicity tour, hear yourself giving a keynote speech at a writing conference, and picture yourself working with your personal publicist and secretary. Can you see it? Now imagine how you're going to get from here to there. That's what you call long-range planning.

Where Do You Fit In?

What kind of career do you want to have? Do you want to write a book occasionally? If so, that's a fine goal. Do you have just one book burning inside of you, but no more? That's okay, too. Make it a great book and you'll feel proud the rest of your life.

Do you have a torrent of creativity just waiting to pour from your heart? To you the prospect of writing 20 or 30 books seems like a cinch. If that's the case, you'd best plan for the long haul. You are a good candidate for a professional career in writing. In any event, no matter what your goals, you should write them down and make plans to turn your dreams into reality. To quote the old motivational adage—if you can conceive you can achieve. And writers are great conceivers.

Where Do You Want to Be in 10 Years?

One of the best ways to plan for the future is to ask where you see yourself 10 years from now. If writing is in the picture, great! That means you really do have a burning desire to be a writer. When you picture the future, try to be as specific as you can. If you are unpublished, your goals might look something like this:

➤ To have at least one completed manuscript.

➤ To have at least one published novel.

➤ To have 15 published category romances.

➤ To have 10 published category romances and a proposal for a single-title historical.

➤ To have made the Waldenbooks and *USA Today* top 50 best-seller lists.

➤ To have completed and published two volumes of a multi-generational family saga.

➤ To be a *New York Times* Bestselling author.

You see how varied your goals can be. You need to be clear on exactly how ambitious you are. Your ambition will determine the steps you take now. If you want to be a *New York Times* Bestselling author in 10 years, for example, you had best approach writing very aggressively and, of course, professionally.

You *Can* Get There from Here

The beauty of the writing profession is that you truly can create something out of nothing. Let's say you want a writing career, but you don't have one yet. You don't even have a book published. Heck, maybe you don't even have a book written. But you can still get to the top if you have talent and work like heck.

So how do you *really* go from ground zero to being a huge best-selling author? Push beyond your comfort zones. Constantly.

In what ways? It varies depending on your personality, but here are a few possibilities:

➤ Become friendlier, more confident, more outgoing in your networking efforts.

➤ Write more books, spend more hours at the typewriter, be more disciplined.

➤ Face your own weaknesses as a writer and overcome them.

➤ Take more risks with your characters' emotions, or reach deeper levels of insight.

➤ Accept your worthiness and your ability to dine with the kings and queens of the industry.

➤ Give yourself the freedom to ignore reviews.

➤ Risk failure, and learn to fly in the process.

➤ Be more supportive of your writing friends, give more and watch how (amazingly) you receive more in return.

> **Stop the Presses!**
>
> Editors often say that unpublished writers seem to think there is some secret formula or a hidden path to success. In truth there is no secret. The best-selling authors of today once were like you. So don't become paranoid and think that success is only for those who have the right connections or secret knowledge. Success is for those who work hard enough to achieve it.

Understand Your Strengths

Ultimately, the key to a long-lasting career in writing is to find what you do well. Once you find your strengths, exploit them. Do what you do well as purely as you can. That's the way you make it easy for readers to find you. Trends will come and go. Hot new authors will seem to zoom past you and then fade into the sunset. But in the long run, if you act professionally, write to your strengths, and be true to your characters, you will succeed.

The Least You Need to Know

➤ If you want to be a pro, start acting like one.

➤ Join professional organizations like Romance Writers of America.

➤ To be a pro, meet your deadlines and gracefully do revisions.

➤ Try to get to know the staff at your publishing house, but never go over your editor's head.

➤ Have specific goals and communicate them clearly to your editor and agent.

➤ If you want to be successful, you'll have to handle the business side of writing as well as the creative side.

Chapter 22

Promotion Tips

In This Chapter

➤ Why readers buy certain books

➤ How to stand out from the crowd

➤ Three layers of the promotion pyramid

➤ The real reason books get upfront store placement

➤ How to create a killer press kit

If a book sits in the bookstore and no one buys it, did it really exist? Of course it did! It was simply overlooked. It either had a bad cover or bad placement on the shelf or a lousy title or was released during the worst snowstorm of the century. Or maybe it simply wasn't promoted.

Who's job is it to promote your book? Your publisher's publicity department. Does that mean you can leave your baby in their hands? Not on your life! In this chapter you'll see how important promotion can be to the health of your book ... and your career.

Books, Books, Everywhere

Everywhere you turn there are new books. You can find thousands of titles in book-stores, drugstores, airports, and wholesale stores. You can order them on the Internet, through mail-order catalogues, and through book clubs.

Walk into the romance section of your local store and you'll see an amazing array of titles—*Her Best Man, The Other Amanda, Sisters and Secrets, Second Star to the Right, Princess in Denim, Bad Company, The Color of the Wind, Bride of the Lion, The Last Warrior.* One after another shiny new cover sits on the bookshelves waiting for takers. How do you make sure your book stands out from the crowd? You try to create an imaginary neon sign that says "Buy me."

Write On!

The back-cover blurb is critical since it's one of the first things readers look at before purchasing a book. Some authors are so concerned about their cover copy that they write it them-selves. This honor is usually re-served for experienced authors, but if you have a knack for snap-py copy writing, you can ask to participate in writing, or at least in proofing, your cover copy.

Reasons Readers Buy

There are several factors that go into the average reader's decision to take a book to the cash register.

1. They read the blurb on the back cover and decide they like the story.

2. They flip through the book and like what they see.

3. A friend has raved about the book (and didn't lend her a copy!).

4. They are looking/waiting for the author's newest book.

How many of these factors can you control? Very few. You can help write the cover copy if your editor is agreeable. And you can write a great book, but that won't necessarily guarantee rave reviews if it doesn't come to the attention of readers. About the only thing you can control are the promotions that go into your book. Be forewarned, though, that promotions can be expensive and the results are virtually impossible to quantify.

The Promotion Pyramid

There are four main areas to focus on when it comes to author promotions. If you stack them on top of each other you would have a pyramid. In general, beginning authors start at the bottom of the pyramid and work their way up as their career pro-gresses.

Reaching Readers

The first and most obvious way to promote your book is to reach out to readers. It makes sense since they're the ones buying your book. The question is, how do you reach them without spending the national budget? Here are a few ways romance authors try to touch base with fans:

➤ **Book signings.** Appearances at independent bookstores and chain stores, as well as at Wal-Marts and other department-store-type outlets.

➤ **Fan conventions.** Appearances at conventions held by organizations like *Romantic Times* and *Affaire de Coeur.*

➤ **Bookmarks and postcards.** Sent directly to readers or bookstores.

➤ **Industry magazine advertisements.** Ads in magazines like *Romantic Times, Affaire de Coeur,* and *Romance Writers' Report.*

Stop the Presses!

As soon as your book is published, well-meaning, but naive friends will ask you when you're going to go on a book tour. Promotional tours can cost tens of thousands of dollars. Publishers reserve that kind of investment for authors who will certainly earn back the money in sales. So don't hold your breath waiting for a 10-city tour.

Broaching Bookstores

The second level to focus on as you expand your efforts to promote yourself is the bookstores. A bookseller who believes in you can hand-sell a lot of your books. That's why romance-friendly bookstores are an author's best friends.

How do you reach out to bookstores? Through personal contact and mailings. You can visit area bookstores, call others by phone, and do mailings to romance-friendly stores. Mailings can include any number of items: a loose book cover, a postcard announcing your book, an informational flier, a printed excerpt, bookmarks, or galleys, to name a few.

Write On!

It's a good idea to bring "Autographed Copy" stickers to your book signings. You can sign books that are left over and slap on a sticker. Bring bookmarks, too. You can make up simple but informative bookmarks yourself at Kinko's, or have thousands beautifully produced at a printer. Do what you can afford. Both can be effective selling tools.

Dealing with Distributors and Buyers

After you start to develop a readership, you'll hope to gain the attention of the romance buyers for the chains and distributors. All you really need to know about distributors and buyers when you're first starting is that they are the ones who get your books into the stores.

A handful of distributors are responsible for most of the accounts to the book chains, grocery stores, wholesale clubs, etc. Each distributor has a romance buyer. The major bookstore chains have their own romance buyers as well. These are very important people. These are the ones who have the power to order your book by the thousands.

The more distributors who buy large quantities of your book, the more widely distributed your book will be to all the important markets. For instance, a first-time author might find her novel in her local B. Dalton, but not at her local grocery store. That's because grocery stores have fewer shelf pockets and the ones they do have are usually filled with books by top authors. First novels aren't always distributed to every chain store, either. As your career progresses, you will hopefully see your books in more and more outlets. Distribution grows as your career grows.

Write On!

The best way to build name recognition is to get as many books on the shelves as possible. So if you have to choose between promoting the heck out of one book or writing another, you're probably better off writing another. If your publisher only wants one book a year, however, then spend your extra time on promotions. After all, a lot is riding on that one book.

What Works? What Doesn't?

There is no end to the amount of time and money you could spend promoting your novel. At some point you have to ask yourself: Are my efforts working? Is my time and money being well-spent?

Generally speaking, your time is well-spent as long as it doesn't take away from your writing time. As for your money, well, you shouldn't spend a fortune promoting your book. Money can't buy success in this business. Isn't that reassuring? At least it is to those of use who aren't millionaire writers!

A Splashy Spread

The decision on whether to advertise or not is a difficult one. Some authors choose to take out ads in industry publications like *Romantic Times, Affaire de Coeur,* and RWA's *Romance Writers' Report.* These ads reach fans and romance writers alike, but they can be expensive. A full-page color ad in *Romantic Times* costs more than a thousand dollars.

Do magazine advertisements make a difference in sales? No one really knows. Taking out expensive full-page ads can certainly give everyone the impression that you're a successful author. Whether it makes a difference at the cash register is open to question. Some authors who make the biggest splash in magazine advertising seem to fall off the face of the earth a few years later. Other authors like Heather Graham, Bertrice Small, and Virginia Henley, who faithfully advertise their books, have thriving careers. Are the two factors connected? They apparently think so.

The important thing is to consider your budget and your priorities. If you can afford to take out ads, it can't hurt. It may help, especially in this tight market. If you can't afford ads, don't worry about it! Some publishers are convinced that magazine advertising makes no difference whatsoever.

Weaving a Worldwide Web

Creating a Web site on the Internet is an inexpensive way to promote yourself. Once you create a homepage promoting your books, you can link it to other sites and list your Web address in your books. Some writers don't bother to promote themselves on the Internet. They argue that people who spend enough time on the Internet to discover your Web site have no time left to read books. No one knows for sure how many books you will sell by having a presence on the Web. But it's a cheap way to tout yourself and it makes it easier for fans to get in touch with you. An avid reader who sees your Web address on the back of your book might take the time to log on to your site and e-mail you with praise, while she might not otherwise take the time to send a fan letter to your publisher.

If you're interested in creating a presence on the World Wide Web, network with other authors about the easiest and cheapest ways to create a site. Companies like Power Promotions at www.powerontheweb.com specialize in creating author Web sites. If you're not ready to create your own site, you can still roam the Internet and chat with fans on various romance sites. Readers who meet you in cyberspace might be more inclined to buy your next book.

Bookmark Your Success

A number of authors have bookmarks made to promote their books. Some are professionally produced and show the cover artwork in full color. Others are cranked out by the author at Kinko's and serve more as an informational tool. You can use bookmarks to advertise the name of your book, the release date, a rave review or a brief plot summary, the *ISBN* (*International Standard Book Number*), as well as any previous or upcoming titles.

So what do you do with bookmarks? Hand them out to friends, book clubs, libraries, and stores. You can distribute them to bookstores nationwide for a nominal fee through the *Romantic Times* Bookstores That Care network. You can also hire an author-oriented promotions company like Creative Promotions in Ridgewood, New Jersey, or an author's consultant like Judy Spagnola in Cherry Hill, New Jersey, to distribute them for you.

The advantage of these sources is that they have each identified romance-friendly stores. If you're going to distribute bookmarks yourself, you'll have to pinpoint your target audience since it would be too costly to mail bookmarks to every chain store in the country.

Baubles and Trinkets

Some authors also do giveaways. They give out trinkets, like refrigerator magnets or key chains, bearing the name of their book or a catchy slogan. These items work best if they're tied closely to your story. One of the best I've seen was Eileen Dreyer's promotion for one of her medical thrillers about a series of hospital-related murders. She sent bookstores pens shaped like a syringe with the name of her book printed on it.

Trinkets can be costly and may or may not be that effective. Analyze the pros and cons before you spend a fortune. You can even ask your publisher's sales executives for advice on what they think will be worth your investment.

A Sneak Preview

Bookstore employees always say the thing that helps them sell books the most is an advanced reading copy. That gives them a chance to read your book so they can enthusiastically recommend it. An advance reading copy is commonly known as an ARC. An ARC is a bound copy of your galleys. At around $10 each, they're costly for publishers to produce. Publishers usually print just enough ARCs to send to reviewers. If you're lucky, a couple hundred ARCs (or even a few thousand) might be sent to choice bookstores.

It's too expensive for most authors to send out galleys themselves to bookstores. They can cost $20 or more each in copying fees. Preferring a cheaper approach, some writers send out a sample chapter. These can be made into attractive little booklets with minimal effort at your local printer.

By the way, sometimes publicity departments forget to send review copies, or they send them too late to make a magazine deadline. So follow up to make sure the reviewers you care about receive a copy in time to make their deadline.

Speaking of Romance ...

Joan Wolf is a critically acclaimed author who writes one historical romance and one medieval mystery a year for HarperCollins. She says that even when you have a big-time agent you have to make sure your books don't fall through the cracks when it comes to promotions. "You always have to keep after them," Joan says. "Catherine Coulter said to me not long ago, 'Nobody cares about your book except you.' This is from a big best-selling author. When you come right down to it, nobody cares about your book like you do. You keep on top of it, it's going to get promoted."

May I Have Your Autograph?

Book signings offer an opportunity to establish personal connections with booksellers. If you go to the trouble to do an event at a store, you will make a lasting impression on the store owner. And if you behave yourself, it will be a good impression!

At some point, however, you have to ask yourself if you should do a gazillion signings or if you'd be better off spending that time writing your next book. Unless you're as well-known as someone like Nora Roberts, you may not sell that many copies. Bookstore customers these days seem to be jaded about celebrities, and the presence of an author isn't that big of a deal anymore.

I once did a signing at a Wal-Mart with three other authors on Valentine's Day. The manager set us up in the lawn and garden center of all places. Collectively we had about 400 copies of our books on hand and between the four of us we sold one book. Yes, one! A man searching for grass seed bought a copy of my Elizabethan novel, *Romance of the Rose*. When I offered to dedicate it to his wife, he informed me that he was buying it for himself! Bless his heart. Maybe he thought it was a gardening manual! Nora Roberts may sell hundreds of books at a signing, but lesser-known authors sometimes sell only a handful.

If you're not a household name, it can be just as effective to sign copies in a store without setting up a signing event. Scribble your signature on the copies in stock, slap on "Autographed Copy" stickers, meet the staff, thank them for their support, and be on your way.

Fanatic Friends

It helps if you have enthusiastic friends who can tell the whole world about your new book. Be sure to alert everyone you know that you have a book coming out. It's handy to have bookmarks for this very purpose. People tend to forget titles—a bookmark in hand is a handy reminder.

After your fourth or fifth book, your friends' enthusiasm may wane. Still, it's important to let them know when you have a new book out. You may be surprised to learn that they aren't cruising the bookstores every month waiting for your next release. However, they'll buy it if they know it's out there.

"Wish You Were Here"

You might consider sending postcards announcing the release of your book. And skip the ocean scenes from Hawaii. Show the cover of your book. Network with writers to find the printers who will give you the best deal. The color reproductions of book covers look beautiful on postcards.

Some authors also send out solicitation postcards to book buyers, distributors, and bookstores urging them to order lots of copies. These postcards usually go out about four months before the book is released during the *buy-in*. Such a mailing is designed to nudge the buyers into placing a big order. However, some important chain store buyers and distributors have gone on the record saying that they get so many solicitation mailings that they throw them in the trash without a glance.

Write On!

Some authors send out newsletters instead of postcards. That way they can update readers and booksellers on all the writing projects they have underway. Plus, fans like to hear personal tidbits about their favorite authors.

Schmoozing with Press Kits

A press kit is a tool every author should create sooner or later—the sooner the better. When you start to approach newspapers or TV stations for coverage of your book, you'll seem more professional if you hand them a press kit. Reporters are always grateful when they are handed organized information. And that's what a press kit is—an organized introduction of you. What should a press kit contain?

➤ A brief biography that highlights your writing-related accomplishments, your education, and your background.

➤ A 5 × 7 black-and-white photo. Be sure to write your name and the name of the photographer on the back. Photo credits are always given in newspapers and magazines.

➤ Reviews of your book.

➤ Copies of past articles about you. If you don't have any, don't panic. You will eventually.

➤ A list of your books, even those yet to be released. Mention the publisher, release dates, and ISBNs.

➤ Other items to include when available: press release, list of awards, articles about the genre, a fact sheet about the genre from RWA (which you can get from the Web site www.rwanational.com), a book cover, bookmarks, and other promotional materials.

Love Letters

The **buy-in** or **sell-in** is the sales pitch that happens roughly four months before a book's publishing date. The sales reps visit buyers and show them your cover and talk up your book. That's when buyers put in their main order. They can update it or increase the order later if they think there is enough demand for your book.

Some writers spend a lot of money having a press kit professionally produced by a publicist. It's a good investment. If you can't afford that, though, you can produce a perfectly adequate one yourself with a little elbow grease. Get a good-looking folder and tuck the above items inside in an orderly fashion. You can even get creative and paste a copy of your cover or a picture of yourself on the outside. Photos can be cheaply reproduced for this purpose through companies like Composites International in Alsip, Illinois (708-597-3449).

Speaking of Romance ...

It may be the publisher's job to promote your books, but you're a cottage industry and should invest in your own business. "Publishers only have so many resources," says Kathleen Onorato of Creative Promotions, "and usually the funds to promote new or mid-list authors are limited. It is to the author's advantage to supplement the publisher's efforts. Don't think of it as doing the publisher's job."

Approaching the Media

Getting coverage in the media is a good way to reach a lot of people. I know I've certainly purchased books by authors who've been featured in newspaper articles. The great thing about news coverage is that it's absolutely free! The not-so-great thing about it is that it can take a lot of effort to get. And once you get the coverage, you may not be happy with the way a reporter interprets your comments. Many journalists take a tongue-in-cheek approach to romance novels. I used to be a TV reporter, so I know how these things work from both sides of the fence.

Here are a few things to keep in mind when you try to get coverage of your book:

➤ Start early. It can take months for a newspaper editor to decide she has the space to do an article about you. If you don't contact her until you've reached your *pub date* or the week your book comes out, you won't get any coverage until your book has already been cleared from the shelves.

➤ Think about an angle or hook that might interest editors. You can always get a "local person done good" article in your local paper. To get coverage in the paper in the big city nearby, though, or if your hometown is a big city, you have to be more creative than that. Does your story involve a specific neighborhood or local history or does it tie into an upcoming holiday or event? Pitch that angle when you phone or write the editor.

➤ Don't be afraid to call editors, but keep your call brief. Pitch your story succinctly and confidently.

➤ Send press releases when and if you have the time to create them. They're very useful, but not absolutely necessary. You can often get coverage in papers through a press release even without doing an interview. (See Appendix F, "Press Releases," for an example.)

The Publisher's Role

You've got a lot to think about in terms of promotions. Just what, if anything, does the publisher do? When you have publisher support, the publicity department can do much of what we've outlined so far. But publicity departments are often overworked and too busy putting out fires to handle every detail you'd like them to. Theoretically, the publisher will give you just enough promotional support to help you earn back your advance. Remember, that's why some agents push so hard for big advances!

Co-Op Advertising

An effective way for publishers to promote romance novels is through the in-store publications produced by B. Dalton and Waldenbooks that are aimed at romance readers. In this newsletter-type publication, the books that are reviewed and featured are there, in part, because the publisher paid for them to be there. Artistic merit has little to do with the selection of titles.

Take B. Dalton's *Heart to Heart* publication, for example. If B. Dalton places a big order for a romance novel, the chain will doubtlessly want to feature the book in *Heart to Heart* to make sure the copies move off the shelves. So, B. Dalton will approach the book's publisher and ask the publisher to pitch in co-op money to help pay for the ad. The publishing house can't just decide to place an advertisement because it wants to. The size of B. Dalton's orders has to be big enough to justify the coverage. Make sense?

Write On!

Smart writers know that in order to succeed you have to promote yourself in-house. First you have to sell an editor on your worth. When she buys your book you then have to make believers of the executive editor and publisher, as well as the publicity team and sales force. It can take a few books to make inroads, but once the whole publishing staff is sold on you, they'll push your book much more enthusiastically to the public at large.

Realities of the Genre

Romance novels sell so well that publishers don't have to promote them to make a profit. Writers don't like to hear that because we all want to become stars. And how will that happen if we don't get a big tour and advertising?

It's a difficult pill to swallow, but your publisher may not care whether or not you become a star. Sometimes making a modest profit on a book is enough. So if your publisher isn't going to make you a best-seller, who will? You, that's who.

Here's the Plan, See?

If you want to reach the pinnacle of the publishing industry, you have to come up with a plan to get there. You have to become a master strategist to make sure you take advantage of every opportunity to make you and your books known to the world. Remember the old adage, "luck is what happens when preparation meets opportunity"? Writers have to create their own luck.

Come up with a plan to promote your book, write it down, and share it with your editor. Send copies to the publisher and publicity department. The more people who know about your efforts, the better. Your publishing house may not go overboard to promote your book, but they'll help you when they can if it doesn't tax their resources. For example, they may not pay for a tour, but they'll help set up book signings in any city you choose to visit. They may not pay for galleys, but they'll mail out your copies and/or promotional items for you.

Speaking of Romance ...

Bobbi Smith writes two romances a year for Leisure Books and spends every spare moment promoting them. "When my agent sold me to Leisure he sold me to them as the whole package. 'She's a promoter,' he told them. And I do think of myself as a bookseller." So much so that Bobbi went on an 11-day, seven-state tour of military bases with fellow Leisure authors Evelyn Rogers, Constance O'Banyon, and Elaine Barbieri. They went dressed in military fatigues and called themselves the "AWOLs" ("Amazing Women of Leisure"). The gimmick garnered lots of media attention and appreciation on the part of their publisher.

Face to Face

If you get any inkling whatsoever that your publisher is getting behind you, you should travel to New York to meet the staff. Of course you'll be familiar with your editor, but you want everyone on the team to support you. Meeting in person with the publicity staff is a great way to cut through the red tape and share good ideas about promoting your book. When they meet you in person they become more enthusiastic about promoting you.

Write Well, Write Often

If you're feeling a little overwhelmed by all the "opportunities" to promote yourself, I have one word of advice: Relax. Your career won't crash and burn if you aren't as prepared as you'd like to be when it comes to promotions. It's easy to get caught up in the publicity whirlwind and forget why you got in this business to start with—to write.

The best way to promote yourself is to write often and well. Great books will find an audience, I am convinced. So happy writing!

The Least You Need to Know

➤ You can't expect your publisher to promote your novel.

➤ Don't put yourself in debt doing promotions.

➤ The best way to make a name for yourself is by writing lots of great books.

➤ Approach the media several months before your book comes out.

➤ Promote yourself to your publisher as well as to readers.

Nuts and Bolts
of the Biz

Did you know that Margaret Mitchell considered three other titles before settling on *Gone With the Wind?* The 1936 classic was almost titled *Pansy, Tote the Weary Load,* and *Tomorrow Is Another Day.* Obviously, Mitchell gave great thought to this issue. She must have known then what publishers certainly know now: A title and a cover can make the difference between success and failure in the marketplace.

You probably hate to think of your creation as a commodity, but that's what it is. The publishing world is a big business like any other. If you doubt that, wait until you get your first contract. Contracts can run a dozen or more pages, and they're filled with intimidating phrases like Termination upon Bankruptcy and Liquidation, Force Majeure, Examination of Accounts, and Submission of Proof. Ugh. Doesn't sound very romantic. But even the romantic at heart need to stay on top of the basics of the business. In this chapter, we'll examine some of the most important issues affecting your career—including titles and covers!

Advantages of the A-Team

We've already talked a little about the importance of publisher support. If it's so important, then why doesn't every author enjoy it to the fullest extent? The answer is simple: Not all books are created equal in the eyes of the publisher. Some get special treatment. And it's all determined by the book's position in the publisher's lineup. The one glorious exception to this principle is in category publishing. Issues like position and publisher support for any given title don't apply. Every category romance gets an equal shot, though admittedly some lines are more popular than others.

Single-title authors have a host of concerns. The amount of promotional support they receive from their publishers, for example, is determined by their position on "the list." Each imprint has a list of a half dozen or more titles that are released each month. Books at the top of the list get the most promotion and those at the bottom get virtually none. The top slots get the best placement in industry catalogues and the biggest pitch from publisher sales reps. Here are a few terms describing the various positions in the lineup:

Stop the Presses!

Don't expect your publisher to put into your contract details about where your book will be on the publisher's list or how much money will be spent on promotions. Promises are made, and usually kept, but rarely are they put in writing. Your agent can ask for a side letter, but they're usually drawn up only when the promotion plan budget is $100,000 or more.

➤ **Superleader.** That's the very top of the list and it's usually reserved for superstars like Stephen King, Tom Clancy, Sandra Brown, and LaVyrle Spencer. Books in this slot often have print runs of a million or more copies. The name of this position varies from publisher to publisher, but you get the gist of the idea. This is the big time, folks! Books in this slot get television, radio, newspaper, and magazine advertisements. The authors also go on national tours.

➤ **A-lead.** This slot is reserved for someone who is considered a best-seller but who is not necessarily a *New York Times* Bestseller. Print runs for books in this slot can range from 150,000 on the low end to 700,000 or so on the high end. These authors have the clear commitment of their publisher. They may not get media advertisements or book tours, but they get other tangible support, like lunches with major book buyers and signings at industry conventions. They also get good placement in bookstores and sales catalogues and a big push from the sales reps. Publishers sometimes have B-leads and C-leads as well, or even another category between the Superleader and the A-lead.

➤ **Mid-list.** A number of spots halfway down the list are reserved for books that, for whatever reason, aren't earmarked for special treatment. The author may be new, or someone who hasn't yet broken out of the pack in terms of sales. These books often get no promotion, no special placement in the stores, and are the last to be pitched by the sales force.

That's the basic breakdown of publishers' monthly lists, though the names of the positions vary from house to house.

Mid-List Blues

There has been much gnashing of teeth over the so-called death of the mid-list, and it's an important issue to you because many first books are slotted in the mid-list. So what's the problem?

As a corporate mentality has overtaken the publishing world, books are increasingly expected to make a profit quickly. Once upon a time, unknown authors started out in the mid-list and stayed there while they built up an audience and eventually moved up the list, but that's becoming increasingly hard to do. The corporate owners of the publishing companies want instant profits, so they load up the shelves with the *back list* titles of big-name authors like Danielle Steel. That leaves little room for unknown writers on the mid-list to find shelf space, much less an audience.

What can you do to deal with this problem?

1. Have your agent push for the best position possible on the list when you negotiate your contract. Publishers never commit to list positions in a contract, but they often will let you know what sort of plans they have for your book.

2. Ask your publisher to put more money into your cover so it really stands out, and ask for better in-store placement. In order for your book to be prominently displayed, your publisher has to purchase placement at the front of the store from the bookstore chains.

3. Write a damned good book and hope word-of-mouth sales will put you in a position to move up the list with your next book.

4. Consider selling your book to one of the lines designed to introduce new authors to the market. They frequently offer lower advances, but come with good covers and/or advertising support designed to give the book a fighting chance.

Love Letters

An author's **back list** is the sum of her previous titles. For example, when you go to the store to buy Danielle Steel's newest release, you'll probably find additional titles from her back list as well. An author's back list remains in print only if the titles continue to sell well enough to warrant reprinting (going back to press for more copies).

The Harlequin Machine

If you are writing a category novel, you don't have to worry about positions and mid-list and in-store placements or covers. They generally receive the same quality of covers, though the elements of some are more engaging than others. And they all receive equal distribution. That's the beauty of the Harlequin-Silhouette system. That's why writing a category novel is less fraught with risks than writing a single-title romance. The only other publisher of series romances, Kensington, sells the Precious Gems line on a nonreturnable basis exclusively to the Wal-Mart chain, so issues like placement and lists don't apply in the same way.

Sell-Throughs

Once you become published, you'll start to hear a lot about sell-through. What is a sell-through? It's the percentage of books sold. Let's say your publisher prints 100,000 copies of your book. If 50,000 copies sell you have a 50 percent sell-through. If only 25,000 copies sell you have a 25 percent sell-through. Why is this important? Because in the age of computerization authors live and die by their sell-throughs.

Write On!

Not only do old authors take on new names, old names take on new authors. For example, Carolyn Keene wrote the *Nancy Drew* series until she passed away. So how are new *Nancy Drew* books still being released? Other authors are writing stories that are being packaged under the Carolyn Keene name.

The Curse of Computerized Sales

In the days before computers, there was less competition among authors, there was less corporate emphasis on the bottom line, and sales figures weren't tallied as quickly or as precisely as they are now. An author could write half a dozen books or so before stores and the publisher seemed to notice how well she was selling. Authors had more of a chance to develop a readership and improve their sales.

Now, thanks to computerized cash registers, stores track exact sales figures from week to week. If your book does poorly, the buyers for the bookstores know it right away. Let's say a chain like Waldenbooks buys 10,000 copies of your novel, but sells only 4,000 copies. Armed with these exact figures, the chain's romance buyer will, in all likelihood, buy only 4,000 copies of your next book. In that case, your print runs, instead of going up, would start going down.

By the way, a 50-percent sell-through is considered an industry minimum standard. Some distributors say they'll hang onto an author who drops down to 40 percent, but the chain store buyers say they expect 70-percent sell-through.

Same Author, New Name

A number of romance authors with low sell-throughs have found themselves persona non grata at their publishing houses. Their editors turned down their next books simply because of bad sales figures. It's a terrible and tragic turn of events because it has nothing to do with talent and everything to do with the bottom line. How do these authors cope? Some start writing under a different name. That gives them a fresh start. They can fool the computers that track sales by starting over as a new entity.

This approach is usually undertaken with the publisher's blessing and cooperation. If your sales history is sketchy but an editor loves your work, she may decide to launch you with a new name. Without that genuine enthusiasm for your work, though, a publisher will simply choose instead to get behind an unknown author with a clean slate or another veteran with good sales.

What Do Sell-Throughs Mean to You?

Ideally, your publisher will closely manage your print run to avoid a poor sell-through. They do this by basing the print run on orders of your book. Your publisher's reps will go out to book buyers about four months before your pub date. They'll present your cover and pitch your story in a process that's called a buy in. The buyers will place orders, and the publisher will base the print run on those orders, knowing that they can always go back to press later if demand exceeds supply.

Don't expect your publisher to print a million copies just because she loves your story. Those kinds of numbers are reserved for stars like Tami Hoag and Elizabeth Lowell who have fans waiting to buy their books.

In-Store Placement

There are several factors that can help or hurt your sales. One of them is positioning within the bookstore. Obviously, readers gravitate first to books that are placed up front near the door or the cash register in a *dump*. That's where you want your book to be!

Love Letters

A **dump** is a free-standing, in-store cardboard display that holds a large number of a particular author's books. A generic dump is topped with artwork that often touts the publisher's name. A custom dump is topped with artwork from the author's cover. Your books won't appear in a dump unless a store has ordered at least a couple dozen copies.

How do books get chosen for this prime real estate? I'll give you a hint: It's not a merit-based system. Publishers pay big bucks to make sure a title spends a week in the "new arrivals" rack or on a particular outlet's so-called "best-seller" list. Stores that buy big quantities of certain titles will also place them upfront simply to move copies out the door.

One can only assume the upfront placement is a big contributing factor when lesser-known authors appear on the *USA Today* best-seller list, which, incidentally, is a legitimate list you can't buy your way on to. So if you walk into a chain store and see your book prominently displayed, get down on your knees and give thanks to your editor. You have publisher support!

Gotcha Covered

The other obvious factor that will make a big difference in your sales is the cover. They say you can't judge a book by the cover, but readers do it all the time. That's why you want the best cover possible for your book. You could have written the most brilliant love story since *Jane Eyre*, but if it has a lousy cover it will be overlooked by many of your potential readers. What makes a lousy cover?

➤ An ugly color

➤ A title that's hard to read

➤ Silly, bland, or unattractive artwork

The prettiest covers are usually stamped with shiny foil and embossed so that the letters or images are raised. These processes are expensive, but they can be extremely effective at drawing the eye of the customer. That's why publishers invest in these techniques for their top authors.

Flowers and Fabio

You've probably heard by now that Fabio has retired from modeling for romance covers, except for the romances that he purportedly writes himself. There are a slew of Fabio wannabes and look-alikes, though, and many still grace the covers of contemporary and historical romances. These passionate poses will always be popular with a core group of romance fans. Some readers, however, prefer something more subdued.

Many historical covers now feature flowers or "elements" from the story, like a clock for a time-travel romance or a sword for a medieval story. Some publishers believe both types of covers sell equally well. You can express your own preference when your book goes into production, but it may not be heeded. Some publishers will do nothing but *clinch* covers, and some publishers will do anything but a clinch.

Where's My Name?

Don't be surprised if you feel as if you need a magnifying glass to find your name on your first cover. The title will undoubtedly be larger than your name. As you become more established as a recognizable author the lettering of your name will grow larger and will eventually dwarf the title. Publishers know that an unknown author won't sell books on the strength of her name unless she's a famous person. So the title has to sell your book until you become a known commodity. Sounds so personal, doesn't it? Remember, this is big business!

What's in a Title?

If your name isn't going to sell your first book, you'd better come up with a good title for your story. A bad title might sink your ship! One can only wonder what would have happened to these famous books if the author had used the original title:

Love Letters

Clinch is an industry term used to describe the passionate embrace that typifies the traditional romance cover. The women and men on a clinch cover are often scantily clad and in provocative poses. Sometimes this pose is called a clutch.

Stop the Presses!

Don't be heartbroken if your editor dumps your title and picks a new one herself. If she does so, it's because she thinks the change will help the book sell. You don't really have the right to pick the title for your book unless you have a clause to that effect added to your contract, a clause that is usually reserved for established authors.

➤ *Trimalchio in West Egg* = *The Great Gatsby,* by F. Scott Fitzgerald

➤ *Tom-All-Alone's Factory that Got Into Chancery and Never Got Out* = *Bleak House,* by Charles Dickens

➤ *Something That Happened* = *Of Mice and Men,* by John Steinbeck

If you have trouble coming up with a good title for your book, you're obviously in good company! Ask your editor for suggestions. Someone with an objective eye can often come up with something catchy.

Love's Raging Titles

Trends in romance titles come and go. A decade or so ago, lots of historical titles evoked images of torrid romance with words like fury, raging, passion, and tender. Then came the blank-and-the-blank titles: *The Wolf and the Dove, The Kilt and the Heather, The Lily and the Leopard, Falcon and the Sword.*

Category romances these days hit on familiar themes with babies, brides, ranchers, cowboys, father, daddy, and mother. Some titles play on rhythms. Jayne Ann Krentz writing as Amanda Quick has a truckload of one-word titles: *Affair, Dangerous, Deception, Desire, Mischief, Mistress.* Elizabeth Lowell got into the rhythm thing with her two-word titles: *Only His, Only Love, Only Mine, Only You.* The advantage of creating similar structures to your titles is that it triggers the reader's memory: Oh, yeah, I read her last book. It was great. I think I'll get this one.

Some writers seem to have a talent for clever titles. Brainstorming is a good way to come up with a catchy name for your book. Here are a few pointers to keep mind as you do:

➤ A title should have something to do with your story.

➤ It should have a pleasing rhythm.

➤ It should be relatively short, or the print will have to be small in order to fit the words on the cover.

➤ Ideally, it should trigger a pleasant feeling or emotional response that makes the reader want to buy your book.

Changing Marketplace

We've talked a lot about the realities of the business for published authors. But what effect has the changing *marketplace* had on aspiring romance writers?

The beauty of the romance genre is that its creative boundaries seem to expand every year. Authors continually come up with wonderful new ideas and new approaches to old romance themes, and many of these fresh new voices come from the ranks of the unpublished. Truthfully, though, there isn't as much opportunity for newcomers as there was 15 years ago. With the recent spate of corporate buyouts and consolidations, there just aren't as many romance lines now as there were a decade ago. That means there are fewer slots for new authors to fill.

Love Letters

The **marketplace** is an all-encompassing word that describes the latest buying trends that come about through readers' changing tastes in fiction. Twenty years ago sexy historical romances were all the rage. Now readers are demanding more variety in the marketplace.

Growing Readership

Still, romances remain among the most popular of popular fiction novels. As writers continue to push the creative boundaries, the pool of potential readers can only grow. An increasing number of "nonromance readers" are now reading romance because authors like Kristin Hannah and Tami Hoag are crossing over to a whole new audience, carrying with them skills they honed in the romance genre.

Tami Hoag has segued from romantic suspense novels to enormously successful hard-edged thrillers, and Kristin Hannah has moved from traditional romance to women's fiction aimed at a mainstream audience. As these talented authors, and others like them, expand the scope of their fiction and introduce new readers to the fruits of the romance genre, the more opportunity they create for unpublished writers who hope to follow in their wake.

Recognizing Craftsmanship

What does this mean for you? Good news. The market is tight, but that simply means you won't be able to sell a bad book. You didn't plan on doing that anyway, right? There is always room for a great story no matter how difficult the market. You just have to be realistic about how good your work is, and make it better if there's room to grow.

Alternative Markets

If you're having trouble breaking into the romance field, you might want to consider other markets. Sometimes it's easier to sell, and even write, a novel after you have some experience writing elsewhere. It's also nice to have some money coming in while you're waiting for your big break, not to mention a few publishing credits.

A Novella Idea

You've probably noticed anthologies of romance novellas in your local bookstore. I've done a couple, and they're lots of fun to write. A novella is a short novel, usually around 20,000 words, or 100 manuscript pages. Obviously, it takes less time to write one, so you have the gratification of completing a novel sooner than you normally would. They give you a chance to be read by new readers, too. Since there are usually four authors contributing to an anthology, they each bring their own readership to the book.

Authors write for anthologies usually by invitation only. Your editor might call you up and ask you to contribute to an anthology with a particular theme—a collection of holiday, time-travel, or Scottish stories, for example. However, some enterprising authors come up with their own themes and talk their editor into the project. It seems that the only houses that are willing to accept novellas from unpublished authors are the Christian publishers.

Confession Magazines

A surprisingly few number of aspiring romance authors consider writing for *confession magazines,* but it's a relatively easy way to break into publishing. Many of the stories are very well written, though the titles are admittedly absurd, such as "I'm Always Naked When the Postman Rings," "My Dad Is a Priest," or "My Mom Is a Slut."

These stories are all ostensibly true tales, so if you pitch an idea, you have to be prepared to sign a contract stating that the event you wrote about really happened, or you know of someone it happened to, or, well, you get the idea. Writers experienced in this market say they often weave together fact and fiction as long as it's a story that could happen—no aliens or mystical time travel. The stories run from 7,000 to 10,000 words and generally earn $300 to $500.

You'll find a list of confession magazines in *Writer's Market.* There are nine of them, all published by Sterling/Macfaddan. Some are geared toward ethnic readers and others toward blue-collar middle America.

Love Letters

Confession magazines contain stories written in first person that are designed to draw on the reader's sympathies. The content ranges from adventure and mystery stories to emotional, intimate accounts of women who deal with serious problems typical of everyday life.

Erotica

I'm blushing even as I write this, but there is a market for sexually oriented fiction with various unusual specialties. It seems that spanking is a particular favorite, with several magazines devoted to the subject! These publications often advertise in *Romantic Times* magazine. Black Lace, in England, and Red Sage Publishing, in Florida, are two publishers of erotica.

Online Writing Markets

There is a growing number of opportunities to write for online magazines and newspapers. The pieces being bought are short and the competition is reportedly leaner because few authors have been turned on to the market. There is a list of cyberpublications accepting queries in *Writer's Market.*

E-Books

You can now read romance novels on your computer screen or a handheld display called an e-reader. Companies like Hard Shell Word Factory will let you download a romance for around $3 or will sell a romance on a computer disk for around $5. Electronic publishing, or e-publishing as it's called, is in its early stages and is opening the door for many new authors.

The good news is that e-publishers are more open to variety in story lines. They can take contemporary romances, for example, that don't quite fit into the more established category romance lines. The bad news? Well, you won't get an advance. And while you will get royalties, the concept of reading an electronic book hasn't taken off with readers yet. Right now e-books aren't easy for readers to find, but you can purchase them by logging onto Web sites like www.hardshell.com.

Speaking of Romance ...

Lynn Miller is president of a television and interactive media company as well as a romance writer. Here's her take on why you don't see more romance novels adapted for the big screen: "The power of the romance novel is internal, meant to be absorbed privately. Television and feature films are external media that show emotion through action. Only rarely, given the amount of romantic material out there, does a novel contain the type of premise, plot and characters that can straddle both worlds."*

From Here to Hollywood

Many novelists dream of writing a screenplay, but Los Angeles is overflowing with frustrated aspiring screenwriters. If you want to see your work on the screen, you'd be better off trying to have one of your romance novels adapted for film or television. Frankly, that's a long shot as well. Romance novels have largely been ignored by the predominantly male producers in La-La Land.

However, there is an increasing number of romances being optioned and even produced, mostly for television. Debbie Macomber's novel *This Matter of Marriage* was one of a number of Harlequin romances produced for The Movie Channel in 1998.

Often the books that get produced are the ones that are read and championed by a big star. Granted, a famous romance novelist has a better chance of having a star pick up her novel than you do, but that shouldn't stop you from trying if you believe you have a terrific and unique story. You can send a copy of your novel to a movie star who might be appropriate for a leading role, though they're hard to reach. Your agent should be able to track down an address for you. As I say, it's a long shot, but it doesn't hurt to try.

Stop the Presses!

You can visit Hollywood and meet with movie executives, but be careful about sharing ideas too freely. More than a few novelists have pitched ideas that they thought bombed only to see them pop up on television a year later. If you do go to Hollywood, arrange the trip through your agent.

Book Packaging

Did you ever wonder how semiliterate sports stars produce beautifully written autobiographies? Chances are they were connected with a professional writer in a deal put together by a book packager. The writer may or may not have been given credit on the book cover, but she or he sure as heck got paid.

There's an increasing market for celebrity books, "how-to" manuals, and novels based on movies and television series. Many of these projects are conceived of, or at least handled by, packagers. Denise Little is a former Kensington romance editor who is now Executive Editor of Tekno-Books in Green Bay. She says packagers are always looking for experienced authors with a proven track record who can be counted on to write under intense deadlines. You won't get royalties for these kinds of projects, but the flat fees you receive can be generous. That's something to consider if you're a writer "in between" contracts.

Turn-of-the-Century Opportunities

For every door that closes in the publishing industry, another one opens. Just bear that in mind while you're trying to get your foot in those doors. It's important to remember, too, if you have a thriving writing career that takes a sudden nose dive. There will always be readers. People need stories to make sense of their lives.

As the world becomes more electronic and computerized and seemingly distant, I believe writers—romance writers in particular—will become even more valuable. Just remember that as we face a new century. There will always be a market for a well-told story, even if the market looks a little different than it did throughout the last century. I believe that with all my heart, and you should, too!

The Least You Need to Know

➤ Your book's position in the publisher's lineup determines how much promotion and support it will receive.

➤ Publishers want to sell at least 50 percent of the copies printed, which would give you a 50 percent sell-through.

➤ Good covers are critical to the success of a book, particularly if it's by an unknown author.

➤ The traditional market for romances has tightened in recent years, but opportunities in alternative markets are opening up.

➤ Despite the ups and downs of the publishing industry, society will always need writers to tell stories.

Chapter 24

Romancing the Industry

> **In This Chapter**
>
> ➤ A ready-made networking system
>
> ➤ Writers' groups offer more than moral support
>
> ➤ The cyber connection
>
> ➤ The benefits of writers' conferences
>
> ➤ How to handle an editor/agent interview

You deserve to be congratulated. You've had the good sense to choose a genre of fiction that boasts the most friendly, helpful, and knowledgeable authors anywhere in the publishing industry. Why are romance writers so willing to assist one another? We just can't help ourselves! It probably comes from writing about love all day. In this chapter, you'll learn how to take advantage of the ready-made support systems available to aspiring romance writers.

The Good News

It's easy to be enthusiastic about the romance genre. There are so many good things happening in this market. That's in large part due to the fact that romance novels are loved by so many readers. Success always seems to breed more success. But the strength of the genre stems not just from the readers, but also from the tremendous grass-roots organization that writers have built up around the genre.

The World's Largest Genre Organization

With 8,400 members, Romance Writers of America is the largest genre writing organization in the world. It was founded by a handful of writers in Houston, Texas, in 1980, which has been the location of the organization's headquarters ever since. A full-time staff coordinates all the efforts of the RWA board, which include promoting a positive image of romances, advocating author's rights in the publishing world, and holding national conventions.

Speaking of Romance ...

RWA sponsors writing contests for published and unpublished authors. The Golden Heart contest is for unpublished authors. The prestigious RITA Awards are given to published authors. What significance does winning a RITA have on an author's career? "It's wonderful on a personal level," says RITA Award-winning category author Lindsay Longford. "Praise and positive strokes are water in the desert of the publishing world. But the bottom line for a writer, career-wise, always comes back to the question: Are readers buying your books?"

A Chapter Near You

There are 120 chapters of RWA, including an outreach chapter, which is for authors who aren't close enough to attend a local chapter. There is also an online chapter and chapters that specialize in *regency*, futuristic/fantasy/paranormal, romantic suspense, and inspirational romances, to name a few. Members of these groups communicate from the four corners of the earth through snail mail and e-mail and meet at national conferences.

What do local chapters have to offer? It varies from group to group. Some chapters use their time together to critique manuscripts, while others get together to hear speakers and to talk about the business. One group, the Love Designers in Calumet City, Illinois, has dedicated their members' time, talents, and energies into producing a monthly review publication called *Rendezvous*.

Anyone seriously interested in becoming a romance writer should check out the nearest RWA chapter meetings. Here are some of the things you can do at local meetings:

➤ Network with others in the writing business.

➤ Meet other people working toward the same goal.

➤ Find a critique group or partner.

➤ Renew your commitment to writing.

As I mentioned before, I taught myself to write while attending RWA meetings over the course of more than 12 years. The friendships I've made during that time are among the most rewarding of my life. If you'd like to find out about local RWA chapters, call 281-440-6885.

Love Letters

A **regency** romance is one that's set in England between 1811 and 1820, during the reign of the prince regent. The period is characterized by charming phrases and manners and has an avid following among writers and readers.

Because Writers Are Weird

Don't take offense, but writers are a little different. We go off into worlds of our own creations in the middle of the frozen foods section at the grocery store, we forget our children's names, and generally scare our neighbors with the far-off look in our eyes as we pull weeds in the garden. Mind you, that's because we're always creating stories at the most inconvenient times.

An acquaintance once told me that I was the only person she ever knew who could have private moments in public places. So? Weird is good. If we didn't all march to a slightly different drummer, we probably wouldn't have the urge to tell fantastic stories. That's why we need support groups—to find others just like us!

Write On!

If you can't afford a national and local membership in RWA, don't despair. You can usually attend a couple of meetings of your local RWA chapter before you have to join. That might give you a chance to meet and hang out with some kindred spirits.

Support Groups for the Chronically Creative

Writers' groups and conventions can be more than just supportive. They can actually increase your productivity. There is something incredibly motivating about talking with other writers. It validates your aspirations. It takes something nebulous and gives it form. It helps turn a fantasy into a reality. When I network regularly with other writers I get much more writing done than when I remain isolated. It helps me remember my purpose and goals.

313

Speaking of Romance ...

Maggie Osborne, past-president of RWA and the author of over 40 novels, believes strongly in networking. "That's one of the primary benefits of a writer's organization, sharing information," she says. "The better informed a writer is about the publishing business, the better armed she is for the future. Another reason that I personally find writing groups important is that it's a joy to be with people who genuinely understand what I do every day, the problems I encounter doing it, my ambitions and goals, what set-backs mean to my career."*

Strength in Numbers

One of the greatest benefits of networking is that the process helps to eliminate ignorance. Some writers are so eager to be published they'd practically pay a publisher to take their book. It's probably very tempting for publishers to take advantage of that eagerness. It's harder to do when a publisher is dealing with a writer who is knowledgeable about the business.

When you belong to a network of educated and informed writers, you know what kinds of contracts can be expected. So, if a publisher offers you a ridiculously low advance, you can say, "Wait a minute! I know somebody who's making a lot more for the same kind of book!"

Brave New World

It goes without saying that computers have revolutionized the world as we know it, at least for writers. Computers are, in part, responsible for the high volume of fiction being produced by popular fiction writers across the board. You can simply write faster with a computer—or perhaps I should say you can rewrite faster. A computer will allow you to move and delete copy with the click of a mouse. A computer won't pull a first draft out of your head!

By the way, computers may increase the writing capacity of any given author, but it won't necessarily improve the quality. Some writers claim that computers actually lead to poor writing. There is a tendency when working on the computer to edit and delete with wild abandon because all it takes is the click of a mouse. You just might carelessly edit out the perfect phrase that might otherwise have survived if you were forced to painstakingly retype your chapter on a typewriter. In the old days, changing even a word on a typewriter took effort. On a computer, writers may choose words in haste because they're so easily replaced. That's the theory, anyway. Am I going to go back to my Smith-Corona typewriter? No way!

The Internet Connection

If you own a computer with a modem, you can get online and log on to the Internet, which is the other main advantage of having a computer. If you've resisted taking this step, you should seriously consider overcoming your technophobia. The Internet can bring information and advice into your home at the speed of light.

On the Net you can:

➤ Instantly find information from obscure sources that you would not otherwise have known existed.

➤ Talk to other writers and experts who are hard to reach by phone.

➤ Meet other people who share your interests.

➤ Send chapters of your novel electronically to an editor who needs it yesterday!

You can also send chapters as file attachments through e-mail to friends for a critique. Talk about instant feedback!

Write On!

You don't have to have a computer to become a published writer. Shirl Henke and Rexanne Becnel are two prolific authors who write their first drafts by hand. Obviously, you'll have to have your manuscript typed before you send it to a publisher. But writing a draft by hand can be an intimate way to connect with your thoughts, like writing a letter.

Closing the Distance

Logging on to the Internet and chatting with a friend is not nearly as good as seeing someone in person, but for writers who are physically isolated, cyberspace closes the distance. Here are some of the ways that professional and aspiring writers use the Internet to their advantage:

➤ **Live chats.** Writers log on to a designated chat site at a certain hour of the day, type in their messages to each other, and are able to respond immediately. This almost feels like a

Stop the Presses

You might want to think twice about putting games on your computer. Many an author suffering from writer's block has spent hours in front of the keyboard playing solitaire. It's important to spend your writing time writing, not playing computer games or going online.

coffee klatch, but it's a lot slower than real speech. Live chats can be fun, but they are time-consuming. You can download transcripts of a live chat, though, and at your own leisure pan for nuggets of wisdom or good recommendations on reference materials.

➤ **Bulletin boards.** Writers click their way on to a bulletin board dedicated to a certain topic, such as "historical romances," "contemporary romances," "What I'm Reading Now," and so on. They write their comments at any hour of the day and check in later to see who replied to comments or questions.

➤ **Online workshops.** Writers log on to a bulletin board that's conducting a workshop on a particular topic. Participants can interact with the facilitator. Some workshops are conducted through e-mail messages.

Love Letters

Romantic Times is the premiere romance fan magazine. It boasts over 150 book reviews each month and is now delving into the mystery genre. Kathryn Falk, the magazine's founder and CEO, is an innovative Brooklyn entrepreneur who, after acquiring an estate in England, goes by the title Lady of Barrow.

While the Internet admittedly lacks the personal contact found in traditional classes, workshops, and support groups, it's a godsend to those who don't have the opportunity to network in person. It's also a great way to tap into the knowledge of those who might live far away. If your specialty is the Victorian era or the Old West, chances are you'll be able to hook up with other writers who know as much, if not more, than you.

Where to Start

A good place to start exploring the Web is through America Online. AOL has 13 romance boards as part of the Writers Club Romance Group. If you're an AOL subscriber, use the keyword WCRG. If you're not an AOL subscriber, log on to www.members.aol.com/wrtrrams.

Author Cathie Linz keeps track of the best Web sites for authors and romance readers in her *Romantic Times* column "Online Romance."

The Conference Connection

Writers' conferences are a great way to plug in to the heartbeat of the genre. When you're around dozens, hundreds, or even thousands of other writers who share your interests, you'll come away feeling validated and focused on your writing goals.

Speaking of Romance ...

Carolyn Domini is a writer who runs a medieval workshop online. She says workshops enable aspiring authors to learn about writing and make friends at the same time. "They actually become cyber communities where you have a whole town of people," says Carolyn. She says published authors who tap into these cyber communities can learn about what readers are looking for and promote themselves at the same time.

The Personal Touch

Writing is such an ethereal discipline. We sit alone before our keyboards day in and day out, wondering if what we do is real or imagined. Meeting other writers who are doing the same thing makes it all seem real. There is nothing quite like meeting a fellow writer who shares our interests and sensibilities. Conferences are a great place to meet new friends and potential critique partners.

The Real Skinny

One of the very best reasons to attend writers' conferences is to get the lowdown on what's really happening in the business. For example, you'll hear about lines that are folding or starting up, editors who have jumped from one house to another, and lines that are so overloaded with manuscripts they're putting a temporary freeze on submissions. All of these tidbits of information could be invaluable to you. What else can you learn at conferences?

➤ Techniques that best-selling writers used to rise to the top

➤ What kinds of stories publishers are currently looking for

➤ Who has a hot new contract

➤ The newest unknown who is being heralded as the next Diana Gabaldon or Jude Deveraux

➤ Which agent strikes you as someone you'd like to work with

➤ Ideas that are currently overdone

Granted, some of the things you will learn at conferences qualify as little more than gossip, but every industry has the latest "buzz." Writers seem to thrive on this buzz with particular fervor, perhaps because they have few opportunities to socialize with other like-minded people.

The One-Minute Pitch

Many of the regional and national RWA conferences offer aspiring writers the chance to meet with publishers and agents in one-on-one or group interviews. If you're in a group session with half a dozen other writers, you can fade into the woodwork if you're feeling intimidated.

However, many agents and editors will ask each writer to talk briefly about her current project. In one-on-one interviews, you will, in all likelihood, be invited to pitch your idea. The best way to prepare for this is to rehearse. Practice telling your story in a minute or two. Often, agents and editors like to have a peg to hang your story on. So, when appropriate, you can say things like:

➤ My story is in the tradition of Danielle Steel, but features hip 20-something characters.

➤ My story is what you might call a cross between Godzilla and Romeo and Juliet ....

➤ My story is about two lovers who must struggle to find happiness during an espionage caper set against a backdrop of extreme sensuality.

Whatever! I hope your story lines are better than mine, but you get the idea.

Speaking of Romance ...

Michelle Hoppe has been a finalist in RWA's Golden Heart Contest for unpublished authors and has attended national RWA conferences. She says you should be able to describe your book in a sentence or two when you meet with an agent or editor. "Some will exchange personal anecdotes and others will get right down to business," says Michelle. "Mainly what they want to know is who the heroine is, who the hero is, the conflict that will keep them apart, and how it's resolved. Beyond that they don't really need to know too much more."

Advice from the Trenches

Agent Linda Kruger, vice-president of the Fogelman Literary Agency, has been through more than her fair share of agent/author appointments. She suggests that authors organize a pitch on a series of index cards. The cards should contain the following information in this order:

1. Give the title, word count, and category, if any, that your book fits into.

2. Give a short, exciting synopsis of the story, focusing on the "hook," or the elements that will grab readers.

3. & Devote one card each to describing the hero and heroine and what makes them
4. special.

5. Devote a card to yourself: a quick bio focusing on your writing credentials.

Linda says a second set of cards should be devoted to questions you have for the prospective agent/editor. A word of warning, though, if you use this technique. Do not read off of your index cards. They're there simply to jog your memory and to help keep your presentation succinct.

What Not to Say in an Editor/Agent Interview

There are a few obvious things you should never say to an agent or editor. You can come up with a list of your own. Here are a few no-no's to start with:

➤ I know nothing about your publishing house/agency. What can you tell me about yourself? (You should have made an effort to learn something about the publisher/agent before your meeting.)

➤ Give me three good reasons why I should let you have my manuscript instead of sending it somewhere else? (The editor probably couldn't care less whether she buys your book, so don't be arrogant.)

➤ I'm afraid my book isn't very good. I'm hoping you can help make it better. (Editors are looking for confident writers who believe in their work.)

➤ My book is better than anything you've ever seen. (How do you know what the editor has seen?)

Write On!

When pitching a story idea, sometimes "less is more." You want to entice the editor or agent with the high points without bogging them down with the details. Some established authors actually sell their story ideas to their editors by writing the equivalent of a back cover blurb. Prepare your verbal pitch so that it sounds as exciting and intriguing as a romance cover.

➤ May I read one of my scenes to you? (No!)

➤ Here is my manuscript. You can read it on the airplane on your way home. (The editor/agent doesn't have room in her luggage for all the manuscripts that will be pitched to her during the conference.)

➤ I really hate romances, but I thought I'd crank one out until I can write a real book. (Most romance editors love what they do and would be highly insulted to find out you don't appreciate the books they toil over.)

You're Not a Bounty Hunter

If you go to a big conference, you may feel a certain desperate frenzy to become noticed by a publishing house. Just relax. Your job is not to hunt down some poor, unsuspecting editor in the elevator. If you bump into an agent or editor and naturally strike up a conversation, great. But don't force it.

The best you can hope for at a big conference is to get a better idea of what editors/agents might be looking for. If you can get a personal or group appointment, hopefully you'll get an invitation to send your manuscript to New York. Books are rarely read or bought during the conference itself.

Cost Versus Benefit

When deciding whether or not to attend a conference, you have to consider the costs and weigh them against the likely benefits. If you're a brand-spanking-new aspiring author, you may not be ready for a big national writers' conference. You might be better off going to a regional or local conference in your own state or city. Smaller conferences aren't as costly or as overwhelming. You also have a better chance of brushing shoulders with editors and agents in smaller conferences.

Stop the Presses!

Attending a national conference with thousands of other writers can be humbling. Don't lose your confidence just because you suddenly see how vast the competition is. Focus on one or two goals you'd like to achieve, including having fun, and by the end of the conference you'll feel like a winner.

Write On!

Being a speaker at a conference is a good way to get involved in the writing community. Even if you're not published, you might have an area of expertise that would be of interest to writers. Conferences often feature panels on topics like professional behavior, dealing with the media, preparing a press kit, surviving rejection, historical costumes, and creating a Web page, to name a few.

It's Not What You Know ...

The writing business is like any other. Who you know sometimes seems as important as what you know. If you have a published writing friend who can recommend your book to her editor, you definitely have a leg up. If you're best friends with a *New York Times* Bestselling author, there is probably an editor out there who will want to publish your book based on that association, as long as your book is worthy of publication. If you meet an editor at a conference, your book will get more attention than if you send it in over the transom.

In other words, editors and agents are like people in any other business. They sometimes make decisions based on emotional reactions and are often subject to the influence of personalities. That's not to say, however, that connections and personalities will help a bad manuscript get published. It just means that the more friends you have in the publishing industry, the better off you'll be. So start networking!

Can I Quote You on That?

Did you ever wonder how writers get quotes for their covers? They're often procured through these sort of networking-type friendships. If you get to know a popular romance writer whose work is similar to your own, she's a good candidate for a quote once you become published. If you don't know anyone in the romance industry, your publisher can seek out a quote for you, either by soliciting early reviews or by asking another author who writes for the same house.

Publishers generally want quotes from authors whose work is in the same vein. For example, a medieval author probably wouldn't seek a quote from a western writer and vice versa.

Networking Checklist

Networking isn't like joining the Moosehead Lodge. You don't have to wear funny hats and learn secret rituals. You just have to start talking to other writers, sharing information and support whenever the opportunity arises. Here's a handy checklist to nudge you in the right direction.

- ❑ I've sought out a writers' group in person or through cyberspace.
- ❑ I've had the courage to ask questions, even when they seem like silly ones.
- ❑ I've considered attending a writers' conference.
- ❑ I've learned as much as I can about the business before I meet with an editor or agent.
- ❑ I am prepared to pitch my story to an editor or agent.

❑ I am willing to share my knowledge, knowing that this give-and-take is the essence of networking.

❑ I've asked writers whom I like if they'd be interested in sharing critiques or forming a support network.

The Least You Need to Know

➤ You can find the nearest Romance Writers of America chapter by calling 281–440–6885.

➤ Networking provides authors with ammunition to use in contract negotiations.

➤ Live chats, bulletin boards, and online workshops enable isolated writers to network nationwide.

➤ You should prepare a brief and enticing pitch of your story for agent/editor interviews at writers' conferences.

➤ You or your publisher can seek quotes from other authors for your book cover.

➤ Networking is just as important to writers as it is to any other professional in the business world.

Chapter 25

The Last Word (Or Why You Really Can Do This)

In This Chapter

➤ The real secret of novel writing

➤ Making lemonade out of rejection letters

➤ A good time to take risks

➤ The importance of long-range goals

➤ Debunking myths about "real" writers

Writing is an impractical business. Ever was it thus. Still it survives, even thrives. Why? Because some people are compelled to write stories, and other people are compelled to read them. It's a creative transaction that becomes business only after the fact. You create, then you sell. And since you may never sell, it takes a leap of faith to create.

We are essentially creative beings. We need to tell stories. You need to, too, or you wouldn't have reached the end of this book. So let's go out with a flourish. Let's look at all the wonderful reasons why you should follow your heart, not your head, and write that novel germinating inside of you.

How Bad Do You Want This?

Invariably, the people who sit down to write a book are the ones who are compelled to do so. As we've already discussed, it ain't easy. If it were, everyone would be doing it. But if you have a desire to write that just won't go away, that means you need to do it. It's really as simple as that. You don't need a degree, you don't need knowledge, you don't need the approval of a parent, a spouse, or a teacher. You simply need desire. Of course, a little perseverance comes in handy, too!

Stop the Presses!

There is a difference between writing and writing a novel. You can be oozing talent from your pores, but if you never finish a novel, you're not a novelist. You must start and finish a book! Do yourself a favor ... finish that book you've started. Or start the one you've been thinking about. You can do it!

Forget Talent

There are probably a million people in the world who want to write a book, but they don't do it because they're not sure if they have enough talent. The sad thing is that they will never know whether they have enough talent until they sit down and start to write.

Personally, I think talent is highly overrated. After all, where does talent end and skill begin? Clearly, some writers are more talented than others, but raw talent is just one aspect of writing. Some authors have a natural ability to tell a good yarn, some have a talent for tapping into trendy ideas, some have a quirky, interesting writing style, and some have an ability to create a cozy world or vibrant characters. There is room in the marketplace for a variety of skills. Does that mean you have to be the most talented writer who ever lived in order to achieve your dreams of being published? No way!

In It for the Long Haul

I can honestly say that I never received one word of encouragement before I sat down to write my first book. I never had any indication from the universe that I had writing talent or any reason whatsoever to begin a novel. Frankly, I didn't care. I felt that I saw the world in a unique way. Don't ask me why! That feeling was my motivation for writing. I wanted to create a world through my unique perspective. The issue of talent never entered my mind, thank goodness. If it had, I would never have written the first word.

If you want to have a romance published, you have to take a long-range view. You have to give yourself a chance to stumble and fall. You have to give yourself room to grow and watch closely for signs of growth. If you're growing as a writer, then you're on the right track. Only after you've given writing a good shot can you decide whether or not to continue. You can't judge yourself before you even start. The people who succeed in the end, who have the good fortune of being published, are usually the ones who simply wouldn't give up on the dream.

Meant for Bigger Things

One of the best ways to endure any difficult undertaking is to adopt the "I-was-meant-for-bigger-things" approach. It works remarkably well. It helps you overcome rejection and failure time and time again. This is how it works: If you're turned down from an exclusive critique group, say, "I was meant for bigger things." If your article is rejected from the local newspaper, say, "I was meant for bigger things." If your query letter is rejected from a New York editor, say, "I was meant for bigger things." Pretty simple, eh? The thing is, it's almost always true.

In all likelihood, you will find yourself being rejected from the sorts of projects that aren't right for you. When you hone in on what you do best, you will meet with success. So if your romantic short story is rejected by a women's magazine, it must mean you were destined to write the romance novel you've been putting off. If the historical romance novel you wrote to fit into a specific line is rejected, it must mean you were destined to write that big multigenerational romance set in the Victorian era that you've been putting off. Use rejection as a bumper to steer you back on course. Your destiny awaits you! Don't let unimportant failures stop you dead on the road to success.

Write On!

When you get a rejection letter, be sure to reread it after you've had a chance to cool down and think straight. Sometimes authors are so hurt by a rejection letter they don't read it clearly. But sometimes a rejection letter will include praise, encouragement, an invitation to send something else in the future, or a suggestion that will improve your manscript.

Take Risks

There's good news and bad news about a genre as popular as romance. The good news is that it draws talented and innovative writers, and the latest information about trends and the industry is readily available. The bad news is that the experts in the genre have so clearly defined the romance novel that it sometimes scares off writers who might take a different approach. What these new writers should realize is that following the rules isn't always the best way to meet with success.

Invariably, the novels that grab readers' hearts are the ones in which the writer has taken risks, broken the rules, bucked the trends, and written to her heart's content. Since writing is a risky business anyway, you may as well take risks.

Bouncing Back

There is nothing quite as difficult as handing your novel over to someone for acceptance or rejection. Writing, more than any other medium, is the distillation of one's thoughts and being. The words are you on paper. So, if someone criticizes your book, it feels as if they're criticizing you. How do you prepare yourself for rejection, or at least criticism?

You have to vow to bounce back. You have send your book out as many times as it takes until it finds acceptance. Or, start a new book that will inevitably be even better than your first attempt. The crucial thing is to keep going. Have a good cry. Eat a box of chocolates. Then, it's once more into the breach. Often, the people who succeed are simply the ones still standing after the others have fallen by the wayside.

> ### Write On!
>
> There's no better time to take risks than when you're first starting out. You don't have much to lose, at least financially. Once you establish a name for yourself and a readership, you'll be under some pressure to continue writing what's familiar. Write to please yourself and you may find you've also pleased an editor.

Pacing Yourself

There are some lucky devils who are overnight successes. They send out their first novel and it sells a week later for good money. We can only hope you fit into this category. If not, you'll have to learn to pace yourself. The journey to publication is sometimes a long-distance race. If you don't prepare for the long haul, you might run out of steam before you make it to the finish line.

Here are some things to bear in mind as you set out on your journey:

> ### Stop the Presses!
>
> There are two things you can do that might make you feel undue pressure to become published. One is quitting your job to write. The other is getting a degree in creative writing. The education can be edifying, and if it's an advanced degree it might enable you to teach. However, a degree won't guarantee publication.

➤ Many published authors keep working a regular job, so don't plan on quitting yours anytime soon.

➤ When choosing a career, try to pick one that leaves you the time and energy to write in your spare time.

➤ Make your dream of writing a priority, and share it with your family. If they're supportive, you'll have an easier time inserting writing time into your schedule.

➤ Bear in mind that skill sneaks up on you, and you may not realize how much you've improved unless you keep writing.

➤ You can learn about writing by reading novels and books on technique, so don't give up even when you're too crazed to find writing time.

➤ Get a writing degree if you want, but know that it won't guarantee publication.

➤ Accept your current level of writing skills. If you're too green to finish a novel, then finish a chapter. If you can't handle a chapter, write a short story. Sometimes you have to master the basic techniques before you start a long-range project like a novel.

➤ Don't compare yourself to others. All that can lead to are feelings of inferiority or superiority, and both are unproductive. Every writer has his own destiny. Accept yours and have faith that your hard work will one day pay off.

➤ When all else fails, remember that writing is an end unto itself. Writing a book is a form of expression. You hope the world will see it and celebrate its genius. If not, you can still be proud of yourself for finishing a book. It's a rare achievement.

Speaking of Romance ...

Until you achieve your dream of being published, enjoy the fact that you're writing in such a wonderful genre. As *New York Times* Bestselling author Susan Elizabeth Phillips put it, "Lately I've grown to realize how blessed we are to be part of a *good* industry. Our product doesn't give anyone lung cancer or heart disease. We bring people happiness, relaxation, relief from the stresses of daily life. And we reinforce the most important values of a healthy society: caring for others, justice, the importance of family and community. On top of this, our peers are the most generous and intelligent group it has ever been my privilege to know."*

Long-Range Goals

Writing a book takes an interesting combination of urgency and patience. You have to have enough urgency to find the time to write, but you have to have enough patience to know it may take some time before you see your book in print. Most authors have long-range goals (hitting a best-seller list) and short-range goals (I will write two pages every day). The beauty of long-range planning is that:

➤ It tempers the need for instant gratification.

➤ It allows you to improve your skills along the way.

➤ It allows room for acceptance of failure.

➤ It builds character and a tolerance for the delays typical of the publishing industry.

If you're in a hurry, you'd better start writing haiku poetry. Writing a book takes time, no two ways about it. So set yourself some long-range goals and then write as fast as you can!

Dare to Dream

I needn't say much on this topic. If you bought this book, you've already had the temerity to dream of being published. Good for you! What an awesome dream. Dreaming makes sense in this field. After all, when you write a book, you create something that never existed before. You distill words and images from your imagination and turn them into something that's concrete. If you haven't started a book yet, dare to dream of its completion. Then start making it happen. Very few people are ever encouraged to write a novel, so you must encourage yourself. To that end, use your creative imagination to make it happen:

➤ Daydream about who you'll dedicate your book to and where you'll have your first signing.

➤ Picture the cover on your novel and the rave reviews you'll receive.

➤ Find other writers to share your dreams with, and listen to success stories of published authors.

➤ Keep a notebook or journal dedicated to your writing efforts, jotting down goals, dreams, realizations, and successes.

➤ Signal your subconscious that your creativity is important—buy a special pen, a stack of notebooks, a book on nurturing your creative side, or go on a trip to research a new idea. Invest in your creativity.

Writers Are Made, Not Born

The real trick to becoming a writer is to accept the fact that there is no trick to becoming a writer. Anyone can do it. You just have to discard some preconceptions you may be harboring. Have any of these thoughts ever popped into your mind?

➤ Real writers are born under a lucky star.

➤ Real writers are more intelligent or have an above average education.

328

➤ To be a successful romance writer you have to be as attractive as a romance heroine.

➤ To become published you have to have connections in the publishing industry.

Speaking of Romance ...

Margaret Watson has written 14 romances, one published by the now defunct Meteor Kismet line, the rest are Silhouette Intimate Moments books. "Publishing is a tough business," says Margaret, "and it's easy to get discouraged. While talent is very important, perseverance might well be the most important quality you can develop in order to be successful in publishing your book. After selling my first book to Meteor's Kismet line, I went another four years without a sale. But instead of giving up, I continued to write. Not only did this hone my skills, but also I eventually sold several of the books I wrote during this dry spell. So dream your dreams, then sit down at your computer and do the work to make them come true."

Let's deal with each of the preceding misconceptions in turn.

➤ Becoming published has far more to do with hard work than luck. As a reader, you have no idea how much work went into the writing of your favorite novels. A well-written novel appears effortless. Likewise, you have no idea what personal crises your favorite writers may have undergone. Successful writers are people, just like you.

➤ Writing popular fiction doesn't require intelligence that can be measured through scholastic tests. More than a few best-selling authors have been college and high school dropouts. The best novels exhibit wisdom about the human condition, or understanding of the human spirit, or common sense, or sharp wit, or great compassion.

➤ Fortunately, you don't have to look like Sharon Stone to create a character as beautiful as Sharon Stone. That's one of the wonderful things about writing. You're judged by your thoughts, not your looks. Sure, your publicist will have an easier time booking you on a television talk show if you're as glamorous and articulate as Catherine Coulter or Julie Garwood, but a good book will always sell itself.

Stop the Presses!

Some authors take the submission process way too personally. If their first book is roundly rejected, they refuse to start another one. They simply pick up their marbles and go home. There are lots of talented people who will never be published because of this attitude, and it's a shame. There's a fine line between persevering and being unreasonably stubborn. Walk that line carefully.

Stop the Presses!

When you get "the call" from an editor who wants to buy your book, don't get so excited that you give away the farm. Scream "Whoopie!" and cry with happiness. Then say you'd like a day to talk the offer over with an agent, a friend, or a spouse.

➤ I don't know anyone who has been published solely because she has connections in the publishing industry. Of course, that happens, but it's the exception, not the rule. While it's helpful to network with other writers and to meet editors in person, you don't have to know anybody to get a great novel published.

Happy Ending, Happy Writing!

Just as I was writing the last words of this "how-to" book, I received a phone call from Michele Dunaway, a member of the Missouri Chapter of Romance Writers of America (MORWA). She'd just gotten "the call" from an editor. Her romance had just been accepted for publication in the Harlequin American line. Congratulations, Michele! Way to go!

As president of MORWA, I've emphasized the importance of setting goals. Michele said that her goal-setting had played a big part in her success. It proved to me what I've known for some time—that if you have faith and work consistently at your writing, you will achieve success. Success may not always come when you want it. It may not even come in the form you expected, but it will come.

Michele has provided this "how-to" book with the kind of happy ending every romance writer loves. Another aspiring writer has realized her dream. Will you be next? I hope so. In the meantime, best wishes and happy writing!

The Least You Need to Know

➤ The people who succeed in publishing are often the ones too hardheaded to give up.

➤ If you learn from your rejection letters, you'll increase your odds of getting published.

➤ Having long-range writing goals helps you learn to deal with temporary failures.

➤ Nurture your dreams of getting published by visualizing your first book signing and by recording your goals and successes along the way.

➤ Dare to dream of being a published author!

Glossary

anachronism   An error in chronology. If you put a modern term, concept, or object in an ancient setting, it's called an anachronism.

best-seller   A book that has appeared on a best-seller list of some sort. A best-seller that appears on a chain store best-seller list or a distributor's list might only sell in the tens of thousands of copies, whereas a *New York Times* Bestseller will sell hundreds of thousands, if not millions, of copies. So, just because someone is a "best-selling author" doesn't mean she's rich.

bibliography   This is a list of publications a writer has referred to in the text of his or her book. The bibliography is usually found in the back of the book and lists titles and authors. This means that bibliographies are a good place for you to cherry-pick further research books. You can also find bibliographies in the library that are listings of all the works written on a given subject.

Black Moment   This is the point at which the characters—and the reader—think the relationship is doomed. The higher you raise the stakes beforehand, the bleaker that moment will be. Likewise, the higher the emotional stakes, the more satisfying the resolution to the crisis will be. The big resolution is the five-hanky payoff the reader has been waiting for.

blurb   The copy found on the back cover of the book. It's usually a two- or three-paragraph description of the story. The whole point of the blurb is to entice you into buying the book. It's so important to the sale that some authors actually get involved in writing the blurb. However, the blurbs are usually written by freelance writers hired for that task alone.

bodice ripper   A term that critics of the romance genre used to describe the big sexy historical romances popular in the 1970s at the peak of the sexual revolution. Often the heroine's bodice was ripped away, hence the term.

buy-in   The sales pitch that happens roughly four months before a book's publication. The publisher's sales representatives visit buyers, pitch the book concepts, and show them book covers. The buyers place orders based on that pitch, though the order can be increased in the coming months if the buyer sees the need for it. The buy-in is sometimes called the sell-in.

characterization   Your representation of a human being. It's the sum of all the brush strokes a writer makes in order to paint a three-dimensional, fictional person.

Christian publishers   Publishing houses that print religious fiction and nonfiction exclusively. The books are typically sold in Christian bookstores and through other religious outlets. Bethany House Publishers and Tyndale House are two of the more than half-dozen members of the Christian Booksellers Association (CBA) that publish romances.

clinch   An industry term used to describe the passionate embrace that typifies the traditional romance cover. The women and men on a clinch cover are often scantily clad and in provocative poses. Sometimes this pose is called a clutch.

confession magazines   Magazines that contain stories written in first person that are designed to draw on the reader's sympathies. The content ranges from adventure and mystery stories to emotional, intimate accounts of women who deal with serious problems typical of everyday life.

commission   The money an agent earns for selling a book on your behalf. He earns a percentage, usually 15 percent, of your income, but doesn't get paid until you get paid. The agent receives a commission on everything you earn, including income from foreign and movie rights.

copy editor   Someone hired to go over your manuscript line by line. The copy editor is often a freelancer. She or he will focus on grammar, punctuation, spelling, or word usage, editing line by line. She'll occasionally comment on point plots, but that's rare. The copy editor is sometimes called a line editor.

costume dramas   Books that contain very little historical research. In fact, the only way the reader even knows it's a historical is by the costumes worn by the characters.

deus ex machina   A term used to describe an inappropriately miraculous resolution of conflict. It came from ancient Greek tragedies in which an actor playing a god would descend on stage in some sort of machine, as if from the heavens, to decide the drama's final outcome.

dump   A free-standing in-store cardboard display that holds a large number of a particular author's books. A generic dump is topped with artwork that often touts the publisher's name. A custom dump is topped with artwork from the author's cover. Your books won't appear in a dump unless a store has ordered at least a couple dozen copies.

galleys   A proof, or copy, of the typeset pages that will eventually go to press. They're printed on $8^1/_2$-by-11-inch sheets of paper, but the copy looks exactly like it will in book form. Since typos are easy to overlook, the author and a number of other people in the publishing house proof the galleys before the book is printed.

genre   A category of fiction characterized by a particular style and content that readers come to count on. In the romance genre, readers expect a happy ending. Mystery buffs expect the cops to catch the bad guy. In the horror genre, readers anticipate being scared. Each genre has a dedicated following, so disappoint their expectations at your own risk!

hard-soft deal   A deal in which a publisher buys the rights to print your book in hardcover and softcover. Typically, the hardcover version will come out first and the paperback issue will be released a year later, often in conjunction with the release of your next hardcover novel.

high-concept novels   These are books that have a concept or plot that is bigger-than-life, that has never been done before, and that usually takes precedence over characterization. *Jurassic Park,* by Michael Crichton, a novel in which dinosaurs are cloned from DNA and bred for a theme park, is a high-concept book.

idiom   A phrase that's unique to a certain group of people or to a particular locale.

ISBN (International Standard Book Number)   The number assigned to every book in print. The ISBN is listed on the copyright page as well as above the bar code on the cover. Booksellers use this number to order books and track sales.

line   A specific category within the so-called "category romance" industry. Lines at Harlequin-Silhouette include Harlequin Temptation, Harlequin Historicals, Silhouette Desire, and Love Inspired, to name just a few. Each line has a different tone, word-length requirement, and intended audience. Some lines allow for sex scenes, while others don't.

marketplace   An all encompassing word that describes the latest buying trends that come about through readers' changing tastes in fiction. Twenty years ago sexy historical romances were all the rage. Now readers are demanding more variety in the marketplace.

metaphor   A word or a phrase that means one thing, but is used in place of something else in order to make a comparison. For example, her mouth was a rosebud. A simile is a word or phrase that compares two unlike objects, usually with the word "like" or "as." For example, her mouth was like a rosebud. A metaphor is more direct and often more visceral and powerful.

multicultural romances   Love stories that include the flavor and culture of ethnic experiences. The culture might be African American, Hispanic, Asian, or otherwise. The romance, however, is still paramount. Editors of ethnic romances, like other romance editors, are looking for emotion and good storytelling.

multiple submission   The simultaneous submission of a manuscript to more than one publishing house.

narration   The actual storytelling, or the words spoken by the narrator, who is usually an invisible observer. Dialogue is what the characters say, appearing as words between quotation marks. A good book balances both. However, many of today's romances effectively use much more dialogue than narration.

over-the-transom   A term used when an author sends in an unrequested manuscript. If you send your manuscript over-the-transom, that means you've sent it without prior arrangement with an editor.

partial   A portion of the manuscript, usually three chapters and a synopsis. If your chapters are short, your partial can consist of more than three chapters. Usually, editors like to see at least 50 pages of a manuscript.

periodical literature   Any publication released at regular intervals, like magazines or journals.

plot   A sequence of events that hold together and intertwine over the course of a book. The best plots come full circle. Ideas and foreshadowing planted at the beginning bear fruit, or come together, at the end. A subplot is a secondary story line that's part of, but not central to, your book. The subplot should be entwined with the main plot and move the story forward. Otherwise it has no purpose.

prose   A word used to describe natural writing. In other words, fiction that reflects regular speech and rhythm. The term is often used in contrast to poetry, which is a formalized style of fiction. When someone comments on your prose, they're basically commenting on your style of writing.

protagonist   A protagonist is the principle character in a story or novel. It has a more neutral connotation than the terms hero or heroine, which imply a certain amount of heroism. A protagonist may be the main character, but that doesn't mean he or she is sympathetic.

pub date   A shortened term for publication date. This is the month your book will be released to bookstores.

purple prose   A derogatory term used to describe overly descriptive or lush fiction. It evolved from the nineteenth-century phrase "purple patch" that described a brilliant or ornate literary passage in an otherwise dull work of fiction. It literally meant a patch of cloth that possessed the brilliance and gaudiness of the color purple. "Purple passage" was another variation of the term.

Romantic Times   The premiere romance fan magazine. It boasts over 150 book reviews each month and is now delving into the mystery genre. Kathryn Falk, the magazine's founder and CEO, is an innovative Brooklyn entrepreneur who, after acquiring an estate in England, goes by the title Lady of Barrow.

regency romance   A romance that's set in England between 1811 and 1820, during the reign of the prince regent. The period is characterized by charming phrases and manners and has an avid following among writers and readers.

rewrite   The process of honing or polishing your fiction after you have a first draft of your entire book. Or, you might rewrite each chapter as you go along. A revision, on the other hand, is requested by your editor. She asks you to revise your story based on her comments and suggestions.

romances   Novels that focus primarily on the development of a love relationship between a man and a woman. By the end of the book, the hero and heroine should be ready to commit—the required happy ending readers expect. No cold feet allowed!

setting   The time and place of an action scene. Key elements of a setting include the physical surroundings, the environment in general, and the less tangible mood of the chosen place. Setting can be such an important presence that it almost acts like a third person in a scene with two people.

sexual tension   The attraction between the hero and heroine. They're both aware of it, but it often goes unacknowledged. The reader can see it, too, and wonders with anticipation when the attraction will lead to satisfaction. That's how sexual tension can help make a romance a "page turner."

slush pile   The huge stack in which uninvited manuscripts, or manuscripts sent over-the-transom, end up gathering dust until an editor finds time to read them.

spine out   A term used to describe the way books appear on bookshelves in stores. To save space, some stores rack books so that all you can see is the narrow spine. Other stores place books face out so that you can see the front cover.

subgenre   A recognizable type of fiction within a particular genre. It's a subcategory. The romance genre has expanded so much that the number of subgenres seems to grow every year. That's good news for you!

synonym   A word that has a meaning close to another word. The meaning might be virtually the same or slightly different. For example, synonyms for anger include wrath, ire, and soreness.

synopsis   A summary of the novel's events and a cataloguing of character development in narrative form. Writers can use a synopsis to pitch an unfinished manuscript to editors. They can also use it as a guide during the writing process. Some authors write synopses that are four pages long, while others write synopses that are 75 pages long.

unagented   An unagented writer or manuscript is one that isn't represented by an agent. It's a standard industry term used to describe an author who submits a manuscript without an agent. Guidelines usually indicate whether or not a publisher will look at unagented manuscripts.

viewpoint character   The person you choose to focus on during any given scene. The reader will see everything in the environment through that character's point of view.

women in jeopardy   This is yet another romance subgenre. The term can be used to describe a variety of types of romance novels—from a Harlequin Intrigue to a big romantic suspense. The basic idea is that the main protagonist is a female who faces danger throughout most of the book.

word count   The number of words in a novel. The shorter category romances run around 55,000 words. Bigger contemporary and historical novels generally run 90,000 to 120,000 words. Ten or 15 years ago, historical romances often had 200,000 word counts, but paper costs and less leisure time among readers has made lengthy word counts a thing of the past.

Romance Publishers

Note: Publishers sometimes seek out a particular kind of romance, but their preferences often change from year to year. To find out the latest preferences, send for guidelines if they're available. (Don't forget to include a number 10 size self-addressed stamped envelope!) You can often find submission guidelines on publishers' Web sites.

If guidelines or tip sheets aren't available, you're expected to become familiar with the house's preferences by reading its latest releases. Many of the mainstream publishers will accept a variety of settings and subject matter, including ethnic and paranormal romances, as long as the book is outstandingly written.

Avalon Books
401 Lafayette Street
New York, NY 10003
212-598-0222
www.avalonbooks.com

Type: Publishes hardcover sweet romances that appear in libraries.

Avon Books/HarperCollins
10 E. 53rd Street
New York, NY 10022
212-207-7000
www.avonbooks.com

Type: Historical and contemporary romances and women's fiction.

Barbour Publishing, Inc.
P.O. Box 719
Uhrichsville, OH 44683
740-922-6045
www.barbourbooks.com

Type: Conservative, evangelical Christian contemporary and historical novels and novellae under the Heartsong Presents imprint.

Bethany House Publishers
11300 Hampshire Avenue S.
Minneapolis, MN 55438
612-829-2500
www.bethanyhouse.com

Type: Historical and contemporary Christian romances.

Dorchester Publishing
276 Fifth Avenue, Room 1008
New York, NY 10001
212-725-8811
www.dorchesterpub.com

Type: Historical and contemporary romances published under the Leisure Books and Love Spell imprints.

Genesis Press, Inc.
315 3rd Avenue North
Columbus, MS 39701
601-329-9927
www.colom.com/genesis

Type: Multicultural romances under the Indigo, Tango2, and Love Spectrum imprints.

Harlequin Enterprises, Ltd.
225 Duncan Mill Road
Don Mills, Ontario
M3B 3K9
Canada
416-445-5860
www.romance.net

Lines: Harlequin Superromance, Harlequin Duets, MIRA, Harlequin Temptation.

Harlequin-Silhouette
300 East 42nd Street, 6th Floor
New York, NY 10017
212-682-6080
www.romance.net

Lines: Harlequin American Romance, Harlequin Historicals, Harlequin Intrigue, Silhouette Romance, Silhouette Desire, Silhouette Special Edition, Silhouette Intimate Moments, Love Inspired (Steeple Hill Books).

Harlequin Mills and Boon, Ltd.
Editorial Department
18-24 Paradise Road
Richmond, Surrey, TW9 1SR
United Kingdom
+44181-948-0444
www.romance.net

Lines: Romance, Enchanted, Presents, Medical, and Historical Romance.

HarperPaperbacks
10 East 53rd Street
New York, NY 10022
212-207-7000
www.harpercollins.com

Type: Historical and contemporary romances and women's fiction.

Harvest House Publishers
1075 Arrowsmith Street
Eugene, OR 97402
541-343-0123

Type: Biblical-based Christian romances.

Kensington
850 Third Avenue, 16th Floor
New York, NY 10022
212-407-1500
www.kensingtonbooks.com

Lines: Zebra, Kensington, Precious Gems, Encanto, Bouquet, Pinnacle, Arabesque (Arabesque has been purchased by Black Entertainment Network, but submissions still go to Kensington). Kensington publishes historical and contemporary romances, as well as regencies and women's mainstream fiction.

LionHearted Publishing, Inc.
P.O. Box 618
674 Riven Rock Road
Zephyr Cove, NV 89448-0618
702-588-1388
www.lionhearted.com

Type: Historical and contemporary romances and women's fiction. The books are not released in traditional outlets like stores, but through "independent network marketing distributors."

Love Inspired
(look for Steeple Hill imprint under Harlequin listings)

Palisades/Multnomah Publishers
P.O. Box 1720
Sisters, OR 97759
541-549-1144
www.multnomahbooks.com

Type: Historical and contemporary Christian romances.

Penguin Putnam, Inc.
375 Hudson St.
New York, NY 10014
212-366-2000
www.penguinputnam.com

Type: Historical and contemporary romances and women's fiction. Imprints include Berkley Books, Jove, Signet, NAL, and Onyx.

Ponder Publishing, Inc.
P.O. Box 23037, RPO
McGillivray
Winnipeg, Manitoba
R3T 3M3 Canada
204-269-2985
www.ponderpublishing.com

Type: Short and long contemporary romances that don't contain sexually explicit details.

Random House, Inc.
201 E. 50th St.
New York, NY 10022
212-751-2600
www.randomhouse.com/BB/

Type: Historical and contemporary romances and women's fiction. Imprints include Ballantine, Fawcett, Bantam Books, Dell, and Doubleday.

Red Sage Publishing
P.O. Box 4844
Seminole, FL 33775
727-391-3847
www.redsagepub.com

Type: Anthologies of sensual women's fiction.

Silhouette Books
(look under Harlequin listings)

St. Martin's Press
175 Fifth Avenue
New York, NY 10010
212-982-3900
www.stmartins.com

Type: Historical and contemporary romances and women's fiction.

Simon & Schuster
1230 Avenue of the Americas
New York, NY 10020
212-698-7000
www.simonsays.com

Type: Historical and contemporary romances and women's fiction under the Pocket Books imprint.

Steeple Hill Books
(look under Harlequin listings)

Tyndale House Publishers, Inc.
P.O. Box 80
Wheaton, IL 60189
630-668-8300
www.tyndale.com

Type: Historical and contemporary inspirational romances, including novels and novellas.

Warner Books
1271 Avenue of the Americas
New York, NY 10020
212-522-7200
www.twbookmark.com

Type: Historical and contemporary romances and women's fiction.

Electronic Publishers

There is a growing number of electronic and/or multimedia publishers that deal with romantic fiction. Here are a few:

Hard Shell Word Factory
www.hardshell.com

New Concepts
www.newconcepts.com

Neighborhood Press
www.members.aol.com/nppubsrg/welcome.html

Zeus Publications
www.zeus-publications.com

Dreams Unlimited
www.dreams-unlimited.com

Writing Resource Books

There are a number of other excellent "how-to" books dealing with all aspects of the romance writing business, or writing in general. Here are a few:

Falk, Kathryn. *How to Write a Romance for the New Market and Get It Published.* Genesis Press, Ltd., 1999. (ISBN 1885478461)

This is a revised edition of the comprehensive book that the publisher of *Romantic Times* magazine penned years ago. It covers everything from plotting and conflict and the author-editor relationship to the latest trends in the marketplace.

Curtis, Richard. *How to Be Your Own Literary Agent: The Business of Getting a Book Published.* Houghton Mifflin Co., 1996. (ISBN 0-395-71819-8)

A valuable book for anyone with or without an agent.

Holm, Kirsten C., ed. *Writer's Market 2000.* Writer's Digest Books, 1999. (ISBN 0-89879-911-2)

This reference book is updated every year, so get the latest edition. It lists every conceivable publisher and many agents. Aspiring writers will find the examples of query letters especially helpful.

Dixon, Debra. *GMC: Goal, Motivation and Conflict: The Building Blocks of Good Fiction.* Gryphon Books for Writers, 1996. (ISBN 0-9654371-0-8)

This book breaks down the essence of character development in an easy-to-understand way. It's published by a small press and can be purchased by contacting …

Gryphon Books for Writers
P.O. Box 172342
Memphis, Tennessee 38187
901-762-0162

McCutcheon, Pam. *Writing the Fiction Synopsis: A Step-by-Step Approach.* Gryphon Books for Writers, 1998. (ISBN 0-9654371-1-6)

Another easy-to-read "how to" from Gryphon Books for Writers. (See address previously given.)

Zuckerman, Albert. *Writing the Blockbuster Novel.* Writer's Digest Books, 1994. (ISBN 0-89879-598-2)

Published by Writer's Digest Books, this offers insight even to those who have no plans to write a blockbuster novel.

Reece, Colleen L. *Writing Smarter, Not Harder, the Workbook Way.* Kaleidoscope Press, 1995. (ISBN 1-885371-13-6)

This workbook urges authors to increase their output by "pre-writing" instead of rewriting. It has, among other things, a character biography worksheet. You can order it from ...

Kaleidosope Press
2507 94th Avenue E.
Puyallup, WA 98371-2203

Gallagher, Rita, and Rita Clay Estrada, eds. *Writing Romances: A Handbook by the Romance Writers of America.* Writer's Digest Books, 1997. (ISBN 0-89879-726-8)

This was edited by Rita Gallagher and Rita Clay Estrada, two women instrumental in the founding of RWA, and after whom the RITA Award was named. It includes essays from top writers, as does another book from Writer's Digest Books:

Borcherding, David H. *Romance Writer's Sourcebook: Where to Sell Your Manuscripts.* Writer's Digest Books, 1996. (ISBN 0-89879-726-8)

Pianka, Phyllis Taylor. *How to Write Romances.* Writer's Digest Books, 1998. (ISBN 0898798671)

This is another manual from Writer's Digest Books.

MacManus, Yvonne. *You Can Write a Romance ... and Get It Published.* Toad Hall, Inc., 1997. (ISBN 0963749811)

A popular "how-to" book written by a romance novelist who also has experience as a book editor and literary agent.

Grant, Vanessa. *Writing Romance.* Self-Counsel Press, 1997. (ISBN 1551800969)

An author of numerous Harlequin romances looks at all angles of romance writing.

Paludan, Eva. *Romance Writers' Pink Pages*. Prima Publishing, 1996. (ISBN 0761501681)

This book looks closely at publishers. It may be hard to find.

Jaegly, Peggy. *Romantic Hearts: A Personal Reference for Romance Readers*. Scarecrow Press, Inc., 1997. (ISBN 1578860008)

This book is useful to readers who like to keep track of their favorite authors and all their titles. (Note: It's not a recent publication and therefore won't list the latest releases.)

Herman, Jeff. *Writer's Guide to Book Editors, Publishers, and Literary Agents, 2000–2001: Who They Are! What They Want! And How to Win Them Over!* Prima Publishing, 1999. (ISBN 0761519610)

A thorough examination of the industry, including agents' client lists.

Lee, Rebecca Hagan, ed. *Keys to Success: A Professional Writer's Career Handbook*. RWA, 1997.

A handbook published by RWA consisting of articles written by RWA members on topics ranging from agents and editors to career planning. It can be purchased by contacting …

Romance Writers of America
3707 FM 1960 West, Suite 555
Houston, TX 77068
281-440-6885

Romance Reviewers and Publications

There are dozens of publications and online sites that review books or otherwise specialize in the romance industry. Here are a few that published and unpublished authors alike might find of interest.

Romance Writers' Report
3707 FM 1960 West
Suite 555
Houston, TX 77068
281-440-6885
www.rwanational.com

A monthly magazine offering industry updates and writing tips distributed to all members of Romance Writers of America.

Romance $ells

An RWA publication available to the public. This quarterly publication is geared toward romance buyers and readers. It features the latest book releases. Each page features a book with a description written by the author.

Romantic Times
55 Bergen Street
Brooklyn, NY 11201
718-237-1097
www.romantictimes.com

A monthly magazine devoted to romance reviews and articles about the industry.

Rendezvous
1507 Burnham Avenue
Calumet City, IL 60409
708-862-9797

A monthly publication devoted to romance reviews.

Affaire de Coeur
3976 Oakhill Road
Oakland, CA 94605-4931
510-569-5675
www.affairedecoeur.com

A monthly publication devoted to romance reviews and articles about the industry.

Old Book Barn Gazette
Cheryl's Old Book Barn
Route 51 North
P.O. Box 500
Forsyth, IL 62535
E-mail: oldbookbarn@juno.com

A monthly newsletter featuring reviews, author interviews, and industry news.

Calico Trails
1652 Peachtree Lane
Chambersburg, PA 17201
717-262-2278
E-mail: stahel@desupernet.net

A quarterly publication devoted to reviews, articles, and author interviews.

Publishers Weekly
245 W. 17th Street
New York, NY 10011
1-800-278-2991

This weekly publication is the premiere magazine for the publishing industry. It's expensive and dense with industry information and reviews.

Here are a few of the many Web sites that either sell, feature, or review romances on the Internet:

www.barnesandnoble.com

www.amazon.com

www.booksense.com

www.writersdigest.com

www.thebooknook.com

www.likesbooks.com

www.romcom.com

www.booksquare.com/subversion/

www.literary-liaisons.com

webcurrent.com/heartland_writers/index.html

An excellent homepage that has a thorough listing of good links for romance writers belongs to romance author Jo Beverley. The address is www.sff.net/people/jobeverley.

Writing- and Publishing-Related Organizations

There are some important writers' groups that many romance authors join. The first one you should consider is Romance Writers of America. RWA is the largest genre organization in the world and is extremely informative and specific to the romance writer's needs.

As you become more experienced and have some publications under your belt, you will be eligible to join groups like Novelists, Inc., and the Writers Guild of America. Sisters in Crime is for mystery writers, and a number of romantic suspense authors belong to that group as well as RWA.

The Writers Guild of America offers a unique service to members and nonmembers alike. For a nominal fee, you can archive a manuscript in the WGA Intellectual Property Registry. This service can help you prove the date of a manuscript's creation. Most romance authors don't feel it's necessary to take this protective measure against plagiarism, but the service might be helpful for those concerned about protecting their copyright when selling in other markets.

Romance Writers of America
3707 FM 1960 West
Suite 555
Houston, TX 77068
281-440-6885
www.rwanational.com

Novelists, Inc.
P.O. Box 1166
Mission, KS 66222-0166

www.ninc.com
E-mail: info@ninc.com

Writers Guild of America
555 West 57th Street
New York, NY 10019
212-767-7800
www.wgaeast.org

Sisters in Crime
P.O. Box 442124
Lawrence, KS 66044-8933
785-842-1325

Association of Authors' Representatives, Inc.
10 Astor Place, Third Floor
New York, NY 10003
212-252-3695
www.bookwire.com/aar

Press Releases

A press release can be an inexpensive and effective way of getting the word out about your novel. Here are a few things to bear in mind when sending a press release:

➤ It should include the basic information that every journalist wants to know: who, what, when, why, and where.

➤ It should be a single page and easy to read.

➤ Send it out well in advance of your book's release. It can take weeks, if not months, for a news editor to respond to a news release.

➤ For maximum results, your press release should be followed by a phone call. News editors receive hundreds of press releases, and a call from you might result in a closer read of yours.

➤ You can send press releases out for any special occasion: a new release, a new award, or a speaking engagement.

Following is a sample press release. I sent this out preceding the release of one of my novels, and even without a follow-up phone call, it resulted in at least one newspaper article.

For Immediate Release

CONTACT: Ann Kruckmeyer
Phone: 123-456-7890

—BEST-SELLING NOVELIST PENS NEW HISTORICAL—

JOVE TO RELEASE "*A DANCE IN HEATHER*"

WFLD-TV news writer and national best-selling author Julie Beard announces the release of her second medieval romance, *A Dance in Heather,* which will hit bookstores in early May.

A Dance in Heather weaves together a rich tapestry of romance and revenge in fifteenth-century England. *RENDEZVOUS* magazines says: "A glorious love story in every sense—alive and vibrant, enthralling and intriguing ... couldn't put it down until the last page." National best-selling author KATHERINE SUTCLIFFE says: "An alluring, fascinating, and sensual story ... *loved the hero!*"

Beard's first novel, *Lady and the Wolf,* which went into a second printing shortly after its July 1994 release, is also set in the Middle Ages. "In the medieval time period there's a wonderful contrast between the ideal of chivalry and the reality of life, which was pretty brutal," says Beard. "This inherent conflict brings out the best in my characters—their strengths and nobility."

A news writer at FOX NEWS CHICAGO, Beard was formerly a reporter for the NBC affiliates in St. Louis and Green Bay. "After spending all day in the newsroom writing about murder and mayhem, I enjoy going home and creating stories in which love conquers all," she says.

Beard is available for interviews and will conduct autographings in Chicago, St. Louis, and Green Bay in May and June.

This generic press release is a sample of one of several formats you can use. Yours should be written in third person, include one or two quotes, and begin with a catchy headline. It helps if you can enlarge portions of text for emphasis, but it's not necessary. It looks more professional if you use someone else as the contact person, but it's fine to use your own name and number. This press release includes enough information so that a reporter can write an article. Some papers, particularly small ones, will use a press release almost verbatim. Others will use the release simply to trigger an idea for a story and will require a subsequent interview.

If you want help in your promotional efforts, there are a few public relations agencies that specialize in the romance writing industry. Here are a few of them:

Nancy Berland Public Relations
7209 Lancelot Place
Oklahoma City, OK 73132
405-721-3169
E-mail: nberlandpr@aol.com

Creative Promotions, Inc.
344 Cedar Avenue
Ridgewood, NJ 07450
201-251-8182
www.cpromo.com

Power Promotions
4319 Medical Drive, #131-298
San Antonio, TX 78229-3345
830-755-4728
www.powerontheweb.com

Judy Spagnola
113 Covered Bridge Road
Cherry Hill, NJ 08034
856-428-9598
E-mail: JudySpags@aol.com

Index